ONE FAMILY'S WAR

ONE
FAMILY'S WAR

Edited by Patrick Mayhew with an
introduction by
Christopher Mayhew

HUTCHINSON
London Melbourne Sydney Auckland Johannesburg

Hutchinson & Co. (Publishers) Ltd

An imprint of the Hutchinson Publishing Group

17–21 Conway Street, London W1P 6JD

Hutchinson Publishing Group (Australia) Pty Ltd
16–22 Church Street, Hawthorn, Melbourne, Victoria 3122, Australia

Hutchinson Group (NZ) Ltd
32–34 View Road, PO Box 40-086, Glenfield, Auckland 10

Hutchinson Group (SA) Pty Ltd
PO Box 337, Bergvlei 2012, South Africa

First published 1985
© Patrick Mayhew and Christopher Mayhew 1985

Set in Linotron Ehrhardt by
Rowland Phototypesetting Ltd
Bury St Edmunds, Suffolk

Printed and bound in Great Britain by
Anchor Brendon Ltd, Tiptree, Essex

British Library Cataloguing in Publication Data

Mayhew (*Family*)
    One family's war.
    1. World War, 1939–1945 – Great Britain
    I. Title   II. Howarth (*Family*)
    III. Mayhew, Pat
    940.54'81'41   D759

ISBN 0 09 160280 7

Contents

Introduction

We started this 'Budget', as we called it, in September 1939, right at the beginning of the war. It was an idea of my stepmother's for keeping our large family together. Wherever we found ourselves, we would write regular letters for family consumption and send them to her, and she would send us back, in weekly batches, copies of the rest of the family's letters.

Without this Budget, we would quickly have lost touch. Between us, six young Mayhews and two first cousins, the Howarths, we served in the Navy, the Army, the RAF, Special Operations Executive, the FANYs [Field Auxiliary Nursing Yeomanry], the Wrens, the Home Guard, and the Auxiliary Fire Service; and at one time or another wrote home from northeast France, Egypt, Tunisia, Sicily, Normandy and Germany – also from an SOE base in the Shetlands, an internment camp in Ireland, the University of Rochester, New York, and Biggin Hill airfield. Beryl herself wrote unfailingly in every Budget, from the Mayhew family home at Felthorpe, six miles from Norwich.

By the end of the war, we had written between us well over a thousand letters, and when he retired in 1982, my brother Patrick went through them all and edited a large selection for private family publication.

Naturally enough, his book fascinated the surviving contributors. I think we had largely forgotten what the war had been like, and were now suddenly reminded, in the most vivid way, of what had happened to us and how we had felt at the time.

The question then arose – would a shorter version be of public interest? The family was divided. Some felt that the letters were private and should remain so, others that they gave an unusually intimate and authentic picture of the war and could be more widely read. Eventually we all decided to let this shorter version go forward for general reading outside the family group.

The younger Budget contributors were all great-grandchildren of Sir James Paget, a strongly independent character who became Surgeon-Extraordinary to Queen Victoria, and whose descendants (including two bishops and an atheist, all famous in their day) tended to be unusually articulate and argumentative, not least on questions of religious truth. They all shared the same social background: four of the men went to Christ Church, Oxford, and the fifth to Trinity, Cambridge.

Thus although this book is primarily about the Second World War, it may also shed some light on family life and social class in an age which now seems centuries away.

Though I cannot hope to judge the book objectively, I would claim that it brings out very clearly the changes in national mood during the different phases of the war. For readers who did not live through them, it might be as well to recall and summarize these phases.

The first lasted from September 1939 until May 1940, from the dispatch of the ill-equipped British Expeditionary Force to France to its defeat eight months later and its remarkable escape from Dunkirk. During this phase people felt very little enthusiasm for the war. Most of us blamed Hitler for it and thought it inevitable, but the prevailing mood was of resignation. The Chamberlain government gave little leadership and was widely regarded as incompetent, and there was some quite lively campaigning against the war – mainly communist-led – the Russians then being on Hitler's side. David Howarth, Patrick, and I were all in France at the time, and our letters faithfully reflect the general mood of critical, unhappy acquiescence, and also the extraordinary amateurism of Britain's early war effort.

The second phase, from Dunkirk to well into 1941, included the invasion threat, the Battle of Britain and the first heavy air raids. Fighting alone, defending their own homes and led by Churchill, the British rose splendidly to the occasion, and their buoyant spirit is well reflected in the Budget letters. These were great days for the civilian members of the family. They joined, and in two cases commanded Home Guard platoons, organized the reception of evacuees, dug slit trenches, firewatched and were bombed. Felthorpe became a military convalescent hospital, with my stepmother as commandant. In Down House, Uncle Bertie and Aunt Ellie, among their other war duties, acted as host and hostess to an entire infantry platoon; and while David, Pat, and I trained for commissions, the family's thoughts and prayers centred on Paul in his Hurricane, fighting in the skies above us, sometimes directly above us. This phase of the war was the family's, as well as the country's, finest hour.

For the British, the years 1942 and 1943 were psychologically the most difficult. Once the Russians, Americans and Japanese had come in we no longer held centre-stage, and the war was fought far away – mainly in Russia and the Pacific – and on a scale which dwarfed our own efforts, overshadowing even our victories in Africa and the Mediterranean. Though victory now seemed likely, it also seemed a very long way away. In varying degrees almost everyone became war-weary. We felt we had made our contribution and had a right to take things more easily, and to survive. More of the letters being written to the Budget contained complaints of shortages, boredom and illnesses. Writing from Sicily where, without ever meeting, we were serving in the same invading army, Patrick and I report our adventures in an unusually low-key, professional style.

The final phase of the war witnesses the invasion of Normandy, the V-bombs, the liberation of Europe and the first stirrings of postwar party politics. Once the Normandy bridgeheads had been won and consolidated everyone assumed that victory was certain, but almost all of us thought that it would come much sooner than it did. As the months dragged on, our hopes became increasingly mixed with impatience and frustration, and the setbacks – Arnhem, the Battle of the Bulge, the V-Bombs – were hard to bear.

In line with the national mood, the Budget letters began speculating about the future and became increasingly political. What should be done with the Germans? (I am taken to task for fraternizing with them.) Which units of which services will be demobilized first? How should we vote in the coming general election? (Significantly, though the Budget had been pro-Churchill during the war, not one of the younger contributors proposed to vote Conservative.)

This book seems to me to describe war in the most appropriate way, by looking closely at its impact on individual people.
Conventional war histories tell us which battles were won by
which nations – and for what reasons; but we can miss the true
meaning of war when we read about an army fighting rather than
a particular soldier, of a city being blitzed rather than a single
house, of the 'Battle of Britain' rather than of Paul in his
Hurricane, fighting down his fears.

It seems particularly important today to avoid thinking about
war in general terms. The first nuclear exchange will obliterate
all questions of victory or defeat, attack or defence, right or
wrong; only the suffering of this or that particular person or
family (multiplied an unimaginable number of times) will have
meaning.

Is this what Dylan Thomas meant by the strange last line in
his war poem

'After the first death, there is no other.'

THE FAMILY September 1939

The Mayhews

Dad/ Basil	Sir Basil Mayhew, Joint Vice-Chairman of J. & J. Colman Ltd. There are few letters of his in the Budget because he wrote separately to the children almost every week.
Beryl/B	Lady Mayhew, stepmother and creator of the Budget. President of the Norwich Division of the Red Cross.
Dorothea/ Doff	Aged twenty-six, married to 'George' Heywood, Master of Marlborough College. At the start of the war they had one daughter, Susan, aged six months.
Christopher/ Kiff	Aged twenty-four, prospective Labour candidate for South Norfolk and working for the Fabian Research Bureau. He joined the Territorials after Munich and was called up as a gunner immediately on the outbreak of the war.
Pat	Aged twenty-two, was a trainee probation officer working in the Lambeth Juvenile Court area of London. He was living in the Mary Ward Settlement near King's Cross, was a Christian Pacifist and was in the Auxiliary Fire Service.
Paul	Aged twenty, was still at Oxford University. He was a socialist, and a member of the University Air Squadron. He was immediately called up.
Helen	Aged seventeen, was on a schoolgirls' trip to Canada when war broke out.
Clare	Aged fourteen, was still at Benenden School.

The Howarths

Uncle/ Bertie	Dr O. J. R. Howarth. Secretary of the British Association for the Advancement of Science.
Aunt/ Ellie	Mrs E. K. Howarth. District Commander of the Women's Voluntary Service.
Stephen	Aged twenty-nine, was a chartered accountant and was with Hoare's Bank at the beginning of the war.
David	Aged twenty-seven, was on the staff of the BBC and was immediately sent to France as a war correspondent.
Felthorpe Hall	The home of the Mayhews, six miles from Norwich.
Down House	The home of the Howarths, six miles from Bromley, southeast of London.

I

THE PHONEY WAR AND DUNKIRK
September 1939 – June 1940

Felthorpe Hall
Norwich
20 September 1939

'Family all,

'I don't know how it will work out but I think I'm going to try and have about six copies made of every letter of general interest and then you can each have one to read and tear up.

'I'm afraid all the type will seem a bit inhuman but if you've got a better idea send it along. The main thing seems to be that we're all looking for personal news of each other more than almost anything else, and it may be worth sacrificing the handwriting so to speak for the speed of circulation.

'Here life seems curiously full but wonderfully peaceful; I suppose it's having the country all round. . . .

Very much love to you all,
B.'

This letter introducing the Budget was sent out to the family on 20 September, seventeen days after the start of the war which had already brought great changes into their lives.

Chris was already on his way to France as a gunner in the Surrey Yeomanry. His choice of Regiment was somewhat fortuitous because after the Munich settlement, convinced that war was now inevitable, he

'went to the Mansion House recruiting bureau infuriated by the necessity of joining up and resolved to join whatever b—y unit first caught my eye. The Surrey Yeomanry happened to be the only one there.'

He left for France

'feeling very fit and cheerful. I'm allocated to a safer brand of lorry at
the moment – I'm not sure what will be inside it but it might be the
Regimental Cook. If this is so my survival chances (which I will
estimate mathematically anon) rise perceptibly; don't worry about me
anyway – I don't anticipate any real danger for at least three or four
months.'

The Auxiliary Fire Service had been called up the day before
the official declaration of war and Pat found himself

'in a very happy party – a control room run by 3 WAFs, two fire
appliances manned by 9 of us (3 London Fire Brigade and 6 AFs)
and 3 boys as messengers. We had a thrill this morning [3
September]. At 11.40 the whine of sirens and we rushed to get
gas-mask, belt, axe, boots, waders and helmets. Then the final
instructions and out to our appliances to see the balloons go up –
then came the "all-clear". Apparently a single unknown aeroplane
was coming in over the Channel, and they took the necessary
precautions. It was an interesting sensation – extremely little fear but
the hell of a lot of excitement. Rather like the dressing room before
Twickenham Varsity Match.'

Later he was able to report that

'we are getting a little more settled now and we can arrange leave of
3 hours in every 20, but that of course means returning immediately
there's a warning. Yesterday I scrambled along to the top of a
building and in a cloudy but lovely sunset I could count 243 balloons
. . . The only criticism of all this is that it is not dangerous enough.
This may sound rather silly but I really feel very unhappy when I
think of Paul in constant danger while I sit here in reasonable
comfort, waiting for a raid which may not come, for bombs which
may land anywhere but in Euston, and then being fairly safe. And yet
I know I cannot change anything. I must register as a Pacifist but
when conscription comes in I may transfer myself to the RAMC.'

Pat's concern for Paul's safety was misplaced and premature.
Paul had answered his call-up instructions and reported to
Clare College, Cambridge, a city which seemed to be overflow-

ing with the RAF Volunteer Reserve being trained, and here his group

'received two severe blows – first that our commissions are apparently so far away that they're over the horizon and may not come for months . . . and secondly, and much more seriously, came the news that has crushed us. We had imagined in our inexperience of government departments, that our march from the station was merely an unpleasant interlude in an otherwise mechanical existence, and that we were going to leap into aeroplanes and learn to be hawk-eyed baby-killers. Of course, we should have known better; here we are after five years in the Officer Training Corps learning footdrill for 4 weeks or more. We aren't going to be allowed a sight of an aeroplane for at least 4 weeks. If I had an aeroplane I could enjoy everything and "rough it" happily but when you feel you're absolutely wasting your time every petty little restriction becomes more and more infuriating.

'However, I've now acclimatized myself, making my feet form four and my mind work out dialectical materialism. It seems incredible but I have honestly found myself on parade engaging in theological musings; the prospect of a not-so-far-distant meeting with the Almighty inevitably makes one think again of his existence, particularly as for the last 3 years I've been in some considerable mental and spiritual trouble in my indecision. However, belief or no belief, I'm following Pat's example and launching on Comparative Religion as a subject of outside interest, and who knows? perhaps I may emerge with a small nucleus of genuine belief.'

Beryl might describe Felthorpe as being 'wonderfully peaceful' but it had been turned into a receiving home for expectant mothers who would be moved to a nearby maternity home a week before the 'expected date'.

'However we know how these little things can change don't we, so the spare dressing room now has a special floor cloth, a bed made up with rubber sheet, cotton wool in rolls, an odd bundle of frightfully technical looking stuff called "surgical ligatures" which the nurse said we must have, and we're all ready except for Daddy who persists in asserting his inability to take in an "emergency".

'My "Hospital Supply Depot" is taking shape slowly tho' it's an awful nuisance having to scatter it all over Norwich instead of having it all under one roof.'

During a quietish first week of war at Marlborough, Doff
volunteered as a blood donor and arranged to use the cellars
as a babies' and children's air raid shelter. There were great
numbers of troops passing through the town and the greatest
problem seemed to be the disappearance of fish from the shops.
But this changed almost overnight.

'Marlborough has suddenly doubled its population and it's a bit
overwhelming. We've got the City of London School boys here. That
not being sufficient they've dumped 2400 soldiers on us. Goodness
knows where they're all billeted; in condemned houses, hotels,
barns, our pavilions, etc, etc . . . I've offered to take in some children
under 5.'

Helen had gone to Canada on a holiday trip with other girls
from Benenden School and was caught there when the war
started. In the circumstances, Dad invoked the help of a kindly
business colleague who offered her a home with them in
Rochester, New York until she could return to England or until
the war ended; all the family agreed with Dad's reluctance to
bring her back across the Atlantic so soon after the sinking of the
Athenia*.

For Helen it was initially

'all most thrilling and I hardly know whether I want to come home or
stay out here out of your way.'

It was a very difficult time for her; she wanted to come home,
but there was much to be said for going down to the Mabens in
Rochester.

'Mrs Maben brought me a mass of prospecti for the University of
Rochester and they really make the place sound wonderful. The
Eastman School of Music is the most stupendous place you ever
heard of . . . Is Clare going back to school?'

Clare was able to give Helen's 'love to everybody' because as a
fourteen-year-old she went back to school where so much of the

---

* Torpedoed on 3 September with the loss of 112 lives.

daily life was the same as before. But being in Kent added emphasis to new regulations and there was no escaping from the impact of war.

'Last night we had an air raid warning practice just to see that everything went off all right, and as far as I know it did. We have to be most frightfully careful about lights here, and there are ever so many regulations about not opening a window when the light's on, etc.'

And so, by the end of September the Budget had been firmly established and nearly every week for the next six years a copy was sent by Beryl to each member of the family.

Chris was right not to 'anticipate any real danger for at least 3 or 4 months' because for seven months the country was to be at war, but a war which unexpectedly brought little danger to anyone save those in the Navy and Merchant Navy. It was a long period of anti-climax which was finally ended by the disaster of Dunkirk.

During these months the Budget flourished, happily embracing the wider family of the Howarths who were to add greatly to the Budget; with their home in Darwin's old house in Downe (just southeast of London) they were on the direct bombing flight to London and were on the receiving end of countless air raids. The village was declared a 'neutral area' which had its compensations and Aunt Ellie wrote:

'Give me a neutral area for peace; very few cars, hardly any "hikers", no evacuees and no camps. With the petrol shortage we are beginning to feel more like the closely-united and self-sufficient unit that the village must have been a quarter of a century ago.'

Stephen was working at Hoare's Bank in Fleet Street, living partly in a flat in Charterhouse Square and partly at Downe. He was having to be on fire guard from 4.00 a.m. to 8.00 a.m. every morning.

David was in France by the end of September being, with Richard Dimbleby and two others, accredited BBC War Correspondents. In the words of the *Radio Times*:

'They wear uniform although they are strictly non-combatants, and rank as officers. Day by day they will tour the camps, the billets, up and down the line. Every day they will make their records which will be sent off by the fastest possible transport and broadcast here in the News. They will capture for us the authentic sounds of the Western Front, the voices of the men who are out there fighting.'

David described a normal day as being

'something like this – we meet at nine and set off on whatever story we have thought up. We spend the morning recording whatever it is – brigadiers and privates all seem to be equally tickled at the idea of doing a broadcast. We usually get home about 3, and spend an hour or two writing the links for the day's story and getting everything censored. Then in the evening we drive 30 miles to the nearest point by which we can send the stuff by land line to London, and after pottering back we plan for the next day, make records for the American radio people who are here, answer our fan mail (!) and write to you when we feel strong enough. Bed at one. It is hard work but healthy and full of interest.'

Among his recordings was one concert which was

'rather a nightmare. Noel Coward and Maurice Chevalier were both being very temperamental and quarrelsome and on their dignity. We had an awful session in the morning with Chevalier in bed in exotic pyjamas, saying that dear Noel was the greatest artist on the English stage, and Coward gesticulating in dark blue silk pyjamas and dressing gown to match with monograms all over it, and telling us how to run a broadcast, and the British army how to run the war. They are the most hypocritical, conceited, pansy pair of exhibitionists I ever want to meet.

'Dealing with Gracie Fields after that was a tremendous relief. I'm no particular fan, but she has certainly survived stardom without going a bit wrong in the head, as most of the stars I've met do. And with an audience of soldiers she's really remarkable. She makes use of their two main characteristics, a simple sense of humour and that extraordinary sentimentality and played on these so well that last night she had them roaring with laughter, and then within half a minute had genuine large wet tears roll down their manly faces! It was a great occasion.'

Interspersed with the recording of brigadiers and privates, of concert parties, church parades, Polish singers, and spelling bees were moments of excitement and drama; there were situations in which David was in some danger but during this odd period of the 'phoney' war nothing ever seemed to materialize.

'That morning we attended a small party at which Croix de Guerre were being given to some tanks, and in the afternoon Richard [Dimbleby] and I went up to the French advance posts south of the Moselle. This was a brand new experience for us. As we drove gaily along with French officers 4 miles – 3 miles – 2 miles – 1 mile from the German positions we went on looking unconcerned, each knowing that the other was getting more and more excited. Finally we got to a Company HQ which I think was as far as we were meant to go, but while the staff officers weren't looking the Company Commander shoved us in his car and drove off towards the East. We went through a wood which had been shelled (for no visible reason) the day before, through a deserted village and over a hill where a Frenchman said airily "They can see us for the next couple of hundred yards." Then into another wood and up to a barricade where the road had been mined. He said this wood was full of Germans every night, but that they went away or hid in the daytime.

'The French front line was along the edge of this wood, so we went down to it and peered out at the German lines about 200 yards away, across a field. There were a couple of German soldiers wandering about which didn't seem to worry the French – one gathered that it wasn't worthwhile to shoot at the Germans because a lot of other Germans would shoot back. Evidently the Germans thought the same – they could hardly have helped seeing the French – or us – if they had looked. Eventually two Frenchmen stood on a hill on the right and did get shot at but not hit (thank goodness). We were told that if we stayed put on the edge of the wood it was perfectly safe but if we walked a couple of yards forward, it wasn't. These are the rules of Tom Tiddler's Ground aren't they? But at night French and German patrols play a kind of hide and seek with hand grenades in that wood which is not my cup of tea, if I can help it. So we beat it when it began to get dark.

'The next day we spent in the Maginot Line. Although I'm used to mechanical gadgets of all sorts and sizes, I thought the whole thing was staggering, and though I'm no judge I should say it is absolutely impregnable. It's a pity it's not a bit longer, that's all.

'The next day was Strasbourg. I've often wondered what a deserted city would look like and it's just as eerie as I'd imagined, the more so because it's clean and tidy and completely undamaged, with all the stocks in the shop windows and the tables and chairs outside the cafes and not a living soul there except an old soldier and the cats which prowl in the most pitiful way. We stood and watched the Germans across the Rhine – 150 yards away perhaps – and nobody did anything about it. They were firing mortars across the river somewhere but anything warlike is done with an air of apology one feels.

'It is impossible to maintain a balanced judgment about the wrongs of the war out here. We are very much cut off from opinion through being so much pre-occupied with action. Although I still deplore the killing of a German as much as an Englishman, it is impossible, here at any rate, to avoid pleasure in any defeat of the other side, just as one takes sides in a game. I have absolutely no intellect left at present (if you will allow that I ever had any) but I'm not worrying because we're working very hard, and after all that's the best state to be in at present. If I had a day or two off I might be able to take stock a little, and I'd give ten quid for a day entirely by myself. But what is this war to worry about so far? The death rate has not gone up much yet, and there are no signs that the war on land will start before the spring. It may of course, but anything may have happened by the spring; the BEF wouldn't be surprised if it went home without losing a gun, I can assure you.'

Just before the Christmas rush of broadcasts – ten in a single day – David found that the time

'was very full of HM's visit, and the release of the news that there were British troops on the French part of the front. That meant a lot of rather fruitless chasing around in royal processions, and of course the journey to the Maginot Line and back. There was one rather exciting moment when the King was just about to inspect a guard of honour and they were standing at "the present" with me wearing my best salute, all by myself behind them. We suddenly heard an aeroplane coming from behind us which was the direction of Germany, a few miles away; so I and the troops had the peculiar experience of standing there without looking round, and watching the faces of the officers who could see it as it dived towards us. I could also see some French AA gunners ranging on it. In the end it took a good look and went away again. We never discovered who it was, but if it was a German it missed the best target ever; HM, all the French generals you ever heard of, lots of immobilized soldiers, and me.

'I can't tell you how foul the weather is here. It manages to contrive freezing hard with being damp. I suppose I am lucky not to be in a barn like Christopher and others, but our hometown is depressing enough. We all swear we will go a thousand miles to avoid coming through it again after the war.'

Christopher's view of the visit of HM the King was that of a gunner in the artillery and was rather different.

'He passed our way yesterday, inspecting one of the Regiment's gun-pits. We have one gun-pit which is ten times better than any other in the district, specially built for these absurd ceremonial "inspections", I've no doubt. All I know is, I was doing some ordinary routine road-mending with my fellow soldiers on Monday morning; we had paraded at 8.10 for the expedition and were still working at 1.15 having had only ½ hour's break. Just as we were settling down for dinner, up comes a despatch-rider with the command to return immediately home. So we tramp back 3 miles, dinnerless, to be greeted with the news that we must bolt our dinner and march immediately off to this gun-pit to make it fit for HM to inspect. So from 2.15 to dark we shovel farmyard mud out of the Royal Paths. It was pouring with rain and we were thoroughly bad-tempered. The gun-pit didn't even belong to our Battery, and we were by no means the only strangers working on it. If the King formed any impressions from his visit they must have been totally false ones – of mudless farmyards and waterless pits. It all seemed rather hypocritical and stupid.

'Then, by accident, I and a squad who were guarding the Corps ammunition dump saw the procession go by the next day. It was an amusing scene; the small French village turned out to a man, the schoolchildren rehearsing their high-pitched spontaneous cheer, the Mayor peering round the balcony of the "Mairie". But the camouflaged cars passed very quickly, before anyone had time to shout. I hardly recognized anyone, though I stared most at the three cars at the back marked "Press", but saw nothing of David's world-famous nose.

'The general attitude of the troops, including myself, was one of amused, amiable, apathy; any talk of "wild excitement" is propaganda. At least, that describes what I saw.'

At this early stage of the war Chris was almost certainly having the hardest time of anyone in the family, not because of the work or the discomfort but rather because he was the one above all who was not doing work for which he was qualified and which he would find emotionally satisfying.

There was a long delay in receiving his letters from France and the first was not received until 4 October. He apologized for the untidiness of the letter but

'My fountain pen doesn't like writing upside down – but the only chance of writing at all is to be on my back on straw in my billets and get all the light possible from a pocket torch on a bench behind me.

'While on convoy the nights were spent by the roadside – one just took one's blanket, greatcoat and groundsheet, tumbled into a convenient ditch and froze. There was never any water for washing or shaving and not even for drinking. Throughout the trip most of us never took off our boots or shirts.

'Army life would be impossible if one did nothing but work according to regulations and ate nothing but rations; in fact one quickly learns how to make the most uncomfortable circumstances tolerable. If ever you stop my lorry on the way I can always offer you "vin ordinaire" out of my water-bottle, bread and cheese, apples (some given by the French as we pass and some taken from a tree by the roadside) and innumerable cigarettes and sardines. In a comfortable lorry like mine even the longest journey is quite comfortable.'

And there were improvements to follow:

'My lorry is now the acme of comfort; just above my head is a long, roomy shelf, with another piece which hinges in front of it and can be padlocked to the roof. I know none of you will believe it but *I made it all myself*, or nearly all anyway. On it I put my mess-tin, dungarees, *New Statesman*, and anything else, and I've screwed down a box onto it in which I keep food, writing materials and books. So no matter where I am, or how long I have to wait, I can always occupy myself usefully. The shelf is unquestionably my "magnum opus" as far as carpentry goes.'

This display of practical ability rather surprised the family, who had never really envisaged Christopher as a gunner-driver;

to them it seemed a waste. It was therefore not altogether unexpected to hear from him that

'The job I'm on is, as you may well guess, quite absurdly unsuitable. It's not that I should be useful anywhere in the Army; that illusion has long since left me – if ever I harboured it; it's the fact that they've given me a job which calls for every one of the qualities I haven't got – especially mechanical ability, a taste for driving, a willingness to be ordered about capriciously and a capacity for applying myself diligently to matters of the smallest importance. In my present position, though I try my best, I am simply the answer to the enemy's prayer.'

Pat remembered well sharing a £5 car with Chris at Oxford and of all the family he was the most surprised to hear that

'a week or so ago I actually did a repair job on the road. It was just a trip to —— with the Quartermaster for stores, but halfway there the old lorry made suspicious noises and then stopped. Consternation in the driver's seat; quiet, expectant and misplaced confidence in the Quartermaster's. The family well knows my recipe for breakdowns; pause for 20 seconds, hoot loudly, pause another 20 seconds, pray briefly but vehemently and try the starter again. However something more elaborate was clearly called for on this occasion, so I cried "Petrol Feed", jumped for my tools, opened the bonnet (slight pause) and unscrewed the first nut to fit the spanner I happened to be holding. On this occasion it was a nut near the carburettor, and on unscrewing it I found a small piece of gauze, obviously meant to be a filter, filthy dirty. I cleaned it ostentatiously, screwed it back (twice of course, once without washer, once with), jumped back to the driver's seat, prayed, and pressed the starter. She WENT. You could have knocked me down with a feather. To this day I couldn't say whether it was the filter-cleaning or the praying that did the trick.'

There were some advantages in being a driver – you did not, for example, have to go and dig gun-pits, trenches and dug-outs in the 'front-line' – but it was work which involved Chris in very long hours of duty, did not require any particular intelligence and, happily, a

'change of job came just as the novelty of lorry-driving had begun to wear off.

'Now I add and subtract degrees, minutes and yards as a "GPO Ack". It is definitely a change for the better and suits me fine. Gunnery qua gunnery is most intriguing and I'm looking forward to knowing more anon. My job is to assist the GPO [Gun Position Officer] in giving the guns the proper line, range and angle of sight on the basis of information and directions from our observation post and the Battery's command Post. The important thing seems to be, to be accurate over calculation, to be impervious to other people's nerves and temper, and to keep the 6′2″ top of one's head from the beams of the dug-out (the first two of course being dependent on the third).

'I now live in our "forward" area which means a decided lowering of standards of comfort. Two-thirds of the Battery is crammed into a single set of farm buildings, in the middle of the flattest, dullest, most solitary stretch of ground imaginable. There is a large barn for eating in and for lectures or a concert; strikingly beautiful inside – simple, lofty, strong, well-proportioned, but a veritable draught factory and always freezing cold.

'Surprising to record, our spirits seem higher here if anything than at the base in the mining town. One feels more important next to the guns, on a possible battlefield.'

His life in France was of course not entirely confined to driving or GPO Ack work, to billets and the cold; all of these were dominant but there were many side lines and Christopher found himself conducting the Battery's male-voice choir ('picked, I suspect, because their buttons were clean'), editing the Battery magazine and producing rather scurrilous and very funny skits for Regimental concerts. He was also a member of the very good Surrey Yeomanry Rugby Team, but even on this subject he could not resist a passing criticism of the ridiculous.

'My old keenness for the game is coming back and we undoubtedly have a very promising team. One feature of our games which amuses me intensely is the way army discipline reaches even to a football field. You are "detailed" to play rugby just as you are detailed to clean up the cookhouse. At the appropriate time a sergeant cries "Fall in the football team" and you hastily fall in in threes and are transported to the ground. I thoroughly enjoy the game and wouldn't miss one for worlds, but I can't help wondering what would happen if I said I didn't want to play – court-martial no doubt. Then, on that hypothesis, if I played badly I could be court-martialled too. In fact if I disobeyed our excellent captain (an officer) and kicked when I was told to pass out, who knows but I might be called on to account for my mutinous play before a squad of brass-hats.'

Chris was the only member of the family in France and he received many parcels of food and clothing and books:

'Here are the recent arrivals; a magnificent "tuck-box" from the Master and Mistress of Marlborough.

'Another immense and succulent parcel last night from Norwich. Thank you ever so much and many thanks come from my room-mates also. Last night was spent with one hand clutching a bottle of red wine, the other a stoneless date, my pocket torch balanced on my chest, and *Back to Methuselah* propped against my knees, the whole being supported on my bed of straw; almost the "good life" in fact. Also there came the *New Statesman*, the *Spectator*, *Post* and Freud's *Psycho-pathology of Everyday Life* (special thanks bro' Paul). These weeklies really are a blessing. I stop my lorry in some outlandish spot, deposit my twelve tins of anti-gas ointment or sardines or something, open a *New Statesman* and am transported forthwith to the well-loved world of Bloomsbury-cum-Oxford Circus-cum Parliament Square.

'Then there was a second tuck-box from Marlborough College with a second helping of the Headmistress's inimitable cake.

'If an army really marches on its stomach, the Surrey Yeomanry will be unstoppable.'

Apart from enabling each one of us to keep right up to date with all the activities of the other members of the family, the Budget – simply through the speed of its delivery – made it possible to interchange ideas, protests, challenges, even anxieties. Raise some issue in a Budget and two weeks later one or more members will have joined in; Paul and Chris joined in anger on the subject of the Church and the Forces. Paul started it.

'On Friday, when we were all summoned together, a King's Messenger delivered and enlarged on the Bible as a source of comfort, but the Messenger (a Captain) was terrible to the point of blasphemy. After the first sentence I began to take notes and, at the

risk of boring everyone, here they are, rehashed; it must sound
fantastic but I can vouch for every single word, and when you
consider that it was delivered by a very educated Captain, endorsed
by our RAF Chaplain it may make you think how hypocritical the C
of E is being. After reading the message the man said "The value of
the Bible to an officer on active service is indeed very great, and
firstly it is because so much strategy can be learned from it." What a
reason for reading the Bible of all books. He went into details about
Israel's return which seemed to mix Zionism with British Israelism,
quoted Isaiah about "a haven of ships" to explain the building of
Haifa in 1932 (honest) and finally produced a gem. Moses on his
deathbed having spoken about "treasures in the sand" he used this to
argue that it was prophesied in the Bible that the British should build
the oil pipeline from Iraq to Haifa. I simply didn't believe my ears on
hearing a very questionable imperialist deal thrown at the feet of
God, but I swear on oath that it's true. He then hit me when I was
already prostrate in confusion by asserting that "The War Cabinet
consults the Bible about its strategy and troop movements" (picture
Winston) and without raising a giggle from anyone except me,
produced the most wonderful prophecy of the war. Somewhere in
Isaiah he found a passage about an alliance of Gomer, Ethiopia,
Libya, Gog and Magog being overthrown by the chosen race.
Ethiopia and Libya are obviously modern Italy, Gomer is thought "by
some people" to be the etymological origin of Germany while (I
swear that he said this) it is interesting to note that on cheap wooden
pencils made in Russia the trademark is "Gog". Voilà, our dirty little
war is a wonderful crusade, ordained by God with the agency of
pencil-manufacturers. Unfortunately, only by implication did he
assert the final heresy that we are the chosen people.'

This drew a reply from Chris:

'I was greatly amused by Paul's account of the King's Messenger's
sermon. No, Paul, we've had nothing like that so far; non-committal,
rather formal, semi-philosophical and very short (as we're standing,
sometimes in the rain) are our sermons. I agree wholly with you that
the King's Messenger's line was unpardonable. My chief complaint
about our Church Services is that the Army, far from retiring for a
few minutes, presses itself further and further into our thoughts and
actions – not from the point of view of the sentiments expressed in
hymns and sermons (though that's bad enough) so much as from that
of organization and ritual. We march in loudly (left-right-left-right

pick up the step there), the padre is marched in, Gestapo-like, by a
squad of officers (he looks out of place with a hope-I'm-not-
detaining-you air, I'm reminded rather of a mayor on a football field
for a ceremonial kick-off), and with military efficiency the "religious
fatigue" begins. The Sunday before last, just as we were about to sing
the first hymn a sergeant actually shouted "Properly at ease there".
Worse still, nobody seemed either shocked or amused by it, which
shows the atmosphere for the whole thing. I keep on expecting to be
told "On the command PRAY, all ranks will turn their thoughts
sharply heavenwards" or something like that. It's a disgraceful
travesty of Churchianity.'

Doff was able to join in:

'We had the Bishop of Southwark here this weekend . . . he also
wanted to know what sort of sermons the boys are getting so I
explained to him the attitude of the boys towards religion as best I
could, and then read him Paul's description of the King's Messenger.
Well, he'd just had an interview with all the Chaplains-General or
something, and had a few choice words to say about the RAF one, so
he pounced upon this description and asked if he might have a copy,
on the strict understanding that no names were mentioned. So I'm
letting him have one. I may do a service to the whole of the fighting
forces! This Bishop is frightfully "anti" polished buttons, etc for
Church parades and is trying to abolish same. So, my Bros., you may
have unwittingly done a great service to your fellow-countrymen.'

In a lighter vein Chris wrote describing food and drink:

'The keynote is simplicity; breakfast, lunch, tea and dinner are
served simultaneously, just as the convoy is about to move off and
consist of one tin of corned beef and two packets of army biscuits.
Simplicity for the caterer, yes, but what about the consumer? A
tremendous problem arises – how to divide the ten biscuits and the
one tin into the different meals. Often have I longed for Stephen's
advice on this point; what should I do, Stephen? Eat $\frac{1}{3}$ the meat and
$3\frac{1}{3}$ biscuits at each meal or have a symbolic biscuit at tea-time
leaving the beef and 3 biscuits each for the other three meals, or eat it
all at once, or throw it all into the ditch and starve?

Stephen, of course, replied.

'Having been addressed in print by Christopher I feel I should lash out myself, and first, I must tell you that high living is not at present in my line. Indeed since the war started there is no more than one outstanding meal in my memory, when I had a pheasant with a really excellent Château Lafite 1929 and some Taylors 1912 to follow, staying at Magdalen about a month ago.

'Apart from that I had a dozen oysters at the Constitutional Club on Wednesday, supporting Conservatism of course, but I always make a point of talking left-wing very loudly in that place. Otherwise life is a dreary round of Lyonses with income tax at either 7/6d in the £ or a £ in the 7/6d, it hardly seems to matter which, and beer about the price of whisky, and now one is doled out three minute and quite unsweetening lumps of sugar to a cup of coffee in the ABC that penury forces me to frequent.'

All Christopher's letters were of course being censored and Dad was worried that he was jeopardizing his chances of getting a commission by the strength of his criticisms of the Army. The sort of letter which gave substance to Dad's fears was written just before Christmas.

'It appears that my military career may be about to undergo a dramatic change. They've been going through the Battery for potential officers, and I was one of the many who were recommended: we were asked if we'd accept a commission if offered one. I decided I would. I joined the ranks originally for several good reasons but these reasons seem to have lost their force now. I shall have had at least four or five months experience in the ranks on active service; have performed all the humblest and most menial tasks the Army has to offer, not excluding potato-peeling, sweeping out the cookhouse and cleaning the latrines, and in general feel I've had a very good worm's-eye view of the Army.

'The only thing that made me hesitate was doubts about my military capacities. For there's no doubt about it family – I was never meant to be a soldier. Four strenuous months hasn't made the slightest difference. I dislike the life and spirit of the Army intensely. I'm not arguing that there's something wrong with the British Army qua army; perhaps it's the best possible spirit and organization compatible with its task of winning the war, though sometimes I doubt it. All I'm saying is, I loathe it. I loathe being told exactly when to get up, exactly what to wear, exactly how to fold my bed clothes and overcoat. I loathe people looking me up and down on parade, commenting on my boots, perhaps, or telling me I haven't shaved enough. I loathe being marched to my meals, my games, and even to my prayers. I loathe the attitude "it doesn't matter what you do as long as you all do it together" and the equally familiar expression "There are no excuses in the army". I loathe in general the army's mania for uniformity.'

With the family now widely dispersed, Beryl immediately undertook major Red Cross responsibilities in Norwich. At the same time she worked hard to hold the family together and to keep Felthorpe as a well-loved home to which from time to time we could so happily return. We could all visualize the new Felthorpe scene, even when she wrote:

'Well, well, the Horrors of War have arrived even at Felthorpe at last, and on Sunday I dug out the old bicycle, pumped it up with much sweat of my brow, and pedalled off to church. I might add that it rained hard and I had to pray on exceedingly wet knees; however virtue was rewarded and no rheumatism has resulted.

'This morning I made a tour (a bicycle one so thank goodness the village is not more straggly than it is) of my evacuees. The dirty heads are clearing up, no one else has caught the infection, and everyone seemed happy so it was quite a cheery morning.'

And always there was that very special feeling of coming home to a Felthorpe welcome:

'On Friday I spent most of the morning getting the house really gay with flowers, michaelmas, chrysanthemums, a dahlia or two and an odd "last rose of summer" still blooming; I quite enjoyed the change. Then I hopped into Norwich for a few bits of fatted calf. Visited our biggest Working Party, patted them all on the head, thanked Heaven (not audibly) I was only there to talk and not to sew, and betook myself to Thorpe to meet Pat and Paul. Pat had said he might have to come in uniform so I leaned on the barrier looking for a trim figure (quite incredibly handsome in navy blue with lots of bright buttons and a most becoming cap) but far along the platform came two ruffians – head and shoulders above the crowd – quite unmistakable half a mile away tho' Paul had produced a grey cap from somewhere and was chewing his pipe which Pat has told you is an extraordinary sight; I don't know why, it just is.

'We got home, had a hasty cup of tea and sallied forth armed to the teeth to chase the wily Felthorpe covey of partridge from its lair. There were no fewer than 3 coveys on the stubble by Clark's cottage and we got in reach of one. Then we walked through the woods towards the lodge for pigeons and finished up in Mill Hill. Total bag was 3 pigeons, 2 partridges, 1 pheasant and a rat.'

By mid-October the day had come when Beryl had to take her Red Cross exam:

'I think, I *think*, I've got thro'. First he told me to bandage a fractured fore-arm; my brain was a complete blank after those committees, but it was alright except that I tied the man's thumb in when it should have been left out. Then I sat down at his desk and he said "What are the signs of fainting?" Visions of Guides at Church parades rose before my eyes and I said the face would be pale and the skin cold. "What would you do?" Visions again of unbuckling belts, removing ties, and I translated this into the technical "Loosen any tight clothing, see that they have plenty of air, etc." and he seemed satisfied. "The signs of haemorrhage" thank heaven had been learned off by heart and came back to me but the last was a beast. "What antidote would you use for ammonia in the eye?" "But ammonia's a corrosive" I said weakly and only just stopped myself from adding "don't give an emetic". "Yes, Yes," he said kindly "but is it an acid or an alkali?" Well heaven knew that, I didn't. I told him to get the patient to open his eye in a basin of lukewarm water, then put in a drop of castor oil, bandage the eye and take to a Doctor but still he wanted to know what I'd put in the water. "Boracic Acid" said I, burning my boats. He heaved a heavy sigh of relief, which I think meant "thank God the woman's guessed right", smiled upon me and bade me go. There were such lots of things I could have told him, all the names of his bones, where to stop bleeding – oh, masses of things, but whoever heard of anyone getting ammonia in the eye?'

On another occasion Beryl found 'how useful one's Guide training can be, and how unexpectedly it comes in'.

'The two new mothers arrived from the other side of the country one afternoon when I had to be in Norwich, so I did not see the five children that they brought with them. They seemed decent enough people so just imagine what I felt like when the school teacher sent up a note on Friday evening to say the school nurse had been to inspect that afternoon and all the new lots' heads were bad, two of them crawling. My heart descended into my boots, but it was clear that if the infection was in this house too it would have to be dealt with and nothing short of "head inspection" by me would meet the case. I decided in my own mind that I'd have to stick to a demand to see for myself no matter what protests were made, but luckily, tho' rather upset, they were both perfectly amenable, so armed with an old comb, a bowl of Dettol and a strong light, I carried through the hunt – and drew a blank.

'Next day I got all the paraphernalia out from Norwich and the young came up from their billets to be coped with by their respective Mamas – the house reeked a bit with the oil you have to use – but anyway it was a reassuring stink.'

Both Dad and Beryl were involved in every aspect of the work of the Red Cross.

'When I got home about 6 I found the Red Cross had been chasing Dad all the afternoon (without success) to report 38 men landed at Yarmouth from the *Willowpool*. It was too late to do much that night beyond making sure people there were looking after them, but we got to Yarmouth at 9 next morning to see what the Red Cross was doing and could do. It was all most interesting. The "Shipwrecked Mariners" have a house on South Quay which is usually used for rest and recreation and here we found most of the *Willowpool* men, and a few from previous wrecks; they had been fitted out with clothes and railway warrants by the "Shipwrecked Mariners" and were leaving for their homes, mostly in S. Wales. The *W.* struck a mine which practically cut her in half, mercifully all the men got to their boats and after a 3 hour row reached a lightship; from here the lifeboat was telephoned for, and fetched them into Yarmouth. They are incredibly cheerful and determined to get to sea again! At the Hospital we found the ones who had been hurt, also a ward of about 25 soldiers from a neighbouring camp. While we were there 3 more men were brought in from another wreck, absolutely frozen, one was being "thawed" with a kind of cradle over him (under the bedclothes) fitted with electric lamps.

'Dad interviewed all the people in charge of the three places and then got busy to fill in gaps with things not provided by other Societies. We went to Boots and got little spongebags fitted up with comb, soap, toothbrush, paste etc. for each man. A shoe shop for a supply of slippers to each Home, a gift of towels and pillowcases to one Home as their supply was inadequate, and, of course, cigarettes all round. The sea was a dirty grey and looked too beastly, there was a bitterly cold NE wind and I was devoutly thankful that Helen was hundreds of miles inland.'

On that day Helen was in bed recovering from a cold. She had been having a very full life, with a fair blend of entertainment mixed in with a lot of hard work at the University of Rochester, which earned her a letter from the Dean.

'Dear Helen,
   'We are glad to be able to congratulate you on your excellent average for this semester. Your name has been put on the Dean's List which is an academic honour of which you can be very proud indeed. We hope that you will maintain this good academic standing throughout your college course.'

   But all the time there was a deep longing to get home.

   'You [Dad] suggested my staying out here for two or three terms but honestly – I don't think I could do it, and unless there is a particular reason why you don't want me home, I dreadfully badly want to get back by Christmas.'

   But the decision was taken that it would be better if Helen stayed in America and she gained a lot of comfort from the thought that Paul was likely to be sent to Canada for training.

   'I hope Paul does come out to Canada, it would be a terrific thrill, but the only drawback is that they are sending several of the boys over to Vancouver. Take care that you stay in Toronto, brother.'

At the end of October Paul was still in Cambridge and although he had managed to pass through the deep frustration of not being given an opportunity to fly, he was nevertheless bored and sometimes depressed.

'I am still in Cambridge. That makes six weeks that I've twiddled my thumbs in this old-world town, and tempers are beginning to get frayed, but curiously enough your little discontented Paul is perfectly happy. About three weeks ago I felt very bored but I am now past boredom, much as a cow must feel after 12 hours of chewing the cud, and the heavy blanket of entirely indifferent contentment has descended on me. The days seem to slip by fast enough and as I point out to everybody a week here is a week less in France, and probably a week more of existence. In fact, since my air-efficiency is so staggeringly low, I've come to the conclusion that I may be here for weeks more, but it's all in the lap of the Air Ministry and I'm content to leave it there. When I'm told to go somewhere, I shall go, and there's an end to it. My colleagues, however, are simply furious. Keen, eager air-aces to a man, they're simply itching to patrol the Rhine and no amount of persuasion will convince them that Cambridge is altogether pleasanter. Linked with this enthusiasm goes the most remarkable and rather unthinking self-confidence. Every officer here seems to picture himself coming out of the war alive, and indeed demobilization and its aftermath is one of the main topics of conversation. I, on the other hand, am convinced that if the war lasts more than 18 months I shall be a casualty (but really quite unscared by the prospect) but when I suggest that only about 10% of us here would survive a 5-year war I'm laughed to scorn. They may be right, but I fear they're only trying to bluff themselves.

'I've been to see *Dawn Patrol* again. It's full of beautiful heroics, but through it all runs the absolute imbecility of war. As soon as I begin to think I get depressed; it's not that I'm personally afraid of death – I'm not, and only a bit scared of dying. Personally I'm in as good a position as anyone, I haven't any overwhelming attachment to life, and coming from a large family I don't know any hearts that will break over my departure. But all this doesn't bring one peace of mind. I'm simply overwhelmed by the stupidity of man in throwing to the winds everything that might be great and glorious in their world and instead indulging in thoughtless and hopeless self-destruction. More particularly, I know I'm in the wrong place myself; emotionally and logically I am convinced that war is not and never can be morally right or in any way advantageous, and that whatever other people may think, I should personally in no way support it. And yet it all comes back to the plain fact that I haven't the guts to do anything about it. It doesn't need courage to fight, it does require courage to resign your commission in war-time (it's probably impossible anyway). I'm not content to drift through this war "doing my duty" and I can't see any real mental contentment for me before peace and/or death, but the alternative is just too much for me to face and I'm afraid that disillusioned drifting is to be my fate. I know well enough that I've wasted what few years of discretion I've had so far, and I'm going to waste the few that remain. Taken all round, rather a failure of a life, whose loss will not be very great. But I can't pretend I'm very happy these days.'

But everything began to change for the better when, in mid-November, he was posted to the RAF College at Cranwell.

'Canada is now out of the question, I think, and I shall stay here for four months, which will finish my training except perhaps for a little gunnery practice. Of these four months two will be "intermediate" training and two "advanced". My total flying hours will probably come to only about 150.

'Otherwise – it's good. In an interview with the Chief Flying Instructor we were asked whether we wanted to fly single or twin-engined machines. I put in a very strong plea for single, and temporarily succeeded. I shall fly Hawker Harts and very light fighter-bombers, with a maximum speed of 160–170 m.p.h. Provided I'm not transferred soon I shall remain on single-engined machines for ever, i.e. my active service will be reconnaissance (suicide), dive-bombing (dangerous but exciting) or my beloved Spitfire. This is very pleasant as they are all admirably moral, the first two only being used for military objectives, so pray that I don't get transferred.

'I thrive. With a) peace and b) summer this would be almost the greatest life on earth. One does about 1½ hours flying sometime in the day, and some good mental work the rest of the time.

'We are right in the wilds here. The nearest town is Sleaford, but it's a dim, dirty and dull little borough 7 miles away; consequently one lives very much on the premises. Yesterday we got off at noon and feeling rather fat and sleek I walked there; on the way five people offered me lifts, which was rather comforting but I steadfastly refused them and walked. There was a half-gale sweeping across the flats, a few specks of rain, a deserted road, bare trees and a generally sombre appearance and I simply loved it. Downwind starlings flashed past at about 70 m.p.h., my hair got typhoon tossed, my feet got sore, the clouds simply raced across a leaden sky and I felt very good. Arrived in Sleaford I bought some presentable cigarettes, had a bad tea in front of a roaring hotel fire, and took a bus back, with my lungs blown out with air, my feet beautifully tired and my whole being longing for a hot bath.'

In all ways Paul's outlook was beginning to become more positive. After a few days' leave at Felthorpe he wrote:

'The journey back lasted a very long time, 4½ hours for 90 miles. But it was very peaceful and the buffet at Ely was open. Whenever I travel by train now it's almost inevitably in the blackout and I've found that I'm perfectly happy sitting in the dark and thinking. Yesterday I realized how pleased I was really to be earning my own living. I grant you it's fantastically exceptional (I might almost be said to be earning my own death) but nevertheless I do like to think that I've ceased temporarily to be a mere dead-weight on Father and can now support myself through all possible situations. In many respects I think it is this that makes me reluctant to return to Oxford if it's a short war. I loved last year more than any other in my life – a large circle of very good friends, a lot of interesting and stimulating mental work, the right amount of physical exercise, a delightful irresponsibility, good music, fairly intellectual conversation on tap, the Union, and round everything the indescribable and inimitable atmosphere of Oxford. Yet now that I have launched out into the world with a vengeance I can't really conceive going back there unless the war ends in a month.'

But now that he was at Cranwell there was the joy of flying, and especially of aerobatics.

'There are some funny sensations at times, such as hanging perhaps 6″ out of the cockpit with all your weight on your straps in the middle of a roll, while your feet suddenly try to leave the rudder bar and kick you on the chin. Strangely enough I find it more than enjoyable, particularly when you're up solo and can climb off on your own somewhere to about 5000 feet and think there's nobody within a mile of you in any direction, and there's just you and the sun and the blue sky, with a really powerful machine under your control and simply asking to be thrown about the sky. A loop or two to start with because they're peaceful and easy, and then anything you can think of. Oh, if only there wasn't a war on at the end of it all, I should simply love it.

'On the assumption that one's not a good horseman till one's fallen off, nor a good yachtsman till one's capsized, I may now be on the way to be a good pilot; I didn't crash, but I feel rather ashamed of myself. Here's the whole epic: –

'I was sent up solo at 9.00 a.m. to do 1½ hours aerobatics, steep turns, forced landings etc just round the aerodrome. Now, to start my excuse, I must say that I have never done any more practical navigation than local map-reading (no cross-countries or anything) and that the weather conditions were poor, with clouds about 2500–3000 ft and a fairly heavy mist that restricted visibility to 1 mile at most. Anyway, I took off, and found that the clouds were too low for aerobatics; this rather damped my enthusiasm so I did some steep turns, practised forced landing approaches in pleasant-looking fields, and generally fooled around. Twenty minutes later I found myself in an unknown part of the country. This wasn't very worrying as I knew I couldn't be far away so I started going round in large circles till I found something identifiable. Eventually I found myself over a town which I guessed (rightly) to be Grantham from its very large railway station and aerodrome. Now comes the really shame-worthy part: I have never been to Grantham before and had never even looked at a decent map of Lincolnshire (Grantham being 18 miles away) so I had simply no idea how to get back. However, I seemed to remember hearing that the bearing from Grantham to Cranwell was 220° so realising that I was faced with a mapless "cross-country" I set off. Actually there was a map in the cockpit, but it was prominently marked "for use in emergency only" and being over Grantham was scarcely an emergency, so I didn't use it. I have never tried to fly a compass course before and had no idea of the wind speed, but I didn't do too badly. After a quarter of an hour when I should have been past Cranwell there was still the interminable sameness of Lincoln below me. By now I was really cold; like a fool I had left off my "teddy-bear" and my fur boots and I was gradually freezing. Moreover I was beginning to wonder just how large a field must be before an inexperienced pilot could get into it successfully; in fact life was looking moderately gloomy. I was very cold and visibility was no better when I saw a simply enormous town, so I whipped out the map, and found that to have a chance of identifying it I should have

a)   to fly immediately above it risking balloon barrages and AA
b)   to fly at about 1000 ft, this being ultra-illegal.

'So, with my heart in my boots I did both and by means of canals and railway lines decided that it was Leicester of all places. Then I realised that 220° was not the bearing from Grantham to Cranwell, but from Cranwell to Grantham. So, with an utter disregard for the law, but an urgent desire not to lose myself, I got home by map-reading and following the railway lines, and by pushing the little lady along did 48 miles in under 20 minutes to get home 5 minutes overdue. I reported with my tail between my legs, only to discover that instead of being a darned fool for getting lost, I was a blessed hero for finding my way back.'

Paul expressed concern about Christmas at Felthorpe because 'Here I am, a disloyal officer returning for ten days leave and feeling more and more civilian with every hour that passes, and lo and behold, a complete Major-General is sprung on me to share my festivities'. Beryl had written:

'The "Major-General" [General Sir Bernard Paget] who has begun to crop up in various letters is a Paget cousin. Dad found him, or remembered him, I forget which, and wrote to ask his good advice when Pat wanted to leave the AFS and join the RAMC. Now, most curious, he's been sent to Norwich to command the 18th Division and is staying at the Royal Hotel. Complete with his wife [also a Paget by birth] he came to lunch on Sunday and proved quite unorthodox and most charming; they are coming to stay a week at Christmas with Julian, aged 19, now putting in a year at Christchurch, and another lad of 15. It seemed too cruel to leave them stuck in the Royal over Christmas as they all have country tastes and hate towns, and if the first week is a success, we hope that anyway the boys will stay on for the holidays.'

It was a huge success and everyone was delighted with the 'discovery' of the Pagets. Paul wrote:

'The Pagets are good fun, particularly the Major-General who is simply charming, entirely unorthodox, and the most level-headed man I have ever met. The males of the family have taken to late arm-chair discussions which are normally unknown at Felthorpe simply for the pleasure of hearing him talk, and if his colleagues were like him I should have no fear either of the conduct of this war or the settlement afterwards.'

However, overall he found Christmas to be

'a sorry festival, with only half the family here, and no Howarths; the house seemed terribly empty – no Christopher cracks, no Helen laughs, not even a Heywood kiss, and we missed you all terribly. If we all survive this muck, a real family reunion is called for.

'Pat has now returned to Hants and he knows not what. He's got a hacking cough, and a uniform, but in spite of it all seems fairly happy, though he'd like to know what's in store for him. His favourite game now, after a week's intensive training, is to make sweeping generalizations about the Service mind. It makes me feel quite a veteran.'

Within a matter of weeks from the start of the war, and in the absence of the expected air raids, there was a reaction against all the defence forces, with a newspaper headline about 'Patriotism at £3 a week', and Judge Metcalfe sending a man to prison with the remark that 'there are too many Auxiliary Firemen anyhow'. There seemed a reasonable chance that many of the sub-stations would be disbanded and that Pat would be unemployed. As he already felt that his effort could not be compared with that of his brothers he began to think in terms of joining the Royal Army Medical Corps. But there were still some very satisfying experiences in the AFS.

'At 1.01 this afternoon I sat down to lunch.

'At 1.02 this afternoon I left my lunch and rushed to my trailer for the bells went down and business was on. Two trailer pumps were ordered to go to a fire up the top of York Road, by King's Cross and Mayhew found himself and his crew roaring down the Euston Road with one of our resident firemen (LFB) in charge – demotion for Mayhew but as it was my first fire I was completely satisfied. Besides, have you ever been in a car with complete priority? It is really most gratifying and exhilarating – we roared down the Euston Road and in the distance we could see a pall of smoke which meant that at least it was not a false alarm. As we came closer it was clear that it was a decent-sized fire for to the naked eye there were 6 trailer pumps and 3 LFB appliances already in the road.

'We drew up and Arthur (our LFB man) went in search of the officer-in-charge. He found him and we went along to man a branch (nozzle to you). We were in a yard about 20 yards by 7 facing a 4-storey warehouse. There were an incredible number of hoses lying around and we were wading about in 4 or 5 inches of water. The first floor was well alight and there was plenty of flame and smoke; each floor was slowly collapsing.

'We went in at a doorway on the ground floor and were about 4 yards in the building directing our hose on to the roof or ceiling and on to some packing cases. It is a great feeling of power you get by knocking over a packing case by sheer water-pressure. There was a considerable danger of the ceiling falling in on us, which all added to the excitement.

'We were just in the middle of it all when news of an air-raid came through. There had been no general alarm; just a private LFB and AFS alarm. We had to get our gas masks and generally prepare ourselves, but as the fire was dying down the powers that be decided to send back all but the bare minimum.

'So we returned. There are some highlights I remember – working next to a leaking hose with water pouring down my coat – water streaming down the back of my neck – water coming through the ceiling above at so hot a temperature that one had to move from under it, great fun, and worth weeks of training.

'Then Dad came in and we showed him round, discussed everything, and managed to get off for tea. Very pleasant to see him, and secretly he was longing for another fire, to see us off and to follow. It was all very good fun and I now feel a veteran.'

By the middle of November Pat had made his decision.

'I intend at 11.15 this morning to resign from the AFS. Actually I will give a fortnight's notice, but as far as I can remember I signed no contract and should therefore be able to quit.

'But enough of this. A great pal of mine came up before the Bristol CO Tribunal on Friday last and was registered unconditionally within 3½ minutes. It cannot have been very difficult for the judges because he is a registered member of the Society of Friends and has been a member of the Peace Pledge Union for 2½ years. But he was able to get some amusing (?) statistics out of the *Peace News* which he saw there: –

> Up to Nov. 1st there were registered
> unconditionally as COs:
> In Manchester, 6 cases out of about 70
> In Bristol, 49 cases out of about 80
> In London, 0 cases out of 90.

'Rather odd. On his tribunal sat a quaker and two other very open-minded people and the result compares favourably/ unfavourably (strike out to taste) with Judge Hargreaves of London whose latest pearl of wisdom is "Even God is not a pacifist for he kills us all in the end."'

On 9 December Pat registered at the Norwich Labour Exchange as a conscientious objector. He had not been looking forward to this

'because for the first time in my life I will be publicly entering an unfashionable minority; also I have been to quite a number of Labour exchanges in my life and without exception they depress me. Being a Paget however I have that appalling love of argument for argument's sake and therefore I think the tribunal might be quite good fun. The only difficulty being that I'm not an extremist – I believe in euthanasia, and if I saw a man on top of Selfridges about to drop a bomb into a crowd of shoppers, and if I were on the top of the Marble Arch, and if I had a rifle with telescopic sights (rather improbable all this!), I would shoot to kill – showing a profound lack of faith in the power of prayer. Does this mean that I should fight in a war? Judge Hargreaves will say "yes" and I will say "no" and we'll be off. (His latest "But you find in the Book of Revelations that God ordered a war in heaven".)

'I called at the Norwich Labour Exchange – a very definite improvement on the normal London one; it is not so dirty, it is better shaped, and it is pleasantly arranged into "booths" so that by lining up and waiting you cannot miss your turn. My turn soon came and feeling rather miserable I informed the man that I wished to register as a CO; this was apparently not his job so they shuffled me along to the end booth where another man took charge. It all seemed quite simple, as far as I could see the only difference was that my particulars were taken down on a blue card while the normal was a yellow (I'm surprised Ernie Brown [Minister of Labour] hasn't changed this round!). In the end they gave me a card which registers me as a CO for 14 days, in which time I have to apply to the local tribunal to have my case heard. And so I left the LE and everything looked lovely, the fresh air through your hair, the shoot in the afternoon, the hunger, and above all a wonderful sense of mental peace. Life was really settled again and I am glad that I am now publicly classified with the pacifists. On Tuesday I am to report at our local RAMC centre for a medical examination and enlistment.'

Pat did not in the result appear before a tribunal; he later received a letter:

'with reference to your application for registration as a Conscientious Objector.

'I am to inform you that, since you are already a member of the Armed Forces of the Crown, it is not possible to proceed with your application . . .

'I have however to draw your attention to the undertaking recently given in the House of Commons by the Secretary of State for War, that a man who volunteers for service in the RAMC and intimates that he has a conscientious objection to combatant service, will not be required to undertake such service.

I am, Sir, . . .'

'It's 5.20 on Tuesday Dec. 12th – the last occasion during this war that you will receive a letter from your civilian brother, cousin, nephew, uncle, etc. Today I presented myself at our local recruiting office and was seen to straight away and asked my name. I gave it and it was put down three times and I was passed on to the Ministry of Labour representative who put my name down six times. Upstairs for a medical examination. I had to wait a few moments but when once the medical trip started I take my hat off to the Army for their efficiency; you passed from one cubby-hole to another with a different doctor testing different parts of you in each. In No. 2 I was asked why I was joining the RAMC and my plea of being a CO was greeted by "well, we are all entitled to our opinions – I hate war but we've got to fight." I didn't answer for there is none. In No. 5 I was asked why I was going into the RAMC and my revelation of c/o'ism was greeted by the remark "good man" and he then went into a long quotation from a book discussing the deliberate insularity of pacifists.

'And so I passed from the medical to the enlistment where a dear old sergeant accepted my being a CO very well, and so on, until the very last fence with everything going perfectly, we got to the oath.

'Now I don't object to the King and no one told me in what way I was compelled to "defend His Majesty, his heirs and successors, in person, crown and dignity against all enemies." But the wretched oath then goes on "and obey – the Generals and officers set over me". Well in the normal course of events I'd obey, but I'm not prepared to be transferred to a combatant unit even if the King says so himself. This I pointed out and found a hornet's nest; they could not guarantee me no transfer and I didn't think I should pretend to obey what I had no intention of obeying, so they said they would write to the War Office (!) and I went to lunch. Here I met Dad and B. who seemed to attach no importance whatsoever to an oath and could see nothing dishonest in taking it. They were so convinced as to the pettiness and futility of worrying about signing anything that I went back after lunch and duly got fixed up. It will add perjury to my many other crimes, but that doesn't seem to matter nowadays.

'And so I joined up, as disloyal and protestant a member of His Majesty's Service as is likely to be found. I depart tomorrow for the central RAMC Training Depot at Crookham, Nr. Fleet, Hants – I only hope it's not too dead-alive.'

Later he wrote:

'I have been quite staggered by the extraordinary friendliness of the other privates; we are all here at the will of the Government and very few indeed are at all interested in the war or the politics of the war. There is none of this bogus sentimentality that is nowadays lavished upon soldiers and the general atmosphere is extremely healthy – I am encouraged by the cheerfulness and the patriotic apathy of the group.

'At tea-time I was sent, as C of E, to see my "padre" – a pleasant enough man but wearing that blasphemous union of the clerical collar and the battledress. His speech was worthy of his uniform, being an atrocious mixture of religion and army – which I believe to be almost impossible. For example "I always say that a good soldier needs the same qualities as those of the good Christian – The Grace of God, the guts of Jesus Christ, and the gumption of the Holy Ghost." He gave the impression of regarding religion as the best means of stopping knee-knocking while under fire.'

Pat was able to get home for three days at Christmas and was able 'to heartily recommend the Bernard Pagets, they are eminently worthwhile'.

Doff and George spent Christmas at Marlborough.

It had not been an easy first term of war. George had been extremely busy with the two schools, and Doff had had to continue to be a hostess, mother and housewife in a large official house under ever-increasing difficulties.

'This week has been much the same, boys to dinner, boys to tea, boys to gramophone-concerts, in fact nothing but boys, with an interlude for a sherry-party.

'We're going to have a fearful day tomorrow – it starts tonight really with a dinner party for six rather sticky people.

'This weekend we've had staying with us one Dr Bailey (late Public Orator of Oxford) who is one of the judges sitting on the Bristol tribunal. He told us that they decided beforehand that they would never argue with the objector's point of view, and they only wanted him to prove to them that he was genuine in his belief.

'Tomorrow we've got the Bishop of Dover and his wife coming for three nights and I was only informed this morning. I was only allowed 2 lbs of butter this week instead of my usual 6 – what a life.'

The difficulties were mostly connected with staff and food:

'I trot down town every day and haggle with the grocer over butter and bacon, of which there's a definite shortage. Are the troops eating a prodigious amount of bacon these days? I'm unable to find any in Marlborough this week, and the butter's lousy and the meat expensive.

'I've asked the German refugees to come in to dinner on Christmas night as I want to try and give them a traditional Christmas with a tree, turkey and carols. It's one of the many things I have to thank the parents for, the knowledge of what Christmas really ought to be. It's going to be done exactly the same for Susan for as long as I can manage it' –

an undertaking which, no matter how great the difficulties, was kept throughout the war.

The first six months of the war was a period of anti-climax; and there was a general feeling of boredom and frustration running through the civilian population and the Services. This was reflected in some of the family letters. Doff wrote:

'Oh, I wish the war was over – I wonder when we're going to do something, it makes me mad all this reconnaissance business, we lose planes and men and they must know most of Germany backwards; – that's a stupid remark but I'm feeling like it. War's so utterly and completely futile, it accomplishes nothing and it's a sheer waste of life. Personally I don't believe the world will be a better place when it's over; Hitler may be destroyed but there'll always be someone else,

and so we shall go on. Every generation for the past 4 has been
through a war, and I'm jiggered if I'm going to produce children
who'll have to go through another.'

Christopher wrote:

'But as for any news – the trouble is, I'm now so much in a rut that
I can't even appreciate and describe the peculiarities of my everyday
life; for after six months in the BEF life is ceasing to seem peculiar at
all. Surely it's perfectly natural that 35 men should live together in a
cowshed? and that they should have less living-space relative to their
numbers than the pigs in the building opposite? Surely "homo
sapiens" must by his very nature, eat standing up and sleep on straw?
Surely button polishing is creative work of great importance? Surely
order is finer than freedom, alcohol than art, receptiveness than
curiosity and a clean uniform than a pure heart?'

The peculiarity of this 'phoney' war was commented upon by
Helen from America.

'I had a letter from a friend of mine who has just left Benenden
and she pointed out that there was really practically nothing going on
at home and that life is running a pretty normal course.'

But although, as Helen wrote, life was running a pretty
normal course, it was not an easy winter for anyone; it was one of
the coldest for many years. The New Year saw the introduction
of rationing and the issue of ration books. As from 8 January
each person was entitled to

> 4 ounces per week of Ham/Bacon
> 12 ounces per week of Sugar
> 2 ounces per week of Butter

In March meat rationing was brought in and there was a weekly
entitlement to 1/1d or 1/2d (6p) worth of meat per head.
Clare wrote from Benenden that

'It may interest you to know what we are doing. Bacon – we are
having it ordinarily, and those who like it can have almost as much as
they like because very few people do like it. Sugar is just put on the
table and we are left to our own discretion how we share it out. Butter

is the most complicated, margarine is always on the table and we are allowed as much as we like; so far we have each had a small pat of butter put on our plate, but this I believe is going to be changed; each person is allowed three pats a day and at each meal there are going to be several pieces on a plate, so that we can eat our three pieces how and when we like.'

Beryl wrote that

'all the papers have letters about telling the Neutrals England is not starving yet, so Helen please note and spread it abroad that I've just had an egg and a rasher of bacon for breakfast, butter on my bread and a lump of sugar in my coffee. The making of large damp chocolate cakes to send to Pat is a little more difficult.'

Pat had written from France:

'Six of us have formed a sort of tea-club! We are tired of tinned salmon and no jam, so we buy French bread and jam, etc. Could you therefore in future parcels concentrate solely on jams, pastes, biscuits, etc? They'd be highly appreciated. If rationing can take it can anyone make me a slightly-damp, plain, chocolate cake – no icing and damp.'

A few weeks earlier he had written:

'Family, it is La Belle France for Pat, and what a hectic piece of muddlery by the Army! Here's the story.
'On Saturday my particular job was dry-scrubbing my dormitory and this I was doing with just sufficient effort to pass army scrutiny when a corporal walked in and said "Do you want to go away?" I said "To France?" – he said he didn't know where, so I said I didn't want to go away and went on with my scrubbing. Now it so happened that I had to change my gym shoes at the stores and had been told to go up that morning, so at 9.45 I wandered up that way – almost entirely because I was tired of dry-scrubbing – and I duly had to pass the Orderly Office. As I went by I was hailed by a raucous "Hey, you" and scenting the manner of our sergeant I duly halted and signified the fact that I had heard. He then said "are you a Nursing Orderly?" Well, I didn't want to be a nursing orderly proper but a stretcher-bearer and as I had only been in the RAMC three weeks I replied rather cautiously that I was being trained as a NO but he leapt

at it with a "Thank God, you'll do; join that party over there". I found
that I was being posted to a Field Ambulance. Well, at 9.45 I was
dry-scrubbing and at 10.45 I was in a lorry bound for Fleet and then
by train to Newbury. Quick work!'

Pat joined the 145th Field Ambulance and very shortly
afterwards sailed to France. He was on the baggage party and
found to his surprise that

'It was a real blessing for there were only about 30 pieces to move –
all very heavy but soon finished, and it carried with it the infinite
pleasure of reserved seats as we had to travel together. The result was
that we travelled to the port, six of us in a first-class carriage! The
voyage over was rather less fun because it consisted so largely of
waiting; it was 4 hours on board before we moved and then we waited
six more hours for dark and escort, and it was rather gloomy. I got a
lucky berth on top of the baggage which was comparatively
comfortable but quite incredibly cold. I slept about 3 hours that night
but time and again I had to get up and walk about because my feet
became really painfully cold. The unloading of the baggage was pure
agony as we had to carry it all up instead of down; however,
eventually we got it all off the boat, then a shortish train journey and a
great victory for the baggage party for while we went by lorry with the
baggage, the others had a 4-mile march at the end of a tiring day.'

In due course the Field Ambulance settled into a small mining
village outside Henin-Lietard, the troops being billeted in the
local cinema. Pat soon became very involved in running a
canteen with one other-rank colleague, and being responsible
for creating and training – with the officer-captain – a Unit
rugger XV. It was a peaceful and potentially boring situation and
inevitably from time to time his letters harked back to probation.

'It is for London and probation that my heart longs – these and the
family. God, this does seem a futile negative sort of life; just a waste
of time, pleasant enough but quite valueluess.
'Incidentally, I read a long paragraph in a five-day-old *Times* all
about the Social Services in wartime and I found myself wondering
and praying that all this evacuation may be a blessing in disguise – I
shall never forget a conversation I heard between three people at a
shooting-lunch in December; they had become aware for the first

time that slum children really did have lice, really were underfed and were not even "house-trained". What will the effect of this slow awakening of the upper, ruling class be? Can it die again or will it lead to a real re-housing programme, to a determination to see real family allowances, to the starting of some Dental Health Insurance, to free education throughout all classes and the abolition of juvenile employment. I can only hope so, but with little confidence. Is there really any chance of "a land fit for heroes" – not the "warrior" heroes but those who keep a sense of humour on 6 children and 35/- a week?'

He had a deep anger at what he saw as the Church of England's negative stance on all the matters which he believed to be of truly Christian importance:

'Not since the war began has Lang [Archbishop of Canterbury] publicly recognized the honesty of the CO, far less has he supported him. A moderately able speech on Education seems to have been his major contribution to this war for Christianity – if it is a war for Christianity why are not the priests here with us, going into the front line and killing and dying as Christian Crusaders instead of sitting at home and saying prayers for kids who've been conscripted and sent here to "defend Christianity"? – a hypocritical lot are our C of E, they're even a reserved occupation being, I suppose, too holy to kill but used to encourage others to do it for them. They've set Christianity back years and countless years.'

Because there was no active war and little of interest in the daily life of the Ambulance, and perhaps because there was no one to talk to among his friends about his hopes and ideas, Pat used the Budget to unburden himself and he realized that he was creating a wrong impression at home. Dad referred to 'his heaviness in his soul' but Pat denied this, firmly claiming that his last letter

'was caused, I suppose, by a sub-conscious home-sickness due to my knowledge that Chris and Paul were at home. It was not a very serious bout of nostalgia nor was it very prolonged, but I let myself indulge in that masochistic pleasure of day-dreaming – it is interesting to watch others fall into the mood, to lie on their blankets and start to talk about Birmingham, their girl, of the cliffs of Devon –

it is a perfect example of Bitter Sweet, for while we are quite happy
here, reasonably comfortable with very little to complain of, I think
we all count the days to peace and a return to normal.'

In fact he was busy and living quite a full life; the canteen was
proving to be a seven-day part-time job and he was playing a lot
of rugger. He found

'a little club of local boys run under the auspices of the Church. They
are all Catholics and are aged from 14–18. I find that my French
must really be quite good now as I can discuss serious subjects with
them; I always spend at least an hour a night at this club.'

He was also taking Esperanto classes from the young son of
the proprietor of the local cafe where he went for occasional
meals and in the evenings.

For a few weeks the Ambulance left its central-heated cinema
in a mining village to take its share of outpost duty in front of
Metz. It was based in

'a glorious village in the very best San Michele style. A valley with a
trout stream, strawberry fields flanking the stream, and leading up to
this lovely village, clean and unsophisticated, centred around the
church and living as a unit. Above the village we find the vineyards,
giving way to the hills, moss and violets, and from the hill the fine
view over the plain underneath, or on to the wooded hills across the
valley – all the trees seem to be silver birch or oak and it really is an
absolute dream village. For the first time I have understood the
spiritual motive power that inspired those country poems of Alfred de
Vigny – eaves, swallows, sunsets, blossoms, bees, all were there and
also the first cuckoo of my year. Lovely place.'

During this period Pat was moved into the Orderly Room –
not a success – and later into the

'Medical Inspection room, learning the methods of recording and
passing on the various Admissions and Discharges (A & D) from our
hospital. It's quieter work, more interesting and personal. Quite apart
however from the actual work in the MI room there is also a good
opportunity of learning a bit more about medicine. I have been able
to watch a certain amount of elementary surgery and although I

apparently go as white as a leper and feel miserable, I have not felt at all inclined to sickness or faintness, and I find that I improve each time that I see something done.'

While he was in charge of the canteen Pat became a Lance Corporal and for a time, until some senior NCOs were transferred to the Ambulance, he was made a full corporal. This brought forth a typical comment from Chris:

'Pat, hearty congratulations on the second promotion. I wonder whether if I proclaimed myself a conscientious objector and refused to fight, the Army would promote me and double my salary. It is most thought-provoking that I, who am at least loyal to the Army's cause (if not blindly loyal) should still be a gunner after 12 months, while you, having formally and vehemently repudiated the Army's entire "raison d'être" should in less than 4 months be rewarded with two promotions and a double salary. Do you think if I went one further than you and fought *against* the British Army, the War Office would make me a Sergeant?

'We do have different ideas in the family. Here are five sentiments from the Budget of Feb. 22nd, all excellently typical of their authors, with which I do most profoundly disagree.

From B. "Six blissful days to spend in the woods – what more could the heart of man desire?"

From Pat. "Either we should be Quakers or at most a revolutionary body within the Roman Catholic Church."

From Doff. "Thank you so much for the potatoes, they are most welcome."

From Paul. "I'm fed up – at being given five days more leave."

From Helen. "We intend to go round all the stores and furriers in Rochester. Boy! Are we going to have fun!"

'Now for myself if there are three things in the world to which I am indifferent they are woods, fur coats, and potatoes; if there are two things I shall never be they are a) a Quaker and b) a rebel in the Roman Catholic Church; if there is one thing I crave above everything else, it is more leave. So keep it up family, it's stimulating.'

By the middle of January Chris was due for leave and

'Having melted down my lump of ink and reluctantly taken off my left hand glove, I am ready to write my last pre-leave weekly letter. It really is cold, even worse in the billets, it seems, than outside. The snow filters straight through the roof in a fine mist and the draughts are appalling. Frost gathers on one's blankets, spoons stick in one's mess tin, damp clothes can be stood upright, everyone coughs and/or talks in hoarse whispers. However, I feel perfectly fit now myself, so long live Saturday evening when I shall arrive at Felthorpe in the best of spirits.'

On 30 January Beryl was able to write

'in right festive mood for Kiff is home at last. Last night Dad and I listened to the six o'clock news and VERY nearly burst into tears when they got to the announcement that leave for the BEF was "off" once again. However he had sailed (according to plan) that morning and about 8.00 the welcome telegram came through that he was safe in London and would be home today.

'The kindly providence that watches over the family then just surpassed itself and produced a phone call from Paul to say that conditions were so bad all his lot had been given five days' leave and he'd be home today too! And he is!

'Kiff's train was only about 1½ hours late and he arrived looking extremely clean and even smart in Pat's best overcoat. He looks rather thin, and tired under the eyes, but has a bit of a tan and really looks a great deal fitter than when he used to rush home from London to spend a hectic weekend electioneering in S. Norfolk.'

But leave ended and

'I think if ever a man is entitled to feel miserable it is when he gropes around Victoria Station in the black-out at midnight, looking for his returning "leave" train. The future appears as completely dismal as the past has been completely joyful, and the immediate prospect – two hours in a crowded train, followed by a march around the port at two in the morning, followed by a rough, crowded crossing, an endless crowded French railway journey and a ride in a crowded lorry, ending at one's crowded billet (no beds available) at 1.00 a.m. the next night – is almost more than the stoutest heart can bear.

'But it was a horrid blow. Felthorpe had been so monstrously enjoyable, the parents and family so shatteringly kind, the fatted calf so prodigiously succulent, that it was hard to bear.

'It was also something of an experience to get such an intimate sight of the horrors of modern warfare. Microscopic pats of butter; spilt atoms of sugar; dimmed street lights and headlamps, and even enemy aircraft not 50 miles from where I was staying! It was with some relief that I shook the dust of East Anglia from my Army boots and repaired to the sanctuary of the Western Front.'

He was later to add:

'I forgot to tell you in a previous letter that one of the thrills of leave was that I shot a pigeon. It was in the drive, the guns Stephen and myself; the morning cold and fine with a stiff SSW breeze. The quarry was sighted in a tree opposite Chambers' cottage and shot while attempting to escape. After a ranging shot I registered a direct hit at range 40 yards, angle-on-sight $15°$ elevation, on a bearing approx $N.15°$. This is the first bird or beast I have shot since I gave up shooting a couple of years ago. Which shows the brutalizing effect soldiering is having on me.'

Christopher's letters home were uninhibited and he never failed to criticize the Army or the Government when he felt that criticism was merited, but the effect of this was that he

'was much interested to hear the other day that for some time past my letters have been subject to a special censorship by a senior officer! Quite right too. Outside the unappreciative family circle, my revolutionary opinions are taken with proper seriousness. Who more likely than I to concoct some secret and seditious plot? – or having secretly concocted it, to write home about it in my Sunday letters.

In one letter Chris wrote about a full-scale thirty-six-hour manoeuvre and illustrated the role of a 'GPO Ack'.

'I just spent the whole time – sometimes with the GPO, sometimes by myself – reconnoitring our positions, "spotting" myself on a map, siting our anti-tank and bren guns, deciding a "track-plan" for our vehicles, laying out our guns on their lines with compass and director, setting up an artillery board, working out "meteor" telegrams, allowing for such niceties as that the wind's velocity and bearing varies at different altitudes, and making out tables which tell you the amount of change you must make in the range and switch of each individual gun to make up for their firing from slightly different positions. Then you are ready for the fire orders coming in by telephone from certain sources.

'All most exhausting, and by the time you've worked out all necessaries for one position – often before – it's time to move on to the next and start all over again.

'If it hadn't been so tiring the scheme would have been enjoyable. When things go well it's a striking sight to see a battery of field guns going into action. Tractors pound their way over rough ground; guns and limbers are swung round into position; teams melt into their respective guns; GPOs yell orders through megaphones; telephones buzz; gun barrels swing up and down; everything is surprisingly efficient and picturesque. At night it can be still more striking – when it is quiet for instance, and you can hear the guns coming up many miles away; a very low growl which comes and goes with the wind, or when you can see the long procession crawling over a moonlit skyline – for nothing looks so sinister as a moonlit gun.

'But of course the picture spoils itself as often as not. Guns get bogged; telephone wires break; people curse; it rains; an iron fence upsets your director; you drop your india-rubber in a puddle, and in any case anything to do with war has to be very striking indeed before it is permissible to admire it (loud popular cheers for grossly indefensible statement).'

Chris had accepted an invitation to apply for a commission and was put down for the Artillery. He found this very disappointing and he was not very excited at the prospect.

'The Army is so damping wherever you are in it. Getting a commission is like changing a third-class for a first-class cabin in a sinking ship – a change for the better no doubt, but not much help really.

'I've seen one of the leaflets the Boche has been dropping on our former base town, where we sang the carols. It points out to our good French friends how much more comfortable and safe we are, billeted with them, than are the "Poilus" in the Maginot and how France's population statistics show that, win or lose, she can't afford a major war yet (a very good point this), and how this war is England's war, not France's (a very bad one). I'm quite sure the leaflets had not the slightest effect on any of the inhabitants of the town I met when I was there.

'In fact of course the trouble is that the French are far more vindictive against Germans than we are, though I get the impression that opinion is already hardening in UK. I've been talking to a great many Frenchmen about what to do with Germany when the war is over. The reply is always "Il faut diviser l'Allemagne" – the only variation being the number of parts into which the wretched country is to be divided. A kind of super-Ruhr occupation is vaguely envisaged. All most disturbing.'

He was put on a course of instruction in signalling which he enjoyed but he doubted whether he would ever be a good signaller;

'I can't resist the temptation to be facetious, whether the medium be flag, lamp, telephone or wireless. Give me a fine clear day, a conspicuous position, and a large white flag and I am lost to all sense of reason and responsibility. Huge long messages, vast mixtures of sedition, libel, obscenity and sheer fatuity are laboriously wagged from hilltop to hilltop.'

Many a day was spent by Chris in a 'Road Party' – a day's outing with a pick and shovel making or mending roads, an exceedingly dreary occupation.

'But today's roadmending was much less tiresome than usual. The weather was fine, the mud docile, the surrounding country pleasant and my companions amusing. Moreover we had the most welcome innovation in our method of work. Instead of working on an indefinite task from nine to five we were given a certain stretch of road and were told we could dismiss when we had finished it. The result was comic. I estimate that more work was done in the first three hours than on the whole of any previous day. On the old system an officer would stroll up and down the stretch of road keeping a perfunctory watch on the party; having no eyes in the back of his head he would leave behind him a trail of talk and cigarettes which only disappeared when he turned round and started back again. Today, however, all was changed. Officers were forgotten; the dinner hour almost resented. Chunks of earth flew upwards, rubble crashed into potholes, wheelbarrows and trucks hurtled along the road – a really comic sight for those who knew the old system. Naturally we finished long before five – my party could have finished by 11.30 and nearly did – and were dismissed as promised. All my previous preference for piece-work against time-work is confirmed, but I fancy that our

military employer, unopposed by any Trade Union, will greatly
increase our daily task in future.'

At that time Doff felt that she couldn't talk about the war – for
what was there to say? – at least in words that could be put on
paper. It had been a very difficult few months since Christmas,
and George had had the continuing problem of keeping the
school running and maintaining standards despite staff shortages, massive administrative difficulties, and a wickedly cold
winter. He wrote:

'I read of the devastating ennui of my brothers-in-law as they sit in
the stalls, pit and gallery of the theatre of war and wait for something
to happen differently from the happenings of today, and all their
yesterdays. I, on the other hand, would cheerfully give a cargo of
blue-bottomed baboons and golden guineas to the man who would
guarantee for me even a week of unvaried routine. The term has now
lasted over five weeks but on no one day of it has the whole of the
staff been well and out of bed; the average number of sick masters
has been between four and eight, for two notable days ten masters
were out of action. The War Office has also smoothed the way for
efficient organization by calling up four masters at different times
since Christmas.'

Both Doff and George had hoped to get up to London to meet
up with Chris when he was on leave; this became impossible but
they were able to spend

'a very pleasant night in London. London hasn't really changed much
has it? I mean, the bus conductors still chat, the shop gazers are still
in full force, and there are a mighty lot of people. We went to a news
flick, quite good; we heard the Finnish Symphony Orchestra playing
Finlandia, with photos of Finland as it was and as it is now, sort of
super-imposed. Very moving.
'We then sauntered down Regent St in the pitch dark and I fell
over umpteen rotting and decaying sandbags, but we eventually
arrived at the Café Royal where we were meeting a friend for dinner.
I was rather struck with London's blackout, it struck me as being
extraordinarily good – far better than Marlborough.
'We dined superbly at the Café Royal. It really is absurd to

remember that there's a war on when we get faced with seas of food all beautifully cooked and served.

'The next morning George went to his meeting and I went and shopped. I bought hundreds of yards of material and lbs of wool in case the war goes on for years!'

The quantity of food that could be obtained at the Café Royal contrasted favourably with Doff's predicament a little earlier:

'SOS! SOS! Can Felthorpe or Norwich supply a starving people with any potatoes? They are willing to pay gold for same. We've enough for one potato per day per person until the weekend and then no hope of getting any more. The town hasn't any. Swindon hasn't any and the lucky few who have some are finding them all frosted or black.'

Beryl was able to help out:

'Thursday I turned my attention to Doff's potatoes – or the lack thereof, and despatched some by post, some in tins, and a cwt. by train. I think the root of the trouble is the controlled price, they can't be sold at more than 1d a lb and at that, I suppose, it does not pay a shop to worry about obtaining them from any distance. Daughter, there seems to be lots in London if you pay carriage.'

After Christmas leave Paul went back to Cranwell and when the weather permitted, put in more hours of flying practice and became increasingly confident as a pilot.

'I've at last begun to fly somewhat better, though I say it as shouldn't. I still get stuck in my slow rolls, stalled while on my back – an unpleasant experience in the extreme – and then coming out in a screaming, unorthodox, inverted dive; but I merely need half-an-hour's dual to put that right. I think my real improvement dates from Monday when I was sent up with a map to practise map-reading. I did this OK for ¾ of an hour and then decided that for the remaining ½ hour I'd make myself a confident pilot or kill myself; so I climbed to about 6000 feet which gives you an enormous distance in which to correct mistakes, and making sure there was nobody for miles, I simply threw the plane all over the sky in loops, stall turns, spins, slow rolls, dives and everything else I could think of; no doubt I did them very badly but it did give me confidence in handling the machine in all kinds of positions except low-flying, which I haven't done myself yet.

'Otherwise only two things stand out, the first on Tuesday when I went up early in a thick ground-mist, flew around for some time and then came upon one of the most beautiful sights I've ever seen in England. There was a shallow bank of mist effectively covering the whole ground from about 2000 ft where I was, and emerging on its little mound, standing entirely isolated in a sea of mist, with the rising sun just touching it, was Lincoln Cathedral; it was really most stirring.

'Finally on Thursday I went on a "height test". This is merely a check-up on your physical condition since you climb to 15,000 ft and you can't get above 18–19,000 without oxygen. It was a wonderful morning and I simply loved it. You have to be careful to keep your ears cleared every few thousand ft or your ear-drums burst, so I chewed gum and sang Brahms and Beethoven symphonies fortissimo all the way up. Eventually I climbed to 16,000 ft so as to say that I had been no less than 3 miles vertically upwards and suffered nothing worse than a headache that was quite painful from 14,000–16,000 ft and then astonishingly vanished as soon as I got down to about 12,000 ft again.'

It was at this time that Paul first took a bus to Belton, near Grantham, where the father of a schoolfriend was Rector.

'I found myself welcomed with wonderfully open arms. Michael was on very good form and sent his love to nearly all of you; otherwise I found the Vicar who is a wonderful kindly old man, the very best type of Christian country vicar, and finally a sister of about 22, by name Monica, of equal charm with the rest of the family. We went and formed 50% of the congregation, while the vicar preached an admirable sermon and Michael and Monica (and of course I) behaved exceedingly badly, particularly for the vicar's offspring. After sherry and an admirable lunch Monica and self went and explored the neighbouring estate of Lord Brownlow. Later we went and skated, or rather they skated while I slid owing to a lack of skates, and so back for a late tea and the new recording of Brahms' 1st on the radio-gram in a delightful little "attic" consecrated to the younger generation. Finally I was prevailed on to stay till the late bus at 10.45 and left most regretfully having sampled a most reassuring amount of kindness and civilization as contrasted with our mess.'

Paul was changing and he realized this when the powers-that-be at Cranwell started to introduce a more rigid discipline, with numerous rules and even compulsory games.

'Strangely enough I find that after six years of incessant grumbling at petty regulations, I now take an attitude like the Gods in Olympus. This may be yet another aspect of my growing indifference to everybody and everything based on a good cynical disillusionment. But I rather think it's the one virtue that I've acquired in 4 months of war – an ability to remain unruffled. There are a number of things that can raise me to the peaks of wrath, but over regulations or lesser physical discomforts I entirely fail to get worried. I don't quite know what it is; partly without doubt a feeling of indifference and simply waiting for what's coming to me without caring what it is; partly that I'm busy and haven't much time or energy left to worry; and primarily I think because I'm at last acquiring the habit of using my spare time. I've cut down my bridge by about 90% and now find that I'm perfectly content to read. In fact the inevitable has happened and my incorporation in the military has changed me; instead of raising the flag of revolt and instead of acquiring the Service mind (I have as yet escaped this monstrosity I think) I have adopted a complaisance and a sort of independence from my surroundings that really delights me.'

By the end of February Paul had passed his 'wings' exam 'with colours flying at a surprising height' and was a qualified pilot. He was beginning to enjoy Cranwell, but this was largely due to the fact that Belton – and Monica – was only half an hour away by car.

'I arrived in time for dinner on Friday and plunged straight into the perfect peace that goes with a village rectory in England. It's this peace I really miss at Cranwell; in Belton the Sunday sermon is the week's great event and the choice of hymns of vital importance. I forget there all the male rowdiness of Cranwell, even the pheasants of Felthorpe, even my own intellectual conceit, and I slip delightedly into a complete lack of worry, save over *The Times* crossword. In the day-time one goes long walks over a surprisingly attractive countryside, walks which are wholly delightful when one considers that everything around you, or its equivalent, has stood for centuries, and that whatever the next ten years may bring, they will stand for thousands of years yet. It's extraordinary how important one begins to think our own particular age is; with millions of years behind us and millions of years in front of us, it's preposterous to think of war "destroying civilization" etc. I suppose that even if human progress were put back a thousand years, which is unbelievable, it would be quite imperceptible in the history of man. A sobering thought – how petty we all are, how inconceivably unimportant each individual appears! I know that Pat at least will rise at this, but anyway to a pagan, it's unquestionably true.'

One of the last exercises that Paul had to do in Intermediate training was his 'cross-country' which involved him in landing at Abingdon aerodrome and returning. This caused him no problems, he flew over Oxford 'dipping my wings sentimentally over Christ Church' and was back at Cranwell for lunch. The afternoon flight proved more difficult.

'The powers that be decided that I might as well get my second cross-country done and sent me off to Duxford (near Cambridge), Bicester (near Northampton) and home. Well, by this time I'd got a superiority complex; it was a supremely lazy day of flying and I enjoyed sitting back singing, and thinking of all the puny mortals creeping along beneath me. So off I soared in approximately the right direction, checked myself over Sleaford and Spalding, concluded my course was right and went metaphorically to sleep. Peterborough slipped by more or less in the right place, and the only question was whether I should get back in time for tea. About ¼ hour later I looked over the side rather more attentively and discovered myself over a hopelessly unidentifiable piece of Fen. However, it was always possible I was OK and being able to see 5 miles in any direction I felt OK. However, eventually I discovered I really was lost, moreover nowhere could I find Cambridge which should have been obvious enough so I cruised round unsuccessfully for a while and then decided to swallow my pride and land somewhere. I had packets of petrol so I went on flying in what I imagined my right direction was until I came upon an aerodrome, and there I landed – at Stradishall, quite the wrong side of Cambridge.
'However, I was rather popular; I reported at the Watch Office and was besieged by all their heavy-bomber pilots eager to fly my Hart. They showed me the insides of one of their bombers which resembles the Great Eastern Hotel in size, then I went and had tea in the mess. Having at length got permission to return to Cranwell I found that they hadn't the right kind of petrol and couldn't get it till

the morning – so I stayed the night. Everyone was charming to me; we stood each other drinks all round, I dined in the mess and slept rather badly in a spare bedroom. After breakfast this morning with the weather perfect, Cranwell was apparently under cloud 200 ft high so an instructor came and fetched me, much to my disgust. I took a sad farewell to all my companions and came back here for the inevitable rude reception. However, such things are not remembered long, and I'm thinking of doing it again sometime; I enjoyed myself immensely.'

By March Paul had progressed to Advanced training which he found a great improvement. It was now assumed that they knew how to fly in all possible conditions and it only remained to teach them to fight. He was now flying Hinds (supercharged Harts) and had his first experience of night-flying.

'It was a clear night but very dark and it didn't look likely that we should have any "horizon" to help us. There were three of us on that flight and as we drew near to the flare-path I think we were all – not nervous, but slightly exhilarated in the face of an entirely unknown venture. It was really extraordinarily exciting and reminded me irresistibly of Hollywood. The flare is only a naked flame and only lights up about 4 ft around it but they form a T leading out across the aerodrome for you to land by.

'Night flying is always chaotically organized and I had to wait an hour and a half before I went up. I "bummed" cigarettes and stamped around, in a vain endeavour to defeat the cold which was steadily sapping my enthusiasm and stringing up my nerves. But at 10.45 p.m. the moment finally came and I climbed with my instructor into my plane. We flashed our recognition lights and got permission to take off from the control pilot; we wave away the airmen from the wing-tips, dimly visible from the navigation lights, and taxi bumpily over the invisible ground to the first flare. Everything is set in the cockpit and my instructor opens the throttle. As we lurch forward and the flares begin to stream past on my left, my feeling is solely one of interested excitement. Is this really going to be as difficult as people say? How well blacked out is our station? Will my bed for the night be in my room or the hospital?

'We've left the ground now, and we're climbing steadily by our instruments. The flare-path has slipped away behind us, and the station is below us. It's very badly "blacked out" and I comment on it to my instructor, but I get only a discouraging grunt back so I desist.

At 1000 ft we turn to the left and see the flare-path again away to the left. Flying down-wind we again flash our lights and get permission to land. The horizon is quite invisible – there must be a slight fog coming up – so we have to fly entirely on our instruments, helped a little by the angle of the searchlights on the horizon, and the stars above us. Then my instructor throttles back and we "rumble" peacefully in.

'We did four circuits dual, and then after a test with my flight-commander I went up solo. My test was to do three circuits and landings and provided I walked away unaided from the last, I was presumed safe. I expected to be rather terrified, but I was nothing but exhilarated; and though my landings were not exemplary, I got through it safely, to retire to bed at 1.00 a.m. with a special dispensation to lie in bed next morning.'

Occasionally, but increasingly rarely, Paul worried that he was losing all incentive to fight for the ideas and ideals that he held at Oxford.

'Soul-searching, it seems, was a luxury that I only had the energy to indulge in peace-time; consciences in particular and spiritual values in general are now so much at a discount that it seems not only useless, but almost profane to discuss them. Even an interest in politics is now thought slightly superfluous. Added to this is the emergence of that streak of cowardice, mental as well as physical, that I have hitherto tried to bluff myself into ignoring. Somewhere at the back of my mind I have an awful dread of serious thought, because I know I should arrive at the inescapable conclusion that on moral, rational and political grounds I should oppose this war with all my strength – and I know equally well that I haven't the guts to resign my commission (probably impossible anyhow), face Mr Justice Hargreaves, and make myself persona non grata at Felthorpe. So there remains for me the Drift, disillusioned and objectless, without spiritual ideals, without many political aims, and still worse without any personal justification. My present existence runs counter to almost every conviction I held a year ago, when I was a convinced Socialist, a sympathizer with a Gospel of Charity and an incipient pacifist. However, in the words of Margaret Sullivan "here's to Drifters"; God knows (I suppose) where we shall fetch up, and I know it won't be where I should like to fetch up.'

But there was an overall feeling of being

'utterly and selfishly content. It's rather horrifying to find oneself contented in war-time, but I can't help it; none of my friends and relations seem to be in any immediate danger (with apologies to the BEF) and I personally am sublimely happy. I imagine myself to be in love (hush!), I'm living in extraordinary luxury, and I simply delight in taking up my little aeroplane. I admit this existence won't last long and I'm due to leave Cranwell, but sufficient unto the day etc. and I'm very contented.'

Paul left Cranwell and went down to Warmwell in Dorset for firing practice; this was not very successful because although the weather was wonderful there was

'a kind of thick tropical haze. It's perfect weather for flying but we're not here for flying, only for firing; and since all our low-lines criss-cross each other like a seaside golf-course, it's highly dangerous if you can't see exactly where you're flying. So we sit on the ground and sunbathe. So far, in nine days we've only had 1½ days firing which were spent in attacking ground targets, at which I was fairly proficient, and "astern chase" when you sit on an aeroplane's tail and shoot off at a little red cone that it trails behind; at this I was monstrously bad, but so was everyone else and we shall get another crack at it.'

Paul left Warmwell on 9 May, the day before the German invasion of the West, and was sent to Old Sarum, Salisbury, for training in Army cooperation. This meant that he was close to Marlborough and Doff and George invited Monica to stay with them; at the end of May Monica and Paul became engaged.

Between January and May there had been major changes in life at Felthorpe and Dad was appointed Sheriff of the County of Norfolk.

It had pleased His Majesty, by and with the advice of His Privy Council to require Dad 'to take the custody and charge of the said County, and duly to perform the duties of Sheriff thereof during His Majesty's Pleasure' whereof he was duly to answer according to law. Beryl reported:

'Dad is busy learning his duties as High Sheriff and going into everything most thoroughly; he's heard that the Judges say Norwich does not treat them with nearly as much respect as other places, so he's trying to borrow a guard of honour from Bernard. Really, of course, it is that he read of a special guard being provided for someone 'cos of the IRA and does not put much trust in the beautiful sword which is to swing by his side.'

Later he attended on the Judge

'looking his part to perfection and more decorative than words can say in his black velvet suit with silver buttons and white lace jabot and ruffles.'

These few extracts from Beryl's letters to the Budget are representative:

'Friday I got some 80 shirts and 20 pairs of socks sorted into sizes, packed into parcels of tens, labelled, listed and delivered them at their appointed places, – only to find there was a new order that everything was to be marked with a beautiful Cash name tape so most of it had to come back to be opened and repacked. Scratched around for buttons for 30 pyjamas, the stuff came a fortnight ago, but the buttons have not caught it up yet. We dined at Crown Point and went to a "National Government" meeting in Norwich in the official capacity of High Sheriff complete with wife; it was pretty dull, the Lord Mayor (Socialist/Philosopher) made a short and excellent speech, Capt. Wallace (Transport) a long and singularly dull one.'

'From the Welfare Hut at Thorpe Station, and yes, I'm still awake! Haven't had a chance to go to sleep as a matter of fact. I "came on" at 10.30 p.m. and a nice moonlight drive landed me in fairly wide-awake, which was lucky as the hut was cram full and doing a roaring trade. Thank goodness the two women with me had been here four times already and poach eggs, spread salmon sandwiches or produce a cup of cocoa without turning a hair. I spotted a moderately safe looking corner with a sink that looked about my line and have spent a pretty solid 90 minutes washing up, drying and emerging at hectic intervals to sell a packet of cigarettes or take the money for a cup of tea – cash registers aren't nearly as much help as I always thought they were, you still have to do all the calculating about change!

'Now there are two men sleeping in the far corner, two sitting over some baked beans, and no more expected till the mail comes in at two.

'Thursday – No, I didn't go to sleep. The mail was a bit late and got in about 2.20. 18–20 men came in off it and the trade in tea and poached eggs was brisk. Then four of them settled off to sleep, but five others preferred to sit up and play dominoes – they were from mine-sweepers, mostly. The Red Cross dozed in chairs, knitted, read, but the chairs were very hard and the huts had got a bit cold. A little before 5 we roused ourselves with Oxo and biscuits and put fresh water on to boil for a new lot of tea and soon after, five of the men had their "breakfast", blankets were stored, beds folded against the wall, the remaining orderly swept up the floor and we had a final wash and clean up. Then I took a silly lad who'd missed his bus last night back to Loddon, and finally got to Crown Point just before seven.'

But the Carrow works and the Red Cross committees were only part of their lives and there were many more relaxed and happier moments for Beryl and Dad, working in the woods and garden at Felthorpe.

'It was a heavenly day and I attacked my border with marked if limited success. It's all very well, I wanted to put it all to potatoes then I could have got on with the war with a quiet mind, but Dad would insist we must leave flowers there, so I'm just torn in two; when the Red Cross committee dithers I think how the shepherds purse is seeding itself unhindered around the delphiniums, and when with joy I'm uprooting ground elder I remember all the pyjamas that ought to be got out to idle workers.

'Saturday and Sunday were blissful and summery, we took the dead heads off the early rhododendrons, disentangled the clematis which always insist on tangling their shoots instead of spreading out, took a lot of dead wood off a beech tree and finally embarked on cutting out the dead wood in the shrubs that the snow and frost more than half killed in the garden – that's a very long job and will last us many evenings and weekends.'

Like so many other people David found the early part of 1940 rather pointless and boring, although there was a lot of work to be done in recording the 'war' in France.

'I suppose I have had a lot of minor adventures, and see more of the "war" on land than most people, but the most dangerous thing I've done is still to drive across the Place de la Concorde in a French taxi in the black-out. Such parts of the front as I've seen are not nearly so frightening, and German troops look at you across the Rhine in no-man's land with no more threatening expressions than the drivers of other cars. That's really not an exaggeration. Long may it stay like that. I still think a land offensive is an uneconomical way of curing even our calibre of boredom, though the prospect of sitting in France indefinitely while the Navy (and the Finns) fight true war makes even me feel like encouraging someone to shoot off a gun and make at any rate a demonstration of getting on with the unpleasant business.'

One of David's recordings was of a Polish choir –

'That was some day. Everywhere we went – and it was about a dozen different places – there were deputations of Poles waiting to welcome us with speeches and bouquets and bands assembled to play all three national anthems twice etc. Also drinks. Every drink you can think of at hourly intervals all day. We were very old by the evening and not quite in our right minds all day, but it was good fun, particularly dinner, where there were four Englishmen and four Poles and we all talked French with different kinds of funny accents. We have four more days with Poles this week, and we are hoping they are not all the same or it will be sick leave not ordinary leave for me at the end.'

Visiting the Poles was part of a ten-day trip starting in Brittany.

'We came back along the valley of the Loire, which was very beautiful with hoar frost on everything and icebergs floating down the river. Our next job was round the Jura and that was nice too except that it was 10° below Fahrenheit – coldish when you're not really dressed for it. I walked ten miles one morning in the hills. It was the first proper walk I've had since I've been here, and made me feel very well.

'Another afternoon I borrowed some skis from the Chasseurs and went out on them skiing. I think that shows your son is braver than you think. I was very pleased to find I hadn't forgotten the little I knew about skiing and I didn't sit down once. Nobody was more

surprised than I. But the prestige of the Empire depended on it, so it
was just as well.

'The coldest moment was at a Prix d'Armes in the mountains. A
General was giving a lot of Légions d'Honneur to people, with a
battalion drawn up in front of him, and I had put myself immediately
on his right so as to make sure he didn't fall over the mike (one did
the other day). So I had to stand in a dignified position for 20 minutes
with the wind blowing in at one ear and out of the other and the temp.
below zero. But worse things happen in war, as we realized when we
went to our sector of the Maginot line later on, and heard how our
sentries in the advanced posts had been getting on.'

When Christopher came home on leave the Howarths managed
to get down to Felthorpe. At the time Stephen had been

'quite busy in a purely secular way; I expect it will surprise you to feel
that secularity still exists, but it certainly does. For many hours a day I
have forgotten the difference between war and peace, which I
suppose Christopher and Pat will envy enormously while I am a bit
shy about it. A troublesome feature of this business is that about 98%
of people must be fed up, those at home wanting to get away, and
those not at home wishing they hadn't got so far; and the only people
not fed up are people professionally interested in slaughter, and
people like David with a really interesting job; and he has to pay for it
by a lot of overwork, I expect, which I always think is an awful curse
after about two days and nowhere near worth any ordinary carrots.
And of course when we get peace we shall all try and settle down
again, which is a virtual psychological, economic, and political
impossibility. I think at the end of this I shall form the Escapists
Club; it will be pretty select if it is to keep its membership under the
ten million mark, in fact select enough to be limited to about 4. It will
buy a boat and sail round the world for eighteen months, calling
occasionally at luxury ports for an escape from escapism, while the
world is set to rights by Christopher and (perhaps) David, who will
not be allowed to join even if they want to.'

Problems were arising in David's BBC unit with differences
of opinion about its size and the scope of the work.

'It turns out that a suspicion we both had was right – that the office wants Richard [Dimbleby] to go and have a look at the Near East; he will be going in a week or two. Meanwhile I think I shall be looking after the BEF and the French Army – the only slight fly in the ointment is that if the war starts in Sweden or in Norway while Richard is in Syria, goodness knows how I shall get away from here. As you know I should be like a lion in a cage if things were going on in Scandinavia and I was here doing nothing but spelling bees, but it's impossible to be sure you are backing the right horse whatever you do.

'At the moment I am waiting for a communique which is supposed to be coming out tonight.

'Well, the communique arrived at five to nine. It was about a raid in which five unfortunate Germans had been killed, so I ran like a hare from the office to the telephone building, spent what seemed like hours trying to find the censor, and got on the phone at least five past. I dictated it to London, rushed back to the office and turned the wireless on and heard it announced as a "message which has just come in" just before ten past. Meanwhile the newspaper people were solemnly telephoning it for their morning papers. That sort of little thing cheers one up.'

With the departure of Richard Dimbleby to the Near East there were tentative plans for the re-organization of the BBC team in France. David came over to London and found that

'the Talks Dept, which I was in before the war, wanted me back so I went off to Skye for my holiday, telling the people here to fix up whichever they liked. Well, I got back from there on the Friday the blitzkrieg started, to find that they had decided to put me back in Talks. So, after all the months of waiting, I missed the offensive when it came.'

Life for both Chris and Pat had continued along the well-known routine until the German forces invaded Holland and Belgium; both managed to write brief letters home on 10 and 11 May.

Chris's letter was headed:

'Somewhere in Somewhere
(and don't read anything into this.)

'I can't tell you anything. But no matter, this won't reach you anyway. Safe and sound.'

Pat wrote:

'Telegrams come much faster than letters, so hold very tight to the old truth that no news is good news.

'I'm incurably well, and oddly enough very peaceful in mind and spirit.'

The speed of the German advance through Holland, Belgium and France was wholly unexpected; their armoured divisions broke through the positions of the allied forces which were cut off, surrounded or brushed aside. There was a general retreat of the British Army towards the Channel ports and the greater part of it was evacuated through Dunkirk and Calais.

It was difficult for Helen in America to have to sit on the sidelines; the extent of the disaster was difficult to believe and she could hardly credit it:

'From this side of the ocean things look horribly grim; the Americans' chief delight is to exaggerate and excite the people and – Heavens above! – they've got me in the jitters! Nazis claim Channel Ports! Calais in German hands, Nazis claim! Allies retreating on three fronts! Nazis claim successful raids on the East Coast of England! I haven't heard from you all for quite a long time, but I've never stopped thinking of you or stopped wondering exactly where the boys were.'

Both Chris and Pat moved with their units into Belgium as part of the Allies' plans to oppose the German advance, but Chris fell ill and became detached from the Surrey Yeomanry as the army medical services coped with his soaring temperature. His efforts to rejoin them were unavailing and he was evacuated; he felt very badly about this but found a fellow sympathizer in David who wrote:

'Stephen and I and Christopher had a very large and British meal at Simpson's last night and when I found C. in just the same state of mind as me, it was very comforting. Neither of us was quite sure whether it was humiliating or tragic or just funny to have sat for seven months making brave faces at the enemy across 200 neutral miles, and then have retired to safety and Simpson's, one with a temperature and the other with a grouse on the day it started.'

Chris wrote of his experiences:

'The Huns, you will remember, got up very early one Friday morning and invaded the Low Countries. I was asleep at the time, but very fit, and perfectly ready to push them back again; and I was bidden to join our Reconnaissance party and advance into Belgium that same afternoon.

'But then there was a slight change of personnel in our Reccy. Party, and at midday (just after I wrote you a note from Somewhere in France), I was told to stay behind and come up with the guns on Monday morning.

'That night I felt I had a chill coming on, and took the familiar dose of hot coffee, ¼ pint rum, and extra blankets. But I wasn't too good on Saturday, and on Sunday, while manhandling the guns on to the tractors, I passed right out. Much against my will, our Sergeant-major reported me to the MO and arranged that I should go into Belgium in the MO's truck at the end of the convoy. So I was taken down to the Regimental Aid Post, my kit remaining with the troop for the boys to take on.

'Comes the dawn, and my temperature is 102.5 and still rising, and the MO can't diagnose it. He refuses to let me come and summons a Field Ambulance to take me away. So as his regiment, flags flying and trumpets sounding, advances to the battlefield, Gnr Mayhew, having sat on some damp grass no doubt, or eaten something which disagreed with him, is transported backwards into France on a stretcher in a comfortable ambulance.

'On arrival at the Field Ambulance depot, I was promptly consigned to a Casualty Clearing station, still further back in France. But my hopes rose when I learnt that my Field Ambulance was itself going into Belgium that night, and would be stationed reasonably near where I judged my unit would be. So helped by a halfwitted RAMC Orderly (not Pat) who did not let my temperature "cook" (he also tried to take my pulse holding the wrong side of my wrist), I induced the CO to take me on my stretcher with the Field

Ambulance into Belgium. So I spent that night travelling Brusselswards – or thereabouts – in an ambulance, protected from the attention of Goering's Air Force (which had given us no peace for the last three days), by a large Red Cross on the roof, though even then everyone was saying that camouflage would be more effective.

'We got to our destination safely; but almost immediately my plot started going a bit astray. I had counted on at least twenty-four hours to recover sufficiently – I hoped for more – before the arrival of the Hun and confusion of battle caused either my unit or my Field Ambulance to shift their positions. But the Ambulance had hardly arrived before it had to retreat again, and soon, alas, we were steadily going backwards while the news from the front suggested that my unit would also be moving. Moreover my wretched carcase refused to play the game, registering temperatures up to 103.5 and getting steadily less war-worthy. The Field Ambulance doctors could not diagnose it, and eventually insisted on my being sent back to a Casualty Clearing Station. I arrived there after a miserable night in an ambulance, trying to sleep and at the same time prevent a desperately wounded neighbour from tearing the bandages off his head. It was now about Friday, and on Friday night I got rapidly better and my temperature returned to normal; but the chances of my finding the 98th were now virtually nil even if I'd been strong enough to hitch-hike, unarmed and without kit, up and down the front. Moreover, the CCS doctors wouldn't let me go.

'After a long ride in the ambulance, much impeded by the stream of refugees, the country suddenly became familiar and we found ourselves back in France again. I had no idea what they were doing to me; my companions were all very light cases like myself and I thought they were going to find us another unit somewhere. I was absolutely thunderstruck when we eventually pulled up at a familiar station, before the most gorgeous shining ambulance train you ever saw! I was now feeling perfectly well again (if not very strong yet), and this was a dreadful humiliation. Everyone was agonizingly kind and admiring, too, just as though I had been holding the Huns at bay and was minus a couple of legs.

'After a very comfortable but record slow journey (about 30 miles in about 24 hours!) during which we were bombed we arrived at a magnificent Base Hospital, just south of a certain port. Here I thought I impressed the doctor that I was fit for duty – indeed I may have – but now the Hun was close on our heels, and others in the neighbourhood, besides the sick, were thinking of England and safety. We spent our only night at the Base Hospital in the cellars (some of us – not me of course – on stretchers), the sinister thing being that we were taking refuge from shelling and not bombing.

'At 3.30 in the morning we were embarked on to a Hospital Ship, accompanied by the noise of machine-gun fire (not directed at us), from the clouds above, and after a comfortable and uneventful journey arrived at the Southern Hospital in Dartford.'

There was an anxious period without any news of Pat, but on 2 June there was a telegram that he was safely back in England. Beryl wrote about this:

'I went to the Club for messages and found one to ring home. Salmon then gave me Pat's wire:

"Pontefract. Feeling fine. Unhurt. Write soon. Pat." '

For about a week the 145th Field Ambulance had moved around Belgium without ever settling or coming into close contact with the war. By the third week in May it had come to rest in a hotel on the promenade at La Panne, a few miles north of Dunkirk, and there it took on a hospital role, receiving wounded men brought in by ambulance. Pat was at that time responsible for recording the details of those admitted to – and discharged from – the hospital. Gradually the troops retreated through La Panne towards Dunkirk and the time came for the Field Ambulance to leave.

Pat wrote of these days:

'Throughout the week the fashionable seaside resort of La Panne had been becoming less comfortable and far less fashionable, for it was only about 7 miles north of Dunkirk and while wounded poured into our hospitals the German infantry drew closer and their artillery was beginning to find the range of the beach. The Unit was beginning to get a little jumpy and nervous, not so much out of fear as out of uncertainty, for no one knew our plans; were we to stay for death or captivity? Or were we to be allowed to make a dash for death or liberty?

'It was therefore with considerable relief and excitement that the companies paraded at 2.15 on Friday, 31 May, for we all realized that at last our darkness was to be lifted and we had all prepared ourselves

for the news, whether good or bad. I think we were all surprised,
however, by the eventual plan that was put before us – each Medical
Unit in the sector was to contribute 4 men and an MO to form one
last hospital to deal with any casualties that might be brought in by
the retiring front-line troops. Volunteers were asked for by the RSM.

'The Unit was perhaps disappointingly slow to respond to this call
for volunteers. Tommy and Norman immediately gave their names
and they deserve enormous credit for the instantaneous selflessness.
In B Coy and HQ the prevailing opinion was that it was too much to
ask of a man, that they should have given everyone a chance by
drawing names from a hat – as with the "Trial by Ordeal" it was felt
that God should be given a chance to decide. Looking back on my
own emotions and those of the men I know, I am now of the opinion
that all this fervent reasoning was insincere and was merely a
camouflage for our true emotions, fear and desire. After a certain
pause, during which the cock had time to crow twice, two more
volunteers were obtained, Taffy and myself. We were pleased that
the MO was to be "Mac" who would stay with us, for his cheerful
informality was bound to be invaluable through what promised to be
rather trying hours. At the last moment we had to add an additional
man to the party, and Frank was drawn out of the HQ hat; it would
have been impossible to have told from his subsequent conduct that
he had stayed by chance rather than by choice, for he never once
complained, was always cheerful and did more than his share of the
work.

'During the morning our hospital (an hotel) had been evacuated of
patients, and it was pleasing after the previous days' experience, to
discover that this time it was really intended to keep it empty. No
plans however could take into account the effect of a well-placed
bomb; it fell about 20 yards to the SE of the hotel, on the beach, and
caused incredible havoc, bringing down all the fixtures, from the MI
room equipment to Leopold's photo, and smashing every window in
the hotel. Over 70 wounded came into the hospital for treatment – I
went on to the beach to collect the identity discs of the dead; there
were 12 of them and I realized for the first time just how blasted
about man can be – it helped to cure my dread of limbless and
faceless men. All the patients were evacuated, but the bomb seemed
an omen, the first explosion in a night of death.

'Saying farewell to the Unit was a sad business, for I do not think
that any of us really expected to return to England, at least until the
war should be finished. Nevertheless it gave us heart, after seeing
those who had straggled on to the beach throughout the week, to see

the 145 march off in its little groups of 25 – not one sign of disorder.

'The hotel seemed very cold and empty with neither patients nor Unit, and though the subsequent rout round revealed a priceless bottle of Amontillado Sherry, it was with relief that we got down to business and Mac and I went off to explore our new hospital. It was what we hoped it would be, an underground shelter on the front, and we were just congratulating ourselves on our good luck when the first shell arrived and burst about 30 yards away on the beach; let it be recorded here that Mac beat Mayhew to the ground by a full half sec: about 12 shells burst and in the subsequent pause Mayhew beat Mac into the underground shelter by at least 5 yards.

'After a few seconds during which we recovered our breath and our pride, it was decided that I should go back to the hotel and collect the other three, bringing back any food that was palatable, unusual and available. I had no difficulty in getting along to the hotel and it was not until we were all rummaging around the kitchen that the shelling began again – it was very close and we ran into the cellar, which was a wise move as they twice hit the hotel. A wounded man was brought in with the right side of his chest blown away; there was no morphia in the MI room, and so, though it was clear that he was going to die, we decided to take him along to the hospital. I left Norman, Frank and Taffy in the hotel in case any more wounded were brought in, but when I returned all was quiet though an ammunition lorry was giving us a Crystal Palace Exhibition down the road. We therefore finally quit the hotel and recongregated at the hospital.

'I think a brief description of the hospital would now be in place. It was built as an air-raid shelter against which it would have been valueless save against concussion and splinters. It was about 20 yards long with alcoves off the sides, and was constructed of ferro-concrete – unfortunately there were squares in the ground-level roof which were composed merely of thick glass; over all this we heaped sand and endeavoured in all ways to make it safer.

'At first there was not very much work to be done for there were few patients and there were 6 MOs and 24 men; we therefore made tea, talked together and loaded and unloaded ambulances. At 9.00 however the German Artillery began their barrage; it seemed that they were endeavouring to lay a line of shells from the sea's edge right through the town to the land-side, and by keeping up this steady and deadly fire, entirely to cut off the troops retreating from the North to Dunkirk; their fire was magnificently accurate – sleep was absurd and so I can vouch for the fact that for the next 8 hours the barrage lifted only for 10 minutes, at 1.50: otherwise shells were falling every 3 or 4 seconds, always along this line. Needless to say our hospital was dead on this line, and we had 3 bursts on our steps down into the shelter and one burst on the roof tearing a gigantic hole in the top and spilling our precious water. Throughout we tried to evacuate our patients who kept pouring in, but at last this became impossible for the roads were impassable and our drivers were dead, or were unable to get through to us. So men died outside, and inside we lied to the wounded and told them we would evacuate them in the morning; and always they wanted water, and died.

'We had been told that at 4.00 a.m. we could draw lots and really leave a skeleton staff for the wounded while the rest could run for it if they chose. We knew that the infantry were behind schedule so we gave them an extra hour and then at 5.00 when we were between our men and the Germans, we drew lots – one MO and 8 men were to stay. We had already agreed among ourselves that there was to be no further volunteering, and that each should fend for himself. I drew a remaining ticket, as I had always expected to do, but immediately another bearer came up to me and asked me if I would change; he said that he was married with a family, and that he considered it infinitely less dangerous to stay and to risk the German treatment than to run out into the barrage which was reaching its full fury with dawn. I did what I think was the only thing I could do; I said that I could give him no opinion as to the relative safety of going or staying but that if he wished I would change. He therefore canvassed opinion among other men and officers, and decided to stay.

'There were therefore 5 of us in the party – Mac, Taffy, Norman, Frank and myself, and waiting for a favourable moment we set out. Mac had time to see the carnage on the beach which he described as indescribable, but apart from noticing the dead lying literally on our front door step, I concentrated all my energies on running, ducking – along under the shelter of the houses on the front, hurdling over their low stone walls, scrambling over the wreckage and ruin, treading over the dead, swearing and praying, we eventually got to the end of La Panne when the first of the Messerschmitts arrived. We darted under a line of lorries that were stranded on the beach and I pulled two heavy tool cases over me, one over my head, the other over my back, and from this comparative safety I watched them dive again and again over the troops on the beach, machine-gunning them with tracer-bullets; it was an exciting, awe-inspiring and wholly murderous spectacle. It was here that we lost Norman – he dived for the lorries with us and got up uninjured but we split up more on the beach and he got lost among the other countless odds and ends of soldiery.

'We went along the water's edge for a while trying to get a boat to take us off, but although there were destroyers lying not far off land there was no means of reaching them save by swimming, so we decided to push on to Gray Dunes where we could see several boats. During this walk the Messerschmitts never once left us alone, for keeping well away from the destroyers and flying very low, they continually swooped over us to machine-gun us. Once I lost my party – 6 Messerschmitts came at us and while the rest were content to take the shelter (purely psychological) of a half-submerged car, I ran for the sand dunes and found a dug-out. It was hopeless trying to find them on the beach, for they were dressed like thousands of others, so I pushed on to Gray Dunes, sitting in one shelter until I could see the next shelter to which I could run. One Messerschmitt was brought down and the pilot got out, hands raised, and was taken prisoner – I cannot believe that he got far, all along the beach there rose a yell of "Shoot the bastard" and a man next to me fired, at a range of ¼ mile.

'Eventually I got to Gray Dunes and by a miracle I found the others and we sat down to plan our best course. There were really only three alternatives (1) To wait on a pontoon until high tide and then to get taken off or (2) to find a boat and row for it (if there were a boat) or (3) to wait on a stranded paddle steamer until high tide and then to be taken off by the Navy. The first course was dangerous from both bomb and machine-gun, the second from machine-gun, the third from bomb. As there were at that moment more fighters about than bombers, we decided on the third course, and got on board.

'The next two hours were profoundly uncomfortable, for there was absolutely no room and all the time the presence of bombers preyed upon your nerves. It was with immense relief that we greeted a boat when it eventually came to take us on to the destroyer. There were 20 walking wounded on board, so 14 were put on the first boat, and 6 were put on the second. Mac was the only MO so naturally he went with them and he asked me to accompany him to help prepare an MI room and to help him dress the wounds – at the time it seemed of no importance for surely everyone would soon be off. No sooner however were we clear of the paddle steamer than the German Air Force began; suddenly from the sky there appeared 23 fighters and 19 bombers; the destroyer to which we were going was sunk in the first attack, for a bomb down the funnel split her in two and she sank fast – the remaining destroyers immediately sheered off and as the

AA personnel on the shore had already embarked, there was scarcely any opposition to the enemy aircraft. One bomber turned over to us and let drop one solitary joking bomb: it was a very clear morning and it was easy to see this bomb falling. It seemed quite clearly to be a direct hit as it was falling quite straight on us and we seemed mesmerized until an officer screamed "Row you fools! Row!" and rowing like men possessed we just passed under it in the few seconds at our disposal, and it burst from 20 to 25 yards in the rear of our boat. The bombers then turned their attention to a fishing smack and power diving on to it, they dropped between 20 and 30 bombs around it without once hitting it, in fact, the balance was in favour of the boat for one bomber dived too steeply, could not pull out and went straight into the sea.

'Our boat was an extremely old-fashioned sort of lifeboat in which the propellor is worked by the combined efforts of men pushing a joy-stick between them; there were twelve such joy-sticks and a comfortable complement for the boat would have been 34 or 36. At this moment, when we were the only boat afloat in the bay there were on board six wounded; Mac, myself and 71 RAs. Even therefore if the army had been a democratic community our two votes would have been of no importance, and we had no alternative to accepting the dictates of the RA and they decided to row to England. We were at this moment under the delusion that we had only about 35 miles to go, though this would be considerably increased just so long as the tiller remained in the hands of senior but incompetent officers. We rowed with despair for continually our helmsman put us back towards Dunkirk; eventually however public opinion overcame orthodoxy and the officer handed over to an AB who told us that we had nearer 85 miles to go, and who cheerily kept us on a course of N.40°W despite the entreaties of a 2nd Lt whose map-reading would have landed us in S. America if we had been lucky enough to avoid N. France. Forward-back, forward-back, working in shifts until we were too tired to think or worry. It was perhaps lucky that we had no oars, for by refusing to look up we may well have given the impression that we were an empty, drifting boat to the German aircraft that were continually overhead.

'Once some member of the crew said that we were running into mine-nets; it certainly looked like a minefield and we were subsequently told that we had in fact passed through a mined area, though some of us are still of the opinion that the disturbance on the placid sea was due to currents rather than minefields; nevertheless the very thought of mines had the effect of sending us several miles out of our way to circumvent that suspicious patch of sea.

'We rowed on until 6.00, a period of 9 hours, when a mist began to rise; we all prayed for an early darkness, for although it would lessen our chances of being picked up, it would at least hide us from the bombers and fighters who had been flying over us throughout the day – without doing us any material damage, but severely testing our morale. As this mist rose there were three Dorniers circling over us and power-diving on a destroyer on the horizon; twice they performed this operation and then they disappeared for a moment; within 2 minutes three bombers came very low over the water, heading straight for us. There was immediately silence throughout the boat; a direct hit was quite inevitable, and we all felt less fear than disappointment that we should have got so far only to fail. Mac had already got his coat off and was undoing his shoes; I started to take my coat off although I knew that to dive into the sea would never save us. The bombers were right up to us and they turned away as though to avoid the blast of their own bombs, and as they turned we saw the markings of the Fleet Air Arm.

'For a moment the silence held and then our relief burst into action, we stood up, we shouted, we waved and laughed and hit each other and while two planes went off to find a boat the third came zooming down over us to give our position, and each time it zoomed we waved and cheered. It was almost over: soon we were aboard the Sun 3, London, drinking tea and congratulating ourselves and the Navy and the Air Force, until we fell down on the deck and slept where we fell.

'We were landed at Ramsgate where we took the wounded to hospital and drank tea and ate delectable sandwiches provided by fair ladies; and so we were brought to Pontefract to rest, sleep, and eventually to rejoin our units.'

Some ten days later Pat telephoned home that he had been given the Military Medal; this brought a delightful letter from Chris.

'From the moment he registered as a CO, Pat was clearly destined for military glory in some form or other. But you could have knocked me down with a feather when I read the Stop Press in the last Budget. The Military Medal! Good gracious me.

'It is the most delightful incident of the war so far. One's faith is simultaneously strengthened in democracy for allowing Pat to object; in the Army for decorating an objector to itself; in Pat himself; in religion for helping him not to run until the time came; even in compulsory games for training him to run so fast when the time did come. In every way it is most edifying.'

The decoration had a special significance for Pat, as he explained in a letter thanking all the Budgeteers for their telegrams and congratulations.

'When we offered to stay behind at La Panne we certainly expected to stay there for eternity and I merely cursed the type of education which makes such volunteering inevitable. When the CO said goodbye to us he told us that we would be mentioned to the War Office but at the time it all seemed rather silly and far off. However, true to my fraternal pledge, from that moment I refrained from doing anything even remotely heroic. I can merely assume that the powers that be were pleased with us and gave me the credit as the NCO in charge of the party – unjust but army. As B. said over the telephone, "I'm sure you don't deserve it, but what fun!"

'Actually the real pleasure of the award lies in the fact that I am a pacifist. For many years the public has proclaimed pacifism to be synonymous with cowardice, and this does have a fifth column effect upon one's defences. Is it true? Is all this theoretical and spiritual idealism merely a crude covering for a faint-heart? There is an obvious mental relief in getting your sincerity recognized by the military itself.'

The defeat of the Allied Armies and the evacuation of the British forces – less their heavy equipment – from France, wholly altered the war situation. A German invasion of England seemed inevitable and it required a rather illogical faith to believe that it would not be successful; but this brought the whole country together and people even declared that we would do better by ourselves. The east and southeast of England became priority defence areas, against invasion by sea and from the air; experience of the catastrophe in France showed the important part played by the German paratroops and there was a wide response to the appeal to civilians to join the urgently formed Local Defence Volunteers. Felthorpe was close to the east coast which was a probable area of invasion and Dad became Parish Commander of the Local Defence Volunteers, later the Home Guard.

'Oh dear [wrote Beryl] I wish I knew how much might safely be written about the Defence Force or Parashooters. I would not like to give anyone the impression that it was not a vast and most efficient affair, but I might perhaps be allowed to mention that it HAS been fun getting it to its present state of perfection.

'As most of you know, Dad is the Parish Leader and you will appreciate how his experience and training fit him to lead the magnificent body of men who have rallied round. The first theory was that it was to be organized through the Police, and it was an awkward moment when it was taken over by the Military and Dad began to wonder what on earth would happen when Carrow [the Colman works in Norwich] sent an urgent call for him to go to London on business and some General said all Leaders were to man their posts that morning! However, it's not too military as you're allowed to resign on a fortnight's notice so that's a bit better.

'I would just adore to describe the Uniform (once you've got it you must keep it on or you break the Geneva Convention), the arms, the training and the quite thrilling plans, but I suppose I must not do anything of the kind, curse it, lest this letter falls into enemy hands.'

At the time of Dunkirk the Felthorpe LDV were

'called out to man their posts all night and hold 'em to the last man! It seemed a bit dull to go to bed as usual, and also Dad had lumbago and I was sure I could make the conditions a bit easier if only I could invent a valid excuse for intruding on their strictly male and military party. Inspiration arrived – where were the RAMC and the stretcher bearers? Echo answered, so the Red Cross hustled into uniform, packed a bag of "necessities" and "comforts" and hastened to the scene. There it discovered a lovely cottage, persuaded the spinster lady who lived there alone to allow a foothold and proceeded to annex the kitchen (a very comfy one) and the front room. A packet of cotton wool and another of lint prominently displayed regularized the position.

'The men filled sandbags and built barricades till nearly eleven so an issue of stimulants to restore their fainting condition was clearly necessary (Stephen – who nobly volunteered to "hold" Norfolk in his absence from Kent and worked like a black – said it was the best beer he'd drunk for months). Then a shift came and dozed in the kitchen while the spinster (in bed and dozing upstairs) felt safe with the Red Cross snoozing in the sitting room and issuing coffee at intervals. It really was as well I went 'cos she'd never have let 'em cross the doorstep if I had not been there.'

Downe was not only on the direct route from the Kent coast to London but was also only a mile away from Biggin Hill, an RAF fighter aerodrome. Uncle Bertie soon found himself equally involved in the LDV.

'They saw fit on my joining the Local Defence Volunteers to dress me up among the first, obviously as the inhabitant of a large house to encourage the others. It has been said before, I believe, in this very correspondence, that there is much virtue in the feudal system. Being without any previous experience, I am in the odd position of saying exactly what I like to my officers, as a private soldier; they swallow it most generously. I rather amused myself getting into the King's Uniform for the first time at the age of 62 (what DID you do in the Great War, Daddy? Certainly not that) and grand-daughter Sally thought it the funniest thing she'd ever seen, to judge by her convulsions.

'They've given me a rifle of the iron age, which I have never fired, and which jams if you put more than three cartridges in the magazine, and weighs a ton. I've indented for a shotgun, my own having long since passed to its rest.

'Stephen also volunteers locally, and is the smartest drill in the whole push – strange how the body responds to OTC training of years ago (My God, you should see me drilling). Our defensive post is a thing of artistry in clay, flint, corrugated iron and what-not, and would probably make an engineer spit flames.'

Although David was in a reserved occupation he had to register and decided that he would join HM Forces 'and try to get into the Navy, just to round off the Budget's presentation of the war'. He was still in London but Stephen was commuting from Downe and on 2 June he wrote:

'I find that we are evacuated. A few days ago my father received a notice to all householders within 1000 yds of Biggin Hill Aerodrome from the police, that evacuation, at any rate of women and children, was considered advisable. So Sally and my mother are in a nearby cottage, while my father camps relentlessly in the remains of Down House. He says that he can't run while the men remain behind; needless to say, no one else in the place, gentry or natives, has made the faintest attempt to budge an inch.'

The cottage was just over a mile away from Downe and Aunt Ellie went to it most reluctantly and only because 'we both felt rather uncomfortable at keeping Sally within half a mile of the aerodrome after a solemn request from the police to evacuate ourselves'. It was, however, only a short time before they returned to Down House.

The war situation became rapidly worse and Chris wrote:

'The news has just come through that the French have given in, apparently in the worst possible way. I was expecting this after what I picked up in London and am not as dismayed as I might otherwise have been. We suffer tremendous losses and the Nazis will be still more powerful and confident. But Hitler has a very long way to go yet and I've no doubt whatever we're going to see him to the end of the journey – if we don't beat him first. The Americans should now come still closer to us, I think, and with our smaller commitments we should be able to hang on till their aid becomes effective. I think they will be sending us money and ships before many more days have passed and that is the beginning of the end.

'Surely we can hold out meanwhile, despite the terrific bombardment we shall get? After all, the Channel is wider than the Meuse – and did not Shakespeare write

> "This precious jewel, set in a silver sea,
> Which serves it in the office of a tank-trap"?

'Even if Britain was overrun, couldn't Ottawa become the Empire's capital? Why not? And why not prosecute the war from there? The war cannot end until Hitler goes. While he remains, a formal cessation of hostilities would no more end the war than the formal declaration of war began it. This war began when Hitler seized power in Germany – he'd almost finished it before it was declared! – and it won't end until he's lost power again, no matter how many treaties are signed first. If a treaty were signed between Hitler and some wretched puppet British Government, it would merely mean abandoning open warfare for underground warfare, and good weapons for bad.'

In this letter Chris reflected the mood of all the family and indeed of the country as a whole; it was the background against which Dad wrote to the family on the 17 June, in the full expectation of an imminent German invasion of England.

'Dear Family,

'We live in difficult and dangerous times. Those of you who heard the 9.00 News last night will have realized that the whole of the German fury might have been turned on this island almost immediately, but apparently there was a split in the French cabinet and though the final decision is not yet known it looks as though the French will go on fighting in France.

'However that may be, the time is not far distant when we are bound to receive the very serious attention of the Germans and in these circumstances I think it is desirable, bearing in mind our large and widespread family, that we should have some organized method of keeping together. I therefore command you, as head of the tribe, to continue to regard Felthorpe as Headquarters for all communications until such time as the chain is broken; then Headquarters will be transferred to Marlborough and we must all keep in touch with Doff in so far as we are able. If Marlborough gets into difficulties then Helen, in America, will become our Headquarters for communication. It is quite probable that she will have to take up this important position, and please God bring us all together again.'

2

THE BATTLE OF BRITAIN
June 1940 – February 1942

The seeming inevitability and immediacy of a German invasion had a stimulating effect upon the members of the Budget.

Within a matter of days of getting back from France Christopher was sent to the 168th Officer Cadets Training Unit at Aldershot.

'I'm here for four months apparently and am to be trained for an infantry, not a gunnery commission – a fact I only realized after my arrival. It's disappointing as I found gunnery interesting and was beginning to know a fair amount about it. But as Intelligence propose to claim me anyhow, it may not make much difference.

'On Monday I had a long (too long for a Cabinet Minister in business hours, but it wasn't my fault) talk with Hugh Dalton at the Ministry of Economic Warfare. I found him even more dogmatic and fierce in office than he was out, but he was very kind and interesting, tho' I never really feel at ease talking to him. He seems incapable of dropping the "political leader" attitude and talking calmly and naturally. I also found a friend of mine, Hugh Gaitskell [later Leader of the Labour Party], as Principal Private Secretary at the MEW. He apparently runs the whole show; I hope so anyway, he's a most refreshing personality. It would be grand if I could get a job halfway between Intelligence and the MEW, as Dalton plainly hinted. Anyway, Dalton stood me some tea, declared sincerely and with horrifying vigour that there was no hope for the world till the young generation in Nazi Germany had been killed off, and then took me with him in a large staff car to No. 10 Downing St, where he was to attend a Cabinet meeting. I rolled up in my gunner's uniform before the famous doorway, arriving just after Amery [Secretary of State for India] and just before Herbert Morrison [Home Secretary]. There was a large crowd; I felt duly flattered but amused all the same rather than angry.

'Coming down in the train I made a series of good resolutions on the subject of my military career. Starting afresh as I am makes this very easy. I determined that my CO's report when I left would say "Mayhew is discreet and reliable and is always well-turned-out". This was to be achieved at whatever cost to truth, independence and spare time: I was to leave the 168th OCTU as the Colonel's Blue Eyed Boy. So far things are going splendidly. I haven't told the truth or spoken my mind for twenty-four hours.'

(In September Chris wrote: 'Just seen the CO's report on me (they make you sign your own report!). Most flattering, and they passed me out in the first-class category. I can only suppose they gave me someone else's papers to sign by mistake. (It makes no difference either way, they're sure to lose them.))

After Dunkirk David's first act was to arrange his release from the BBC and 'balance the Budget' by joining

'the only remaining service, the Navy. I got the BBC to let me go with their blessing and volunteered for the Coast Patrol Motor Boats; who were asking for people with experience of navigation and marine engines. Well, I have a slight knowledge of both, so I spun a yarn which brought a summons to report to HMS *President X*, Lowestoft, as soon as convenient. So here I am on my way with toothbrush, razor and spare set of underclothes as per instructions, in a bag, but without the slightest idea what I'm in for. Whatever the lowest possible rank in the Navy is, I'm it.'

Paul suffered a few days of deep despair when the French surrendered and he wrote his only 'defeatist' letter of the war.

'The latest news of the French surrender leaves one somewhat unwilling to write letters; it is an undiluted tragedy, and our feelings can only be expressed by one of the officers here who, asked whether there was any further news, remarked "What further news could there be?" It seems the end of everything; one's faith, one's hopes, even one's humanity, for I find even my pacific self getting so angry at times that I could and would shoot any suspected Teuton on sight. So much anyway for the French Army "being the best in Europe".

'Now I suppose it's our turn, and though my morale is now pretty good owing to the rise of my temper, I can't believe that there's much hope for us, at any rate in Europe. Against a ferocious and relentless attack, the Channel's not much of an obstacle and with the army presumably un-equipped I don't give much for our chances. Personally I have only two hopes; first that Churchill is more reliable than Reynaud and that we will go on fighting if England is conquered, and secondly that Russia, in spite of our blunders, will now be sufficiently scared to stage a distraction in the East. In America I have little faith; I suppose in God's own time God's own country will fight. But at present their army is smaller than the Swiss, their Air Force is puny and rather "playboy", and I doubt whether we need their Navy.'

This letter caused trouble for him.

'I have been a naughty boy! My civilian and open-minded upbringing nearly got me into very serious trouble indeed owing to a copy of the Budget [to Helen?] being censored. For one ghastly minute visions of everything up to and including a Court-Martial floated before my disturbed eyes. But rest assured – the powers-that-be have assured me that all is forgotten and returned me the incriminating document to destroy. I've lost prestige, but am otherwise intact.'

At the time his situation was difficult and unsatisfying. He had virtually completed his training but did not yet know what branch of the RAF he would be joining. Within a week he had been sent to Stroud 'for a conversion course i.e. getting used to fighters for (I now discover) a fortnight, Adolfo Volente'. He ended his letter: 'Finally, let me apologize for last week's letter. On reading it over I found it ludicrously defeatist. I do think we shall win the war eventually and my personal morale is getting better daily.'

Pat found himself faced with a problem to which he could find no satisfying answer. Once war had been declared his position had inevitably become more complicated. On the one hand he remained convinced that all Christians – including those in his family – were committing 'mortal sin' by being willing to support or join in the indiscriminate killing of war; on the other hand he realized that in the event of victory the opportunity to fight for social justice and the dignity of the individual would have been preserved through that 'mortal sin' of others, of which he was washing his hands. He was in the position of adopting, in regard to war, a 'holier than thou' attitude towards his family and his friends while depending upon their 'less holy' efforts to protect all his other beliefs.

The conflict within himself is revealed in all his letters at the time:

'The country's Christianity is not pacifist and it is extremely National and Patriotic; the Nation is sincerely (?) convinced that Christ is "on our side" against the forces of Darkness. I disagree – we are now both tarred with the same brush, we resist Evil with Evil, and I cannot believe that the Deity weighs up our Evil against the Nazi Evil, and finding ours less backs us up. I believe that God is "disinterested", for we have temporarily abdicated Christianity, and have made the decision to live or to die by war, trusting more in Roosevelt's Cabinet than in the Sermon on the Mount.

'Why not stay in the RAMC? You have got an MM, you will get promotion, you will always be regarded as one of the "right sort of Pacifists" – hold your tongue and slip through comfortably. Well, that is merely another choice, to care what the Public thinks of me or to mind what I think of myself. I have now recognized that there no longer exists any hope of retaining pacifism and "probation"; the country has finally chosen "probation" and is going to fight for it – I believe that in any future after-life we will have to answer for that wrong decision, but I find it impossible now to enjoy the fruits of both worlds; I cannot save my own soul by Pacifism and yet share "Probation" if we are victorious.'

This brought some family reactions. From Beryl:

'Meantime Pat knows how deeply we all sympathize with him in his efforts to decide what he ought to do and that the one thing we shall never doubt in him is the sincerity of his convictions wheresoever they may lead him.'

From Chris:

'Without knowing exactly why, I feel vaguely disappointed at Pat's retreat from conscientious objection. Perhaps it's because genuine convictions are so admirable in themselves, especially when unconventional and unpopular. Or perhaps it's because a CO's principles are so spectacularly different from those of the Nazis. COs don't merely condemn militarism, they refuse to join the army. They don't merely declare their fellow-men their brothers, they also refuse to kill them. They are perfect examples of men defying the first law of totalitarianism, and putting their principles and their consciences before the demands of the State. In a sense they are what we all would be if only politics allowed it.

'They also bear witness that as a nation we really do believe in Freedom of Conscience and in man's not being made for the State . . . we do allow them to hold their opinions and to remain civilians; which, considering the tight spot we're in, is good proof that we have the courage of our convictions. So I have a weakness for conscientious objection.'

On 23 June Pat applied for a Commission as a combatant.

The news from Marlborough was that

'We're all keyed up down here and the LDV is champing at its bit. I'm attending lectures on High Explosive and Incendiary bombs and have got to put out a fire next week.

'George has had some fantastic letters from parents lately; some have already taken their sons away and others are generally flapping. George is being driven steadily mad. One woman came to see him the other day and as he was out I went to explain matters to her, and she fell round my neck and said "Oh, Mrs H. you're a woman, tell me if you'd evacuate your son to Singapore." I ask you, what can a woman say when bounced on like that? – I believe she left without her son.'

On a day of National Prayer, George had spoken to the boys in Chapel:

'It was during the last War that the late Earl Beatty said "There will be no victory until the nation is on its knees." Today is being specially observed throughout this country, at the wish of HM the King and with the authority of the Archbishops of Canterbury and York, as a day of Prayer to Almighty God in this time of War. There can only be one sufficient justification for such a day of prayer by a nation which professes Christianity – that the nation is fighting with a clear conscience for an unselfish cause in which it profoundly believes, and for which it is prepared to make any sacrifice. "My country, right or wrong," may be the cry of a brave man, but it is surely not the cry of a Christian. If we are going to pray to the God of Christianity, we must be sure that our prayers can pass every test of Christian standards. We have heard many times and from many sources, since this war began, that our country is fighting evil things, and I do not see how we can doubt that truth in face of the overwhelming evidence: but of the evils which we are set to withstand the worst and most insidious are, to my mind, the denial of the inestimable value and dignity of individual personality, on which Christianity has always laid such emphasis, and the denial to men and women of the right and opportunity to reverence and worship the God in Whom they believe. There is much in our national and social life of which to be heartily ashamed, and if we are heartily ashamed of such gross and chronic scandals as mass unemployment, malnutrition and abominable housing conditions, and if we are determined to take up, as soon as the chance comes, the challenge of such scandals in our own country, we can, I think, with clear consciences fight this war against the denial of all Christian standards and ideals. And if we can thus honestly view the idea, we can and must with all intensity and devotion pray, not only today but every day, for the strength, courage, endurance and faith which we need and must unceasingly display in thought, word and deed, until the powers of evil have been vanquished and the supremacy of truth, justice, freedom and love re-established among men.

'I need not emphasize the utter beastliness of War: I need not try to describe the disgust and horror which it provokes in me. But when such evils as confront us now are let loose, must they not be withstood by every means? It cannot be right to aid and abet such moral wrong by allowing it to rage unchecked. We must not shrink from the discipline and effort of clear thinking, however painful or humiliating the process and its results may be: we must empty the lumber from our minds and sweep out all cant and jingoism, all false pride and treacherous sentimentality – above all else, let us rid ourselves of any trace of selfishness and self-interest. This ghastly and terrific struggle, in which we are all involved and which may make incalculable demands on each of us, is a fight to the bitter end between fundamentally opposed conceptions of human life and human rights: in the last resort, it is a struggle to decide whether mankind is to live in a world governed and directed by the ideals of Christianity, however imperfectly realized, or in a world where racial paganism will be free to exercise over millions and millions of lives its brutal and inhuman tyranny. On which side do you stand? For you cannot stand out of it: not to be with one side is to be against it. Even if you are not fighting, your attitude of mind affects the issue; the moral is in the end more potent than the physical; what you think and the quality of your resolution from day to day counts one way or the other. Let us honestly, humbly admit and earnestly repent the selfishness, the feebleness, the slovenliness of much in our past lives; let us pray for the vision of a world in which God's Will is done; let us pray, not only for ourselves but for all with whom we stand, that each may contribute to the realization of that vision: let us pray for all that we need to make our contribution worthy of our faith and of our cause, which we now lay before God for His judgment – and then, from this moment, with every power of spirit and mind and body which we possess, without fainting or failing, however perilous, however dark and menacing the circumstances may be, let us together toil and sweat and strive at whatever tasks may be laid upon us, until this tyranny be overpast and mankind can once again tread with thanksgiving and high hope the pathways of Peace.'

Benenden School had been evacuated to Newquay but Clare reported 'even from here about 22 girls have already left to go to USA, Canada, India, Kenya and other places'.

Serious consideration was given to sending Clare over to America to join Helen. Because she was fifteen and a half Clare had to be consulted but this placed her in an almost intolerable position and her letters to Dad show not only her longing to be with Helen but also her sense of being out of things and of no use.

'I want to see Helen just terribly, terribly badly so that I want to go ON CONDITION that I am with her. I hear that you are undecided as to whether I should go or not, but that Beryl and Doff rather say "no, she is more use here". Well when you come to think of it what use am I? I can't do Red X until I am 18 and I am now just 15½, it is the same with everything; and here I am really wasting my time doing nothing even if I do manage to get School Cert; I really don't think it will be any use to me. Whichever way I turn I feel the fates will turn the other. If I go Helen will come back, and if I stay she will probably not be able to get back, in fact I am lost in a sea of "yes" and "no". Now you point out how little I will see of Helen.

'Well I don't mind what I do. I wanted to go to USA but now I just don't know and I don't mind one inch so I think if you don't mind I will leave it to you. Just don't think about me, decide what you think is best, I will be very happy doing anything.'

The problem that Dad and Beryl had to face in regard to Clare was twofold. First they had to accept that in the event of an invasion through East Anglia Felthorpe would surely be over-run, and secondly they had public responsibilities which at that time of extreme crisis were time-consuming and of great importance. It would have been virtually impossible for them to have given Clare sufficient of their time and attention if she came home permanently, or even for the holidays. It was very difficult to judge what was in Clare's best interests because there was an unavoidable risk of her feeling either in the way or unwanted. After a great deal of thought it was decided that she should remain in England, stay on at Benenden, and spend her holidays at Marlborough.

Beryl found the challenge of the war-crisis exhilarating:

'I must confess I find the "present situation" quietly but deeply exhilarating, but probably it's a purely female (and British female at that) sort of feeling which no male could begin to understand. When other people have always done your fighting for you it's an incredible relief to feel you've come to a time when that blessed Ministry of Information poster has some meaning for you at last, and I think George is wrong about history – knitting mittens while other people make it is devastating, but actually making it is a different thing altogether. Alright, I know I'll feel very different when "things go bump in the night", but here and now I wouldn't change places with anyone in history.'

And so, alongside everyone else in Britain, the members of the Budget waited for the invasion.

'Dear me [wrote Beryl], this is a curious war – or anyway the effect has been odd. When you were in Belgium one never seemed to stop thinking about you and wondering what was happening, but now that things really are closer it seems to me I hardly think about them at all. I'm either much too busy making sure pyjamas will be finished as promised or 1001 odd jobs attended to, or else as on Sunday evening Dad and I are paddling in the lake taking off weed and scum, turtle doves crooning in the woods behind us, a family of baby ducks catching flies by the island, and a kingfisher over in the alders – peace incarnate.

'Here we are "feeling safer every day" as news of all your doings pours in, what with David in his fine new uniform protecting our shores and Paul our skies, and here we have started on our LDV Guard Post at last. It's a great pity we have to be so scattered in our various jobs; what a historic defence we could have provided for Felthorpe if only we were allowed to, David repelling the sea planes from the lake, Paul chasing Heinkels from our air, Kiff in command of the artillery – but perhaps the question of supreme command might lead to difficulties and I can believe that the "War Council" meetings might be very protracted.

'Yesterday I had a most successful "women's meeting" as we have no Women's Institute and were being flooded with pamphlets and instructions for the parish. Quite 30 turned up at very short notice which was very good indeed as fruit picking has started and many of them are away all day on this. We started off by discussing the Government pamphlet "If The Invader Comes", a single sheet very much like what the Ministry of Agriculture issue at intervals about "the peril of RATS". It's quite sensible I think, and they all seemed to have read it. Then we talked a lot about salvage, some people give their bones to their dogs but there seems no reason why a grateful country should not have them after that if it wants them. Tins have to be flattened but we are organizing the older boys for this when Dad's sandbags have all been filled and put into position. Opinions are divided as to what to do in air raids, some get up but the majority don't and I fancy more and more will stay put as raids get commoner. I've had a talk with the schoolmistress and she is counting attendances if the children turn up by 9.45 after an air raid.

'Who should turn up on Sunday but David Howarth looking incredibly smart and trim after some of these battle-dresses we're used to, but I gather he was in his "Number One Rig" or "Sunday Suit" which gives him an unfair advantage over those who carry all their possessions on their backs.

'David does seem to be having a wonderful life on his little boat (not so little, sorry); they seem to be amazingly free to do just whatever they think best, draw whatever goods they like from an official store up to the allotted sum each day and cook it for themselves, indent for just whatever they think they need for the boat, and generally get it. I think someone has to stay on the boat and the others within a given mile radius, but this would certainly include Oulton Broad, and I hope he'll be able to sail the *Squirrel*.'

David's promotion in the Navy was meteoric. On 22 June he wrote:

'To my astonishment I have become a Petty Officer after one day as a seaman. You may well raise your eyebrows, but I can assure you they will not be raised higher than mine.

'I got here (Lowestoft) last night and found a dozen other people just arrived for the same job. They were a very mixed crowd, a man from Nebraska, a very Cowes-like yachtsman, some trawlermen, a gentleman tug-skipper from the Thames, and the man who does "any more for a trip round the bay" at Lyme Regis.

'This morning we turned up at the Depot at 9 and signed on and went through various formalities such as "dental inspection" ("Anything wrong with 'em?" "No." "Good.") and a medical ("What colours are these?" "Green, red and blue." "Fine."). Then a Commodore came round and asked us in the vaguest possible terms what we knew about the sea. I was the last and he was rather fed up by then and didn't ask me anything at all. Through all this it had gradually been dawning on all of us that we were no ordinary seamen at all, so when we were told that our pay was to be 42/- a week and all found, plus a "rough-living allowance" when at sea of 1/9d a day, we all managed not to look surprised.'

Two days later:

'Wonder follows wonder very quickly these days for I now find I am skipper of a boat. It's not a very beautiful boat or very large but I am very proud of it. To be more exact, it is a rather old requisitioned motor cruiser of about 42 ft. I have a crew of two, an engineer (also a petty officer) and a deck hand, and as there are three cabins with two bunks in each, we live quite spaciously.

'We have now had our instructions, such as they are. First, we are making all the boats as watertight and grey and well armoured as possible under the circumstances. We have a machine gun and a rifle and I have a revolver. If they try to invade this place or the immediate neighbourhood we beat it out to sea with all the other ships in port and (in the Captain's words) use our own wits and make as much trouble as we can. Not a soft job but better than being on shore. We are given an entirely free hand and a boat and three guns, and that's that. I'm afraid you're right when you say that it all sounds very amateur, and the sort of thing one hoped the British had given up doing. But a large number of small boats, armed, could create more havoc in the dark than a few large ones, I think. You might say we on the sea correspond to the LDV on land, except for having to sign on the line and getting paid for it; and I think the LDV principle is a good one. Anyhow it makes life pleasant, for we are regarded as a kind of gentleman adventurer by the officers, and talk to the Captain (who is next door to an Admiral) in his own language.

'I went out on patrol two nights ago with a speedboat. We were ordered out at midnight, presumably to practise getting all the ships in the harbour out of the narrow entrance in the dark, and in a hurry. I and another speedboat went away first.

'There was no nonsense about this practice – instructions were to get to our patrol positions as quickly as possible. So I opened up to "X" knots. That will seem a pathetic speed to people like Paul, and in fact it isn't much but it was the most ecstatically thrilling thing I've ever done. Can I describe the excitement I wonder? Well, you know the sea on a starlit night, and I expect you know what a speedboat feels like. When you open the throttles she hesitates a split second, as if she couldn't be bothered, and then up go the bows in front of you, she pushes you in the back, and the keel suddenly comes alive as the boat comes out of the water and begins to plane. It's fun in daylight but in the dark! My two crew were clinging on, one either side of the cabin as lookouts. I could just see them and the bows and 50 yds of sea ahead. Astern I could see the gun on its mounting in the cockpit, and then a beautiful symmetrical wake flashing with silver-green phosphorescence. "X" knots is a good lick with the sea full of ships and no lights, and the need for a quick reaction if I or the crew spotted one ahead added to the fun. You can turn these boats much quicker than a car at the same speed because they are designed to heel inwards on a turn, so that you don't fall out, and although you skid sideways if you do it too fast, that doesn't matter. However we got to our station without seeing anything (at dawn I couldn't discover

how we'd done it, the place looked like a sinister Henley Regatta!).
Then we dropped anchor.

'I still get so much naive enjoyment out of being at sea at night
under these conditions that I never want to sleep. I stand, with one
eye on the eastern horizon, expecting I don't quite know what –
motor torpedo boats? Tugs with barges full of German soldiers being
seasick? or the *Scharnhorst?* The other eye, so to speak, and my
mind, is on the large chunks of the infinite with which I am
surrounded; and it induces trite but comfortable philosophical
reflections. My own very small boat, the sea which seems infinite, and
the sky which is, the waves which come out of the darkness and
disappear into it again, to be followed by others, just the same for all
time. Everything one can see is an obvious symbol of the ideas which
for me replace the promise of everlasting bliss, and make me really
not very scared of the possibility of someone suddenly sinking me and
my boat.

'Meanwhile the German planes come over like clockwork, up go
the searchlights, and fireworks on shore, and one sits snugly in the
dark, quite confident of being invisible from the air, and thinks of the
sirens and the damp Anderson shelters which less fortunate people
experience. Then about two o'clock they start coming back. The last
part of the entertainment is our own bombers coming in from the east
at dawn, often very low and looking somehow pleasantly tired and
wanting their breakfasts. Then when the horizon is clear and there is
nothing on it which shouldn't be there, one calls out the crew, pulls
up the anchor, very wet and chilly, and beats it for home, showing the
day's signals in case the army on shore gets too enthusiastic.'

'Hats off to Petty Officer ("Petty" my foot) Howarth [wrote Chris],
the Family's gift to the Navy, chastizer of flat-bottomed boats,
scourge of submarine tank-carriers. His job sounds terribly cold and
wet – not to say dangerous – and on behalf of all those who never go
out of their depths in less than a Channel steamer, I salute him most
respectfully.'

'Thanks to Christopher [replied David] for his salutation which I
shall have earned when I have chastized my first Dutch barge and not
before. In case he is with the infantry on the shore behind me, I'll say
for God's sake hold your fire until you can hear them Heiling Hitler
because otherwise you will be wasting your skill and ammunition on
us. And furthermore remember that if the German Army is anything
like this section of the British Navy, all it will want to do when it lands

is to lie down on the beach with its eyes shut and be given some Mothersill by a friendly hand.

'I gladly give the position of temporary family hero to Paul, and hope never to have to claim it myself. If the flat-bottomed boats appear off this coast, I shan't want to do anything so much as turn my own flat-bottomed boat in the other direction. A remote Broad would be the best place to aim for I think. There I shall abandon ship and retreat on the Felthorpe blockhouse.'

Paul had been transferred to Stroud for a conversion course and was

'unqualifiedly glad to be on fighters. Army Co-op is either inactivity (as at present) or undistinguished suicide; and interesting as it was, it was a rather unattractive future. Now I feel that though the danger over long periods is considerable of course, my expectation of life is by no means bad, and above all I've got the job I've always longed for. I might be put on escorting bombers which is an unpleasant job, but otherwise I seem to have the most moral and the "cleanest" task in the whole war, shooting down bombers over Felthorpe, Marlborough, Belton etc. Apart from that, a fast fighter above the clouds should be a perfect and almost aesthetic enjoyment. We spend our time here, after we've learnt how to fly the things, doing formation-flying and above all learning fighter tactics, both in formation attacks and in "dog-fights". The only offensive weapon that we carry is a cine-camera which registers our success or otherwise. This course should be invaluable as all the "instructors" are fighter pilots who've been in France and really do know their stuff.'

It was while he was at Stroud that he had his

'first crash in the world's fastest fighter. It was a shoddy and unexciting affair, all due to my own damned stupidity and I'm entirely unhurt, the sum of my injuries being the loss of ¼ inch of skin on my knuckles, and a scarcely noticeable bruise on my right shoulder. I was sure to crash sometime, and am not ashamed of having flown 178 hours before doing any damage.

'Anyway, I was chosen for Spitfires to my intense pleasure and had done about 4 hours on them without mishap. However, on Friday afternoon I was coming in to land when I saw another plane coming in simultaneously on my right. So I turned rather to the left and prepared to land comparatively near the left boundary. But here I must have had a blackout (mental not physical) and entirely forgot that they were digging a drainage trench out into the aerodrome from this boundary. It's a smallish aerodrome and given this one fatal mistake the next was inevitable. I touched down close over the hedge and thought all was pretty well until through the dirt spattered over my windscreen I saw the earthworks perhaps 50 yards ahead. That was a pregnant moment, I was still doing about 40 m.p.h. on the ground and had to start thinking. It was obvious I couldn't stop her in time so I considered taking off again, but the hangars on the far boundary seemed unpleasantly close and I preferred a trench at slow speed to a hangar in full flight. So I braked until the tail started to "lift" and tried ineffectually to swing away to the right.

'The trench, I would say, was about 1 ft 6 in wide and 3 ft deep with a mound of earth about 2 ft high on the far side and as I reckon I hit it at about 25–30 m.p.h. you wouldn't imagine that it would cause much trouble but it did. By the Grace of God it didn't turn over or I might have been hurt; I skidded on about 15–20 yards and stopped – stuck-up in the air as a memorial to carelessness and incompetence. The only thing in the whole programme of which I'm inordinately proud is that I found the engines switched off on coming to rest, and yet cannot remember touching them; I can only assume I turned them off automatically as I've always had to train myself.

'I had been jolted most unceremoniously round the cockpit and just sat there slightly dazed and swearing formidably until some workmen dashed up and yelled to me to get out before it caught fire. Once brought to my senses however I moved with commendable rapidity, largely encouraged by a sinister hiss of escaping petrol. Nevertheless, it remained quite unburnt and that is the whole sorry tale of Paul's first and most disgraceful lapse.

'I was very afraid I should be thrown out of fighters for damned stupidity, having at last got to where I want to be in this war. But I was spared that catastrophe, and the incident was finally closed with a very sticky interview with the CO this morning.'

After completing his training on fighters Paul was transferred to Biggin Hill, just southeast of London, near Downe – 'the hottest 100 square miles in the world'.

'We were given our choice so far as possible of stations at Aston Down on Friday. Alas, there was nowhere in either Norfolk or Lincs, and after that I thought I'd try and get near London for many reasons. So when I saw that one pilot was wanted at Biggin Hill visions of tea and cucumber sandwiches with my civilized relations made up my mind for me. As a matter of fact I feel I might just as well be in N. Scotland so far as seeing the Howarths is concerned for we're at 30 minutes (at most) notice all day from 04.00 hrs to 22.00 hrs and about half the time we're at 5 minutes notice.

'I am now a member of No. 32 Squadron (Regulars). The squadron is equipped with Hurricanes (only natural after I've been trained on Spitfires) and for a week or so I'm "on probation" and non-operational, learning the particular Squadron's tactics and convincing all and sundry that I'm an "ace" pilot. I'm very pleased to be on Hurricanes; they're a bit slower (about 350 m.p.h. to the Spitfire's 370) but infinitely more manoeuvrable. I'm not the one to complain if a Messerschmitt can run away from me, and it's encouraging to know that if I go into a steep turn and keep it constantly as steep as I can take it without completely blacking-out, no modern fighter can turn so quickly after me, so that if the aforesaid Messerschmitt is sucker enough to follow me I've got him cold. Moreover, the view out of a Hurricane, (except behind) is better than out of a Spitfire.

'Since I arrived, No. 32 has been in 3 dog-fights (in 23 hours) with casualties on both sides, so my "probation" may be unexpectedly short. The SE coast seems an unhealthy hole.'

Paul's stay at Biggin Hill was very brief; the squadron was pulled out to 'recuperate' and after spending nine nights in seven different places he ended up in Ternhouse near Edinburgh. For the rest of July he was based in the northeast seeing no action but being constantly aware of its imminence.

'It's difficult to describe, but if you can imagine the most important event in your life, and then knowing that sometime, in some form it will happen, maybe now (I'm at 15 minutes notice now e.g.) maybe next week, and always having to be mentally, physically, and sartorially prepared for it, you may get some idea. In addition one only averages 5 to 6 hours sleep every night and of the last 3 nights, I've spent 2½ in my clothes. Don't, however, think I'm exhausted or anything; I'm really on very good form, but I'm beginning to realize why fighter-pilots talk glibly about "wanting" an invasion. Then at least you know where you are, fighting all day and all night with intervals for food and sleep where you can find them.'

Finally, at 5 p.m. on 15 August Dad and Beryl received a telegram from him: 'WELL AND TRULY BAPTIZED'. This was followed by a long letter:

'BLUE' SECTION, 'A' SQUADRON
15 AUGUST 1940

F/Lt   D.H.
P/O   D.C.
P/O   P.M.

'Of all the fighter pilots engaged in battles over England on Monday, 15 August, I have no doubt that I filled the most unheroic role. But since it was in many ways a historic day, and to me personally perhaps the most important day of my life, I make no apology for describing it at length.

'I am a pilot-officer in "X" Squadron, equipped with Hurricanes and stationed somewhere on the northeast Coast. A squadron, for the benefit of the uninitiated, is divided into "A" and "B" Flights and goes into battle in four sections of three planes each. I belong to "B" Flight and on this particular day was flying No. 3 in "Blue" Section.

'August 15 promised to be an inconspicuous day. The weather itself was inconspicuous, for the sun was lost behind thick clouds that stretched continuously at 5000 ft, and below them the country seemed characteristically grey and unexciting. Furthermore "X" Squadron was enjoying 24 hours "release" and there seemed no likelihood of any break in the unending monotony that by now we found so depressing.

'It was at 12.30 p.m. exactly that we knew Field-Marshal Goering had not overlooked us. Above the roar of our "sister-squadron" of Spitfires taking off, the loudspeakers called all "X" Squadron to "Readiness immediately". By a miracle we contrived, in ten minutes, to find twelve pilots ready for battle; some of us, it is true, were dinner-less, one at least was still wet from a bath – but we were ready. At 12.45 p.m. the order was given for the squadron to take off as one force, and in some three minutes 12 Hurricanes were in the air, climbing steadily in formation round the aerodrome.

'None of us could deceive himself that this was not "the real thing". Exceptional as it was to call a squadron from "released" to "readiness", we knew that two squadrons would only be sent up against a major raid. Preparing now for my first aerial battle, I can only confess that I was frightened; after the first three minutes of hectic "scrambling", thought was able to return, and with an almost physical sensation of fear. My stomach seemed to be separated from its normal bonds, and to be working rapidly in reverse; but inevitably the fear was mingled with excitement, and even with relief that at last our seemingly endless wait was interrupted, and I found myself able to view the situation almost dispassionately.

'As we turned out to sea and began the long climb to 20,000 ft fear was still my prevailing emotion, but most vividly I can remember certain thoughts that recurred in my mind. None, to my later disappointment, was conventional: I did not think of my family, my fiancée, or my country. At times such as these, thought becomes something far more personal and immediate. I remember, as we crossed the coast, wishing that I had inflated my "Mae West" less inadequately, and reminded myself that next day I was due for leave; and perhaps most vividly I remember mentally rehearsing the "drill for abandoning Hurricane aircraft by parachute."

'Ten miles out to sea. We are now at 12,000 ft with blue sky above us and a fleecy carpet of cloud far beneath. The engine is running as only a "Merlin" can; the oxygen hisses quietly in my mask. Then almost simultaneously we see them; two miles to the right and 1500 ft above us a long closely packed formation of bombers passes us travelling due west, so close and thick that they appear as a cloud moving across the sky. German, of course, but what are they? They look like Heinkel 111, or perhaps Dorniers – difficult to tell from here. Well, here we go, for good or bad, I'm in for my first fight. Thank God, fear has given place to excitement – and even, I'm afraid, a primitive, pleasurable, blood-lust such as comes with a high pheasant. For 10 months I have been trained for this moment, and by God it's come. Oh, Lord, how I wish it was all over – and yet I know I don't; I wouldn't miss it for worlds.

'My earphones clamour "Red and Yellow sections to bombers; Blue and Green to fighters". So it's not to be the beautiful precision of fighter attacks for me, but the catch-as-catch-can of a dog-fight with Messerschmitt 110. We split up; and as six of us turn in and climb towards the fighters (about 20–25 of them, I should think – odds of 4 to 1. Oh, what the hell! It's been far worse for others) I turn my firing button from "safe" to "fire" and switch on the reflector-sight, until I smile at the similarity to the countless practice dog-fights that I've carried out. Now we're about 400 yards away, climbing in good formation with Blue section leading, and my morale is suddenly shattered by seeing a Me.110 blow up in mid-air – one moment a graceful twin-engined fighter, the next a vivid orange flame and a heavy pall of smoke, while small scraps float idly down like leaves. Poor wretches! If that should happen to me.

'Four to one numerical inferiority, and yet we have the moral supremacy, for on seeing us the Me. abandon the bombers to our colleagues' mercy, and follow each other round in two large defensive circles. Then we are up among them, and for 5 seconds I am utterly, hopelessly, bewildered, until David, leading my section, disappears below me, and I pull myself together. Down we go into a hit-and-run attack on the circle, and break away early remembering to avoid getting entangled in it. "God, they must be insane or hopelessly inexperienced – they're breaking up the circle; and now we're in our element. Who cares if it's 10–3, when one's seen one's opponents make mistakes, and knows that in a free-for-all one's machine is far more reliable and more manoeuvrable, even if it is slower?" A couple of Me. flash across my sights and I give them a burst each to speed their departure without following them. I see Duggie flashing past on the tail of another and envy him his determination. Being a novice, I decide to bide my time and cruise about in the middle awaiting an opportunity. Did I say cruise? That is a euphemism, for if you fly straight for 5 seconds, you'll probably never fly again. So I forget everything I've ever learnt about accurate flying and throw the plane everywhere except straight. "Crippen, just what I've been waiting for, a Me. diving slowly away to my right." A quick turn, that nearly blacks me out, and there it is in the middle of my sights.

'Fear no longer exists, nor any moral principles; this is the moment I've been trained for, and the sensation is such as one felt years ago when the "scissors" worked at rugger. In a fever of excitement and primitive enjoyment I press the button and keep it pressed. Wisps of smoke fly from my wings as the tracer goes away, and with a grim satisfaction I see that I'm scoring hits. The Me. turns into a tight spiral dive, but a Hurricane can comfortably out-turn it, and I follow down firing bursts of a few seconds each. I remember the disappointment I felt as it refused to catch fire, and the dazed relief with which I realized that I wasn't being fired at (I imagine I must have killed the rear-gunner). At 5000 ft, it disappeared into cloud, and I made no attempt to follow it, but returned to the major fray, where I knew David and Duggie were outnumbered.

'The fray no longer existed. Where, three minutes before, there had been 30 planes wheeling and diving, now there was nothing save two Hurricanes almost 5 miles away, searching, like me, for something hostile. Fights carried out at such high speeds break up unbelievably fast, and only continue together for 2 or 3 minutes at the most. Now I was thirsting for blood, so I dived down through the cloud, and searched for stragglers in the cold greyness below. But the sky was clear, and since my ammunition was running low I congratulated myself on surviving my first battle and the prospect of leave, and turned back low across the water, past a significant oil-patch and landed – first down.

'In four minutes my plane was refuelled and rearmed by a small host of airmen, and as I gulped down the last of my cocoa, David landed and taxied back with his thumbs pointing deliriously up – a Me.110. Duggie also had one down, and the squadron as a whole could count seven certain successes against five bullet-holes – a result highly satisfactory in view of our large proportion of untried pilots.

'That was the whole of my inconspicuous part of that day, save for a long patrol half an hour later in an unsuccessful effort to intercept the returning bombers. In our "sectors" about 30 miles long, 32 planes were "confirmed", 21 were "unconfirmed" and 111 damaged; the cost of this was four planes slightly damaged (all returned to their bases) and one pilot slightly wounded. I cannot attempt to explain it, and I believe my fellow-pilots themselves can only accept it as a fact. Our machines are better, our pilots are better, our morale is inconceivably high, and we know that we can and we shall do it again.'

Pat's time in the 145th Field Ambulance was coming to a close; by mid-July the first stage of his getting a commission had gone through. 'Thanks entirely to the personal intervention of Bernard, Hitler permitting, I report at Shorncliffe, Folkestone on August 8. Naturally I shall be horribly disappointed if Hitler decides not to permit, but in that case personal issues would be rather unimportant, so I just pray for 23 days' grace! What an if! It seems inconceivable that Folkestone should be habitable in 3 weeks' time.'

Before going to the OCTU he had seven days' leave, most of which he spent at Felthorpe, and he found

'living at home is like Dunkirk without the enemy. Planes soar overhead most of the day, and battledress and hospital pyjamas lie all round the house. I go out to try to capture a rabbit to raise the meat-ration and I have to be careful not to take lethal 12-bore cartridges.'

During his leave Pat was able to get down to Aldershot to meet up with Chris for the first time in eleven months, and they talked endlessly from lunch until ten in the evening.

'Chris looked remarkably well; he hasn't changed much in the eleven months and can still go into a room full of red-hats and colonels and proclaim very loudly "I'm disgusted with the Army", leaving his L/Cpl brother covered in shame and amusement.'

For his part, Chris found Pat

'much the same I'm glad to say, and bears no traces of the soldier about him beyond the ribbon on his chest. I noted that his boots were dirtier than mine, but my cap dirtier than his.'

It was a splendid day for both of them, despite the difficulty of finding a place in which to have a meal together.

'Unfortunately a big snag arose at the hotel. Some rooms were for "Officers and Cadets only", some for "Officers", and some for "Cadets and Guests only". Into none of these could Pat be induced to enter. Eventually we found a lowlier room entitled "Cadets and Other Ranks only" and here we drank peacefully together. At one moment it looked as though the only possible meeting place for Pat and me was going to be a room off the passage marked "Gentlemen" – and even here I think Pat would have hesitated to enter, so humble is he in uniform.'

Included in the subjects they talked about together was Dad's mild rebuke of them for being critical of the Army and of the Government at a time of such extreme crisis. Pat's criticisms had been mainly of the 'nonsense' in the Army.

'I'm very tired of the Army and find that it all lies in the doing of "silly" things. Surely France and Dunkirk proved to us (to me at least) that if you are busy or on a job then bodily comfort is of no importance. During Dunkirk week I slept an average of 3½ hours a day and ate Army biscuits, corned beef and ½-portion tea, and yet it was easily the happiest and pleasantest week of my army life. Here we have running water (none for the last 3 days at D.), excellent food, enough blankets, cinemas in the evening, beer, cigarettes, books, letters, and yet the unit is really fed-up. Now why should this be so? It's because of the "silly nonsense". For example on Church Parade this morning we had that annoying "Parade shun" – pause – "stand at ease" five times before the service began, as 2nd Lt handed over to Captain, to Major etc. etc. Similarly, why "Hurry along there", or "Right Dress", why do officers always keep us waiting on parade? It's tiring and annoying. Why march to our meals? etc. These things are far more demoralizing than shell-fire.'

Christopher's criticisms had been more profound and more widely based but he found much in Dad's letters with which he agreed.

'Dad is quite right when he says the national morale is higher than it ever has been. Why? I venture four reasons:

a) because we're fighting on the home ground.
b) because the man-in-the-street didn't like or trust the French from the start.
c) because the odds are now definitely against us.
d) because the war has entered a novel stage. Much of the dreadfulness of the war so far has been the 'all-over-again' feeling; this invasion is something new and strangely challenging in a way in which the Continental business wasn't. Digging tank-traps in Hampshire is somehow quite different from digging them in Flanders. It's not just that it's England, but that it's a novelty, something that hasn't already been done by our fathers as well as we're likely to do it.'

But with Dad's opinion: 'I feel that today, in our emergency, we must bury ... all criticism of those in authority, Christopher disagreed strongly.

'You have said this ever since the war began (and before), Father. But suppose the country had felt that way. We should certainly still be being governed by Chamberlain, Hoare, and Simon. They would still be successfully opposing things like the institution of a Ministry of Supply. Churchill would not be in the House of Commons at all – the "loyal" Conservatives of Epping nearly got him out of it as it was. Bevin, Morrison, Alexander and the rest would still be labelled "irresponsible" and "unfit for office". Everyone would be loyally hiding their secret doubts and agreeing that "no alternative

government was available anyway". Sir Oswald [Mosley] and his boys
would still be at large. In fact we would be heading straight to where
France is now. France's collapse was largely due to the suppression
of free criticism of the government and the bureaucracy.

'You say the times are critical, and so they are. But they are no
more critical than when Chamberlain was forced to resign – the first
days of the Belgian invasion – and how many of us regret that event
now? If we've messed this war up so far, it's surely through being too
easy going rather than too critical.'

On 8 August Pat arrived at the OCTU in Folkestone and

'the speed of the Bren-gun carrier which brought me from the station
was merely the prelude to a fantastically rushed first 24 hours . . . this
afternoon I spent an hour learning how to fire a bren-gun and tonight
at 8.00 I go out again on the bren-gun. The reason for all this
bren-gunnery is that on Sunday we go out to man the pill-boxes in
—— harbour. No doubt you can guess the harbour and it promises
considerable fun with air-battles, convoys etc. and even the chance of
an invasion proper.

'I had dinner in the Officers' Mess on my last night with the 145th
– a delightfully democratic evening and I was the guest of honour.
The CO made a speech which really embarrassed me, and I made, I
think, quite a good short reply. Lots of beer, sherry, and port and
back to bed at midnight.'

Folkestone was an exciting place to be in at that time. One
night when Pat was on duty down at the harbour

'About 30 Junkers glided out over us with their engines shut off
and dived down to our local [aerodrome] and dropped a dozen
bombs. I was on watch and saw magnificently. They then dropped
bombs into the town, hideously near our [gasworks] but they missed
it. One plane then saw us, or decided to unload, and three bombs
were dropped. At the time I was about 50 ft above the sea, on a very
heavy stone structure, with a parapet of about 4 ft; I was in the middle
of a highly exposed stretch, doing my sentry beat.

'A shrieking, airy, rushing noise followed immediately by two
more; a beastly noise at a distance and just horrid when it gets louder
and louder and louder until you take a flying leap onto your face
behind the parapet, shut your eyes as though thereby to miss it, think

for just a moment of how silly it is that you should have to behave like an animal, then a deafening report, and another, and another, and God, you're unhurt. Look out for the shrapnel coming down – get your rifle – run for cover – keep under the parapet you fool – damn the AA can't you lay off, you're peppering all round me. Get there at last, make a wisecrack and get your breath back. Christmas, how did it miss me? Look as though you don't give a damn and go on with your sentry beat. Ought I have run? Yes, I'm allowed to take cover when bombs drop but not before. Christmas, that was exciting and really rather good fun; knees are still a bit wobbly, but that always happens.

'Family, I've no idea what that reads like but for about two minutes I've just been re-living the scene, and writing just anything. Actually the three bombs burst 50 ft below me, and horizontally the nearest was about 35 yards away so they were really quite close.

'Paul of course must be our Budgeteer No. 1 for several months now (unless David gets going) and the best the rest of us can do is to hang on until we get again into the middle of it all, but I feel that out of our immobile contributors I have the best viewpoint – seeing a great deal of air-fighting and excitement. We are really in a grandstand seat.

'I saw one fight this week which I think deserves a mention. The alarm went about midday and I rushed into full equipment and ran to perch myself on the top of our "roof" behind some sandbags. Our boys left the "local" and were in the air in time to greet the enemy, consisting of between 20 and 30 bombers. I then had a magnificent view of a tremendous battle which only lasted 5 minutes but during which I saw 8 planes down, and I could not have seen half. The first casualty was a Hurricane which buried itself in the sea about 300 yards away and went straight under; he was followed within 30 seconds by a Junker which crashed in about the same place and burst into a hundred pieces. Both of them came over us very close before crashing and their engines were silent – giving a sense of dignified disaster. I looked behind me then to see a Junker out of control, and 2 parachutes graciously descending amidst a seething riot of planes. Fantastic sight and I stared amazed while two more Germans were shot down; having deposited their cargo the remaining bombers left for home, though I saw 2 more shot down into the sea; and looking back finally I saw a Messerschmitt falling in flames. Seven Germans, one British in five minutes – I was quite speechless at the speed of it all, and the incredible performance of our planes and pilots. The week's totals, which at first sight seem so fantastically unequal, make more sense to me since I arrived here, we are of infinitely superior quality.

'I can remember one rather good air raid (which really passed over us to machine-gun Stephen) – there were countless hundreds of German planes travelling very high and we contented ourselves with a little AA; nevertheless one shell brought down three planes – two in flames. Nice shooting.

'The next bit of news was the convoy – a brilliant and deliberate insult. Have you ever seen a man who sticks out his jaw at you and says "hit me as hard as you like" and you know it's no use? So it was with an odd 30,000 ton convoy sailing through the "German Channel". We saw it far away on a morning of peerless visibility and lowish bombing clouds, and we all stopped working in order to watch, for it was so clearly a compulsory challenge. We did not see the bombing but had a front-row seat for the shelling – rather thrilling and demonstrating admirably just how much sea there is to ship. The destroyers laid a pretty smoke-screen and the shells were, on the whole, profoundly inaccurate.

'The same evening they shelled Dover (and quite a bit further in too – but shush) – terrific noise! You see the flash in France and exactly 112 seconds later you get the most enormous explosion, due largely I suspect to the echo. We viewed it with mixed feelings as they dropped 3 shells into our OCTU (strewth!) the day before.

'Otherwise there is little war news; we're right on the direct daily route of the bombers and we celebrate our 100th raid today – at the moment we're on 99. Our 97th was exciting, an Me. took it into its head to machine-gun our streets. I was in the barber's chair and everything went off at once – Me. cannon, Bren, Bofors, Rifles – an amazing noise. I felt miserable and longed to dive under the chair, but the barber just went on clipping.

'Incidentally I rather hate Paul being at Aunt's [Biggin Hill] because I find I know too much! For instance his local was given merry hell last night – and every time I see a Hurricane down my heart stops until the pilot bales out.'

In one of his letters from the northeast Paul referred to Pat's letter, noting that

'You seem to be a most insidious 5th columnist; it's not good for my morale to be told that "only" one parachute failed to open, or that a Hurricane crashed into the sea and immediately went under.'

Anxiety for Paul's safety was ever-present and was felt most intensely by Dad. In one of his letters he clearly revealed his fears and in replying to him Pat conveyed not only his feelings about Paul but also perhaps a little of the general expectancy that death could be imminent for many others.

'I know only too well what you feel because I also have to put up with the awful fear on seeing a Hurricane shot down or hearing that Biggin Hill is being bombed. I live in the shadow of a telegram from you, as you wait in fear on the Air Ministry. Paul lives an incredibly risky life, but one that has, I think, done him an amazing amount of good; for so many years he has insisted upon being considered the "non-playing Mayhew", and now, when for the first time life starts to be serious he eclipses both his brothers and undergoes the supreme trial of the RAF. He justifies himself not only to the world, but also to himself – for the first time he need have no inferiority complex, no doubts as to his own courage; he has taken the family lead and he is now setting a standard which we never expected to have to follow. I'm sure the RAF has made Paul and has enabled him finally to find his place in the family; the future may be very rough for him, but I thank God that even if the worst should fall to him, at least he has had these 3 months in which to find himself.

'It is now 2.30 a.m. and I'm sitting in a dug-out, having taken over at 1.00 a.m. and expecting to be relieved at 7.30 a.m. . . . . I fancy that Churchill practically promised us an invasion and I'm glad to see that everything points to them attacking Kent rather than Norfolk – I don't look forward to it because life is so eminently worthwhile the retaining, and there is so much that I still want to have a shot at doing or seeing done.

'The weather has been all on our side recently, but today there is a mist and dead-flat sea, so perhaps this is the opportunity – you'll certainly know by the time you read this letter!

'We are staying here come what may, to act as a delaying unit – for we are not a real fighting unit – until such time as a mobile reserve can counter such advance as the enemy may be able to make. Maybe I shall be unlucky, as you may be if they attack Norfolk. Unlike all my collegues here I view the prospect of killing some Saxon son with horror, knowing no alternative but knowing that it must change me, dividing myself against myself. I recognize the fact that I cannot now have it both ways, that some part of me must be broken, and that death alone could save me as a united man.'

*   *   *

Pat's fears were justified because by the beginning of September Paul was back at Biggin Hill. He sent a brief note to the Budget but later amplified it when he had a 'most morale-restoring 24 hours' rest' at Downe, with Uncle, Aunt and Stephen. His excuse for not having written was that

'I really was tired yesterday after 5 days continually on the job. My score has gone up by one Dornier 7; early yesterday afternoon we were sent up to patrol the aerodrome and soon saw the usual hosts of Midian advancing, accompanied by fighters. By the Grace of God the fighters were already occupied so we went for the bombers. I attacked from in front and to the left and the outside leading Dornier turned head-on to me for his own protection. Having thus got him out of the formation I whipped round in a steep turn and went after him. Just as I was nicely in position bullets started flying from behind me, and for ½ a minute I had to devote myself to throwing off what I imagine was a Messerschmitt 109. That accomplished I returned to my Dornier, got behind and below him and opened fire. He started to turn and then very quickly soared up, stalled and went spinning down. I wasn't sure he was finished so went down after him from about 15,000 ft to the ground. Nobody "baled-out" to my surprise and it crashed in a road, very near our PM's lodgings. It hit the ground with a terrific explosion, and when I left the wood was burning furiously.

'Otherwise I have flown and fought and fought. On Wednesday I massacred a sea-plane with the help of two colleagues and fought unsuccessfully with an Me. 109, finishing up by diving 15,000 ft at full throttle after it. I think I was doing about 500 m.p.h. at the bottom and I don't want to do it again. On Thursday we went into a fight at a hopeless disadvantage and I had a large portion of my tail shot away, but I got down quite OK.

'On Saturday I got a Heinkel 111 bomber. We ran into a very big formation with the usual fighter escort, and six of us made a head-on attack to break it up. A head-on attack is very frightening for all concerned and it broke them up beautifully so that I later found 9 Heinkels flying along without any fighters. The rest of my section seemed to have vanished so I attacked the 9th in the formation and set one engine smoking. At this the entire formation turned round and went home, which seemed very flattering to me. My original target was now straggling badly so I used up my ammunition on it and finally left it going in a steep dive with its undercarriage down, its starboard engine on fire and its port engine belching smoke.

Apparently that is counted as "confirmed" though I couldn't see it crash.

'Otherwise I have been bombed with anything from 2000 lb bombs to small incendiaries – no less than 5 times. Twice I was at about 15,000 ft when it happened, once at about 500 ft, once at 5 ft just as I left the ground and saw them dropping in front of me, and once on the ground which was the most frightening. I find it all very morale-shattering and very inconvenient. In addition we've inevitably suffered a fair amount of damage and life is a little primitive. One is permanently in the air or underground, never on the surface like ordinary mortals.'

When Paul had his twenty-four hours' rest with the Howarths, Stephen was working in London but living at Downe; he was deeply involved in the Home Guard and was sent on a

'two day course for Home Guards at Osterley Park. An electrifying two days, based about 85% on Spanish experience as modified by reports of this war. After an hour's lecture of a general nature we jumped straight into the midst of everything, with one on guerilla warfare, delivered by a cripple of about 4 ft 9 in. "Forget the playing fields of Eton and the Marquess of Queensberry" he bellowed "and remember that no way is too dirty to kill a German." With the result that I now know all about how to use a knife and a cheesecutter. Always attack from the back, dear Uncle Basil. If you have to do it from the front, slit him up the stomach – but he'll squeal. He won't if knifed from behind.'

Up to the middle of August Downe had not suffered heavily from the war but on the 18th Stephen wrote:

'I fear that I was a little hasty in describing, yesterday, this place as blissfully peaceful, or whatever it was. Today's programme has been quite strenuous. 10.15 a.m. HGs parade to have a scouting party against our nearest town. 12.45, blazing hot day. HG rapidly approaching Queen's Head; plenty of good-natured badinage about beer. We were within 5 minutes of the sacred engines when up went the Biggin Hill planes, up went the siren, and left-turn in the village instead of right and utter gloom all over the party. However, five minutes later there really was hell to pay. Machine-gunning, colossal explosions every second or two, and suddenly three German bombers hedge-hopping in front of my loop-hole. A minute later, one hedge-hopping straight at us with a fighter on its tail, machine-gunning like blazes. Two of our party in the road lay and prayed and were missed, luckily for them. Columns of smoke to left and right.

'Well, assessing the damage afterwards, the golf course was plastered with bombs, and one house laid out rather badly. We have two duds at the moment between us and the cricket pitch, and others around within about 200 yards. In the valley there is another house laid out badly, about 10 minutes walk away. The village fortunately was missed, but the next one was less lucky and four people were killed in an Anderson shelter which had been left open at both ends. Two more were killed in the opposite direction and we had several shrapnel cases in the first-aid point.

'On the credit side there's one down about a mile away, and another went absolutely sky-high according to rumour two or three miles off. I don't see how any of the four I saw could have got away with it, as they were so low that they are said to have flown under some electric cables or pylons, probably erroneously.'

From that day Downe was totally involved in the Battle of Britain, or more particularly the Battle for London; day after day the bombers flew in over the village and always there was the likelihood of an attack on the nearby Biggin Hill aerodrome. Uncle Bertie wrote, late in September:

'Well, the curfew tolls the knell of passing day (it doesn't, of course, the siren takes its place, at present a little before 8 p.m., we hastily finish supper and clear up), the Dornier winds slowly o'er the lea; the Home Guard outward plods its weary way (those of us on duty to the observation post, a reserve to this very house where it beds down in Darwin's drawing room) – and leaves the world to darkness – except for flak, searchlights, and fires over London – and to me, and a good many other people who one way or another are interested. The rest betake themselves to bed in cellars, Andersons, or what-not (by the way, don't you like the way London has simply assumed the tubes for refuge, despite official bumbledom, which has now had to recognize the practice? Democracy is occasionally capable of governing itself). In our case, besides the cellar which is stuffed with staff and others, there is a ground floor passage in the heart of the house, which gives a sense of security which may or may not be spurious; for myself, after trying this position for two nights, I am reverting to my own bed on the first floor, out of which I may be blown upwards, downwards or laterally at any time. At the moment I feel it's worth the risk, I may be proved wrong, no doubt you'll hear if I am.

'I am no doubt a mild case of claustrophobia; at any rate, my happiest days are those – one in five – spent on duty at the Home Guard Observation post. It has an immense field of view and one can at least see, and not merely guess, what is going on. I happened to be on duty the night they put up the first full-dress London barrage: it was of no obvious use except to cheer people up and hasn't been done on that scale again, though it is no mean show on any night. Bits of shell – now and then a whole one – make us huddle under our tin hats or scoot for cover or, quite illogically, present our backsides uppermost to the elements. Clearly neither we nor the Germans have found the remedy against night-raiding. Time and again one sees the searchlights forming a lovely spider's web and the flak shells bursting all over the place and sometimes apparently right on the spider, but it goes trundling on. Very occasionally, hits have been seen from here; I have seen one. The lights followed a raider right across the sky for miles; he went on straight like a rabbit in a headlight. Suddenly he dissolved into little sparks and was silent – searchlights all out – finished. Quite dramatic it was.

'A nasty idea which obtrudes from time to time is that I see no particular reason why "these things" should end, at any rate in my day. The spectacular defeat of an attempted invasion might cause the German people to find Hitler out; if he doesn't attempt one he'll have something to explain, but that will probably be only too easy. We may succeed in frightening Mussolini. Meanwhile we have to go on making our own magnificent effort, and waiting upon what might be sent in the way of supplies from the United States of America, a country for which I confess a considerable distaste. There, as it seems to me, they speak us fair and take our money while they let us fight their battle for them – not that there is any objection in principle to doing that so long as they do not say (as in 1919) that they won the war, nor send us some half-educated schoolmaster to help settle the peace.

'No doubt one should try to overcome these prejudices, but you know my other one, about politicians, whom as a class I believe to be arrogant, ignorant, and stupid. When Christopher writes to the effect that our victory will be political rather than purely military, I rather think that this is one of the grimmest forecasts I have read about the war. Unfortunately I've felt the same way myself, and encountered the idea in others. It is probably right, but whether it will give peace in our time – oh Lord!'

On 7 September Paul spent twenty-four hours with

'Aunt, Uncle, Stephen and David. It was a hectic time; not only did
Sally run a high temperature, not only did the cook give notice, but
Goering launched his great offensive. About 4 p.m. the sirens went as
usual and I hung around the outside of the dug-out, but then went on
the roof with Stephen to watch a largish fire in the Thames estuary.
We heard a large formation somewhere around, when suddenly we
saw Dorniers coming straight for us in vast numbers. Stephen says he
counted 17 before he gave up, but I wouldn't know because I was
already fighting my way down a dangerously wobbly ladder and
showing none of the sang-froid expected of an RAF officer.
However, later I went out with Uncle's tin hat and watched an
awe-inspiring fight straight above my head between 28 Dorniers and
12 British fighters; but the result seemed rather indecisive. After a
visit to the "local" and an excellent supper Stephen and I, and at
intervals David, yet again climbed to the roof-tops and (slightly
fortified by rum) watched the greatest firework display ever staged by
man.

'A little way down the Thames estuary oil-tanks were blazing
furiously and pouring out dense black smoke for miles. Every now
and then the flames leapt up to at least 150 ft, I should say, and lit the
whole countryside up with the most uncanny vividness. But the main
display was of course the fire in the docks; this was really
indescribable, for over about 3 or 4 miles of horizon the whole sky
was lit up as though the sun were setting and the flicker of the flames
was reflected in the pall of smoke that seemed to cover the whole of
London. Not unnaturally such a beacon was too much for Goering to
resist and there was a ceaseless procession of German planes going
over, dropping their bombs and returning, and the night was wild
with AA gun-fire, the thud of bombs and the dramatic fires.
Personally I shall never forget it, and I think we all felt that we were
watching history being made.'

Stephen wrote of the raids:

'I suppose I'm the only Londoner, so I may as well do my piece
about the sights.

'On Monday when I started for town it turned out that "some
dislocation of transport facilities" meant no trains at all to Charing X,
Cannon St, London Bridge or Victoria, but a limited supply to
Holborn Viaduct; so scorning this I leapt on a bus in Bromley which

rapidly filled to the brim and went dashing up to London Bridge like a taxi, scattering the gesticulating throngs of Catford and Lewisham like chaff. London Bridge was closed to traffic because there was a big fire near the north end and the traffic blocks were perfectly appalling; evidently everyone had decided to use their cars as the railways were so much off, and lots of main thoroughfares were roped off and there were extra buses into the bargain! The best individual bag was, I think, the Bank of England – leave it out if you like Beryl, but it took a knock or two.

'As a result, I feel that the indiscrimination of the bombing has been overdone. It was very bad bombing, but quite a number of important things have been hit by now – I suppose better not say what – and I observe that a disproportionate number of holes seem to exist just by the side of the two railways I have used since the raids started. Also, I'm told, the bombers seem to cruise about to some extent before loosing off, which doesn't sound like indiscrimination, but this is mere hearsay. Whether it is comforting or not, I cannot make up my mind.

'I haven't dared go rubbernecking round St Paul's, but clearly there has been some bad damage there. On the whole, though, the impression is of considerable total damage, but in any given area relatively little damage; there's lots left. And that given that military objectives are more than troop concentrations and aeroplane factories, the Germans are keeping within the bounds of decency. After all, we have announced our intention of defending London, and the place is simply thick with important railways, power stations, gas and water works, docks, warehouses and God knows what, besides disgustingly teeming slums cheek by jowl with all these more or less fair targets. Don't think that I am pro-Goering, but I like my propaganda genuine if it can be, and we can make all the genuine article we want without having to exaggerate.'

Later in the month he wrote:

'All nicely settled down to raids now, I think. As usual the poor old East End bears the brunt of the maladjustments of the social system. In the Deptford–Rotherhithe area, which is the only working-class one I have been through lately, it's the absence of communal shelters, the millions of people, and the fact that the houses lie down in heaps if a bit of shrapnel whizzes past them, which causes the trouble as far as I could tell. Elsewhere as the population can mostly get into private shelters, or at any rate into public ones, and as you don't have more than a dozen houses or so to the acre, things are less impressive.

'The main excitement in the routine to which we have now accustomed ourselves is seeing what ingenious way the Southern will run its trains up to town. One scarcely ever goes the same way twice. Yesterday we edged ourselves gingerly over a viaduct carrying four tracks, two of which at one point were dangling in space. It is now becoming somewhat against suburban etiquette to comment too freely to perfect strangers in trains about visible damage; after all, if it was done last night there's lots that wasn't, and the really odd thing would be if one didn't see something new. The culmination came yesterday when my train, which had shown serious symptoms of despondency on hearing an alarm when nearing home after a record tour round the railway system, sheltered in a shallow cutting for half an hour during the raid. There was a very intense barrage from very nearby guns, obviously bombs were dropped not very far away; planes were overhead the whole time. There were ten people in the carriage; no one said a word, no one opened a window to look out. They just went on reading their papers, men and girls.

'It's extraordinarily interesting to watch the Moralists v. The Rest in *The Times* on retaliating on Berlin; I think the rest win really. No one can expect to square their consciences during a war, since war is essentially a wrong way of tackling a problem, and the only excuse for it is that it is the only way of combating or preventing a greater wrong. That being so, it seems a hopeless mental exercise to try and draw a clear shining line through the fog and say "This side, the act of a Christian; that side, of a barbarian." The only people who can logically and rightly be left out in modern warfare are, I think, those who are non-combatants, will remain so, and whose death or demoralization will not weaken the enemy. On that definition, the bombing of the City of Benares is clearly barbarism. But is the bombing of London? and would the bombing of Berlin be so? I don't think so, I think both could be regarded as matters of military expediency. I am not sure if this type of bombing is worth starting because once you start wholeheartedly attacking civilian morale, retaliation becomes virtually essential as soon as you show signs of success; and after that the war enters on a phase far less controllable by the military or any other authority, far less predictable, and indeed riskier for both sides. However, here we are, wondering whether to retaliate, the other side having started; and I suggest that we should . . .

Aunt Ellie wrote of Stephen and of the problems of living at Down House at that time.

'Stephen struggled up and down to London until last night when it became quite impossible and he had to sleep in the basement at the Bank. Christopher wired to him to meet him at a "prom" on Thursday – I ask you. The result was that they never met, and Stephen had to take to the ditch three times to avoid AA shells whilst walking the last four miles home.

'Stephen's almost incredible calm is quite impossible of imitation by anyone else, though I am thankful to have someone about who is capable of it. Bombs dropping all around him seem to leave him more cheerful than before. I think my own reactions are somewhat intensified by the fact that this house is so noisy anyway that it is quite difficult to distinguish the guns and bombs from anything else at times.

'We are now sleeping some fifty to sixty people here, including 25 privates, 4 NCOs, 2 officers and an indefinite number of Home Guards. The dirt they bring all through the house is incredible but they are very charming.'

Inevitably in the fighting around London and in the many attacks on Biggin Hill there were casualties and Paul wrote:

'The word was given to us to retire from the fray and exchange "Hell-fire Corner" for this amazingly peaceful stretch of Western Shore. A fairly authentic rumour has it that we are only here for ten days and that then we shall return, but even that will be an invaluable rest. Personally I got off very lightly as I wasn't even in action after I last wrote, and my score remains at 2½; but we had a very busy period for our time down south. The squadron in 12 days accounted for about 40 Nazis certain or probable, and ourselves lost about 10 or 12 planes "written off" (and a number damaged but repairable) – 2 pilots killed, and eight injured more or less seriously – not really a bad record. Now we must collect and "train" some ten more pilots and it's going to be very hard work to do it in ten days.

'During the last week or two at BH because the squadron was somewhat depleted and the station not at its best, we were attached only to "aerodrome defence" and only half of us were employed on it, so that we got every other day "released". On one of these occasions I managed to borrow an unwanted Hurricane and 50 minutes later was "shooting-up" Felthorpe to their general consternation.'

Beryl wrote:

STOP PRESS

'Thursday 2.30 p.m.

'A Hurricane has just been making the most hair-raising dives at the House, and we feel sure that it must be Paul. I was writing in the drawing room and dashed out to the lawn after the first, where I was soon joined by Mrs Dunnell. I ran in to shout to the maids to come out and wave but could not find them. I think, headed by Mrs Tubby, they were probably cowering in the cellar! He skimmed the chimney pots at least six times and then to my untold relief he flew safely away!

'Now it's all ears for the telephone in the hope that this means "Leave" or at any rate a station nearer home for a bit.'

'4.15 p.m.

'[Dad] It was Paul and he landed at Horsham St Faiths. B. rang me up and I immediately left Carrow and picked him up. He seems in excellent form and has definitely 2 planes chalked up to him, one a Dornier and the other a Heinkel 111. He also, with his section of 3, brought down a sea-plane.

'He leaves us again tomorrow morning and thinks he will probably shortly be moved from his station, as their squadron has suffered one casualty and several wounded or burned, and they will have to reconstitute again.'

Like Downe, Felthorpe and Norwich had had a comparatively quiet August. Calling herself Caroline (her second name) Beryl kept the Budget informed of all the local enemy activities because the official news seldom gave more than a generalized reference to East Anglia, or the east coast.

But these enemy activities were merely diversions in more prosaic and very busy lives, relieved from time to time by a day's shooting.

'On Saturday morning Dad and I got in two Red X committees where we settled innumerable things, the second one when he was in the chair paid strict attention to business and wasted no time at all – later when we were making a quick lunch at the club, Mrs Carter came up and congratulated him on getting through a long agenda with such dispatch, so he had to confess that we'd got a shoot timed to start at 2.15 (such things have been known to happen even to County Council Committees!).

'We had a lovely afternoon on both sides of the Bungay road. Three officers from the Sherwood Foresters at Drayton turned up; I don't know what they shoot in the Sherwood Forest, but it doesn't seem to be partridges.

'On Sunday evening our Home Guard had a Church Parade with all the other Defence Services; the Wardens and the Fire Party and the Casualty Services met at the Church and just filed in, but the Home Guard did the thing in style, parading at their "Fort" and marching through the village. I was sitting with Mrs Hewitt and the other First Aid people, hoping the HG were not going to cut it too fine, when to my horror and dismay in swept the Rector from the vestry. That was bad enough, but I thought at least he'll pray or just sit still for a minute, but no, with his usual gift for doing the most completely wrong thing possible, he called upon us to sing "God save the King", and we were well into "Jesu, Lover of my Soul" before I heard the HG tramping in behind. Dad's watch was slow and they had no business to be late of course, but anyone but our tactless fool would have had the courtesy to wait for them.

'It was a crowded service but our C of E material seems to make it very difficult for the average person to find things which really express what you want to say. It seemed to me that we kept on singing and praying about "Peace" and I kept finding myself thinking "God, I do hope you realize we aren't asking for just any old Peace." There was very nearly a state of war between our Church Warden (Dad) and our Rector, but thank heaven the latter has written an illegible letter into which we can read an apology, so feelings are cooling down a little.'

It was at this time that the *Daily Mirror* and the *Daily Express* picked up the news of Pat's decoration and they splashed the story of the pacifist who was awarded the Military Medal, under heavy headlines and with comments from Beryl and Dad. It was an embarrassing time for him but it soon passed.

It was at this time also that there were plans to change the role of Felthorpe Hall itself.

'Did I tell you [wrote Beryl] there was a lot of talk about opening hospitals and convalescent homes in these parts after all. The Red Cross came and looked over the house last week and seemed to be very smitten with it, and another party from the Red X have just been over the house again; they seem to like it very much and it looks to me as if the arrangement would go through.'

But the hospital was not to become a reality for another six months and there were meantime many other things to be done.

'On Friday I made a very valiant effort to collect 250 pyjamas and give out 150 waistcoats all at the same time to save petrol. But needless to say it did not work as there were two warnings in the middle. Lots of pyjamas were brought in to each appointed place but in no case all of them, very natural and inevitable, but irritating.

'We can manage about 100 a week quite comfortably, but 250 and those of a new pattern (for women) with a more difficult pocket proved quite beyond our powers.'

But routine and daily incidents were all set aside on 30 September when two telegrams were delivered almost simultaneously, but fortunately in the following order:

'Paul Francis landed here not hurt.
                    Loftus Bryan. Upton Hydro. Kilmuckridge [Ireland]'

'From Air Ministry. Regret to inform you that your son Pilot Officer Paul Francis Mayhew is reported missing as the result of air operations on Sept. 29 1940.'

Doff's reaction to the news was:

'What an anticlimax! On receiving your telegram today I didn't know whether to raise loud cheers or burst into tears. Poor old Paul – it really is bad luck.'

George wrote:

'I must say something to Paul but I don't know what! Should it be sympathetic, commiseratory, congratulatory? I somehow think that it should be sympathy with a dash of congratulation – in that order.'

On the whole it was Chris's telegram on hearing the news which summed up the feelings of all the family:

'GREAT RELIEF FRANKLY DELIGHTED.'

Paul's views on the situation were unqualified:

'I suppose you've already heard this frightful news; anyway numerous people have assured me that they'll get in touch with you and put your minds at rest. I imagine that in some queer way you'll almost be pleased at the prospect of my internment for the duration; but to me it's the most infuriating, god-forsaken thing that ever happened – and the most stupid. I can remember joking about being interned in a neutral country and what fun it would be; but now my sins are visited upon me, and I loathe the whole prospect of the future. That is with all due respect to the Irish, who have been unfailingly kind and sympathetic; but merely that I know now how desperately badly I want to be back in England, whatever happens there. The thought of being cooped up here while you go through the war is slowly but surely going to send me mad. I'd give my right hand to get back to Kent and all its terrors now; and the thought of indefinite captivity makes me suicidal.

'I suppose I must relate to you the abysmal stupidity that has transformed win-the-war Mayhew into Prisoner Paul. But first let me point out the only thing of which I am proud – namely, that my poor figure is of undoubted international importance. Nobody seems quite to know what to do with me, and they're all so sympathetic that they seem most reluctant to intern me. I shall be interned, of course; but I like to think that I'm metaphorically occupying the diplomatic telephone wires.

'For the awful fact remains that I must be unique. The whole story begins when we took off at about 6.00 p.m. yesterday to meet a raid coming up the Irish Sea, presumably for the NW. After cruising round for 20 mins or so, Paul saw a collection of highly suspicious machines miles out to sea near the Irish Coast. I yelled to my Section-Leader but he didn't seem to see them, so I went off in their direction. It took me some time to catch them, and though he started off with me, I arrived alone to meet 8 Heinkels about 15 miles off the Irish Coast going NNW. I made a few ineffectual attacks, but couldn't really press them home because the cross-fire was intense with only one machine attacking. However, it had the desired effect in that they turned SW, jettisoned their bombs and headed for home. I followed them, and reinforcements started to arrive. Eventually one bomber was hit and started to lag with the port engine smoking. So I came in on it and gave it all I had. Both engines then streamed smoke, bits flew off the fuselage, the undercarriage started to come down, and it went into a steep dive. I hear the wireless claims it as "confirmed" today, so somebody underneath must have seen it crash. Then I made my big mistake, and while apparently the rest of the squadron went home, I followed the bombers very fast for about ¼ of an hour SW with a following wind. I have since calculated that I only broke off the attack almost 70 miles SW of Wexford [Ireland] i.e. somewhere out in the broad Atlantic.

'To get home I headed NE instead of almost E as in the excitement of the battle I didn't notice what my position was. In about 20 minutes, I saw land just where I expected England to be, but realized as I approached it that it looked all wrong. For one thing the coast faced SE and again it was flat, instead of cliffed; so I began to think it might be Ireland, however unreasonable that appeared – and though I had no map of Ireland of course I feared it was the S coast. That was serious as my petrol was too low to get me back from the S coast even if I knew which course to fly (I didn't). The sun had set and the evening mist set in. So, still trying to persuade myself that it was part of England, unnaturally strange, I flew up the coast. At 7.30 I knew firstly that it was almost certainly Ireland and secondly that my petrol couldn't take me on an unknown journey in the dark across St George's Channel. So I "crash-landed" in a stubble field with my wheels up. I was entirely unhurt and the plane only slightly damaged.

'I think I probably landed in the most desolate spot in Ireland – and that is saying a lot. So it was sometime before an old farmer's wife appeared complete with offspring and fulfilled my worst fears by announcing "Begad, yes, this is Aireland, surely be to goodness" or something like that. However, I couldn't do anything, so I just waited. The inevitable crowd soon gathered, and the LSF [Irish Home Guard] bore me off to a farmhouse and gave me home-laid eggs, tea, home-made bread, home-made butter and home-made jam. The police, bless their hearts, arrived at 10.00 p.m. and after making a deposition and ensuring that you should be informed of my safety, I was taken to the police station at Enniscorthy (about 4 miles away) and put to quite a comfortable bed at 1.30 a.m.

'But alas, at 4.30 a.m. I was awoken, bundled into a car, and fell asleep again for a 1½ hour journey up here. Since then, I have been treated most luxuriously and generously by "the military" in whose charge I am at present. But I have my own armed guard who never leaves me for a moment, so that it is difficult to forget that I'm a prisoner.'

He was interned in the Curragh Camp. After a few weeks the censors and the Irish mail sorted themselves out and Paul's morale improved considerably once contact had again been made with the family. He had a number of visitors and he was treated with great consideration by his Irish custodians.

Most welcome visitors were Lady Maffey, wife of the United Kingdom representative in Dublin, and her son. It was quickly revealed that they lived in Norfolk and Simon and Paul immediately decided 'that we had met somewhere. Eventually a north Norfolk Hunt Ball at Blakeney seemed most probable. I remember going with Dick Sale and a couple of females. I do try to remember County girls' names but they look so depressingly alike, and so entirely lacking in any individuality that I can't do it. However, we all got along very well and I took a great liking to Lady Maffey. She entered the room and said "I'm Lady Maffey" in the sort of voice that added "yes, and I'm going to cheer you up whether you like it or not." She did too.'

Later

'The Maffeys came to see me in force yesterday – Sir John (for the first time), Lady and son Simon, complete with four incredibly energetic dogs which much cheered the place up. Apart from bringing me "comforts", sweets, fruit, and dozens of back copies of *Life*, they had an immensely cheering effect upon me. They are really a very charming and considerate family. We suddenly discovered that their son-in-law had been at C—— all last winter with me and even shared a room with me for six weeks when I was in Doff's vicinity! I had even on one occasion met their daughter! You can't think how reassuring it is to indulge in good old English gossip for an hour, to remind one that way back in the Stone Age one belonged to a community of more than one that was not strictly delimited by barbed wire.'

The Maffeys were able to bring him a parcel of books which Beryl had sent out and which were received most gratefully by Paul.

'I know how busy you all are but your labour would have been rewarded had you seen me on Monday morning sitting down and making notes on Plato for all the world as if I had a tutorial with

Foster next morning. For the first time since I landed here I was content, as apart from happiness or sorrow, having something really interesting to do and something to make me think. Who also was responsible for *Winnie the Pooh*? Thank you – a real stroke of genius, as was Fisher's *History of Europe*.'

It was at this time that the papers reported that Paul had been elected an honorary member of the Kildare Hunt; the family was scathing about his horsemanship and Beryl considered him to be in far greater danger on a horse than in a Hurricane. For his part Paul declared that he wouldn't get on a horse for £5 but 'it's typical of Irish hospitality; they've never seen me, they know nothing about me, but they feel friendly towards Britain, and they make the un-English assumption that every Englishman hunts'.

With Paul safely even if unwillingly interned in Eire, the family's immediate interest switched to Helen who returned from America at the beginning of October.

'The news of THIS week is of course Helen's safe return to the bosom of her family [wrote Beryl]. One day last week I happened to read the German communiqué and saw they claimed to have sunk a boat called "The Highland (something)" I forget what. It sounded a rather likely size and I carefully refrained from mentioning it to Dad; judge my horror when he woke up early on Sunday morning and remarked he'd been having a nightmare "about Helen in a Highland boat"! Then he went to his bath and the telephone bell rang, and there was Helen saying she'd be in Norwich about 2.00!'

Chris suggested that we should all

'touch wood hard – but what an industrious and resourceful being is the family's Guardian Angel. He wards shot and shell from one of us, torpedoes from another, visits a third on the eve of battle with a most salubrious disease and – perhaps the most ingenious effort of all – gently lands a fourth out of great peril into comfortable internment in a neutral country.

'Welcome home to Helen. After plan and counter-plan she eventually returned at the most dangerous possible moment – rather funny really, now it's safely over – across an Atlantic positively bristling with new-based submarines. Which makes us all the gladder, if possible, to see her safely back. Get yourself a nice gasmask, Sister, and a ration card and an identity card, and a square yard of cellar floor and make yourself at home.'

The decision that Helen should leave America and come home was finally taken once it became clear that Felthorpe was going to be converted into a military convalescent hospital; there would obviously be work there that she could do.

Helen had been becoming increasingly concerned at the expense of keeping her in America, particularly when the transfer of funds from Britain was blocked. She had been writing about getting work in a bank or of obtaining some sort of business qualification. But none of these plans came to fruition and by the end of September she was on her way home.

It was to be several months before the hospital became a reality and Helen quickly became involved in the complexities of arranging billets for evacuees in a small village such as Felthorpe. There was a graphic description of the process in a Budget letter from Beryl:

'After lunch Helen and I collected all the forms, ink, instructions, etc. and betook ourselves to the Church Hall at 3.45 to await our guests. The Rector and Miss Rudd met us there, also about a dozen of the hostesses. From 3.45 to 4.45 we sat and chatted. From 4.45 to 5.45 we chatted and ate some biscuits Helen and one of the children went and fetched from the PO. From 5.45 to 6.45 we listened to Helen playing tunes on the piano to amuse the children waiting with their parents.

'Then at last; just when we were thinking p'raps we might go home a bus arrived and out came our quota. The first woman I coped with seemed a nice clean harmless little thing with a child of 4, "well she'll be easy to place" I thought thankfully, and moved myself to a mountain of a woman sitting rather sadly, so I smiled at a very slick pert young thing of about 20 sitting next to her and asked for her name, the young thing very wisely produced her identity card and with a sinking heart I copied down Zancyger! "My mother cannot speak English" said daughter cheerfully, and told me her Christian name was Jana, her age 15 and the baby was called Leslie aged 9 months. Wondering who in the world would be willing

to cope with this little party I moved to the next and found an even
more shapeless huddle which announced itself as Mrs Larnotz
and daughter Kitty aged 14, but at least they spoke English.

'Returning to the table I found Helen and Miss Rudd had
collected most of the other names and that we had eleven women for
the nine hostesses who had said they would be willing to take women
and only two of these had two children, so there would be lots of
spare billets for children. After our experience last year I expected
women with large families that would have to be divided.

'Old Mrs Stannard – the one who lives opposite the lodge, with a
very kind heart – came up to speak to me, and Miss Rudd and Helen
both swear this is what happened. Me: "Oh, Mrs S. do you think you
could take that poor woman over there, she can't speak English and I
just don't know who to ask to take her?" Mrs S. had a look at them
and turned round to me and opened her mouth to speak, and I said
"Well that's simply NOBLE of you Mrs S. it's a real bit of war work
and I'm sure they'll be wonderfully happy with you". Miss Rudd
swears Mrs Stannard turned to her and said in a dazed way "Am I
taking those?" and Miss Rudd hastened to assure her that she was,
and I had just said how noble and splendid she was being. Helen
scratched out a card like lightning and we pushed the little party off
home promising to come round immediately with the luggage before
Mrs S. should have time to change her mind.

'That fixed up, Miss Rudd said Mrs Larnotz looked the grubby
type that might settle down in old Mrs Peck's rather hugger mugger
establishment so the Rector took her along and we sorted out two
mothers with babies and two with children of 10 and 11 who could go
to the homes off the Holt Road which would have to be used but
would be rather a long way to walk to school. The Rector came back
and took another mother and baby to old Mrs Howes on the
Taverham Road and we settled to send a very smart woman indeed in
a fur coat and a veil with two boys to Mrs Chambers at the Lodge
Farm.

'By then it was pitch dark and quite obvious that eleven into nine
was not going so Miss Rudd took one home and Helen set off with
the other and a very nice small boy to walk them here while I took the
smart lady and the 2 boys to the farm. On the way she enquired
hopefully for the nearest clinic, my heart just sank gently away;
"Clinic?" said I, remembering that awful evening last year with Mrs
Green assuring a very stout evacuee that she must be "expecting"
and the poor evacuee loudly protesting that she wasn't – all in the
middle of the Village St! "Yes" said she, "you see I'm 5 months on

Beryl, centre front row.

Paul

Pat

Uncle Bertie

Aunt Ellie

Stephen

Christopher

David

Doff

George

Paul

Helen

Christopher,
Helen
and Dad

Clare

David

Felthorpe Hall

the way". "Oh, there's a LONG time yet" said I and prayed that Mrs Chambers would not look too closely under that nice fur coat for that night anyhow.

'All five hostesses were simply charming, old Mrs Chambers came out as if she was prepared to tackle six and told the little boys to come along quick as she'd got eggs for tea, Mrs Sleight said beamingly "Why, you must be the little girl I dreamt about last night." Having squeezed 4 women, 2 children and 2 babies into the Austin for the first trip I had of course to go back for the luggage, and all the husbands were waiting in the road when I got back with it to help me sort it out with a torch and make sure they got the right bundles for their guests.

'On Friday morning I rang up Miss Rudd to hunt for a home for her woman (they're expecting a clergyman's family from Lowestoft at the Rectory), and Helen and I set forth armed with billeting forms, assistance forms, ration cards, and long papers with all our instructions. I went in first and had a private word with the hostess, followed by a private word with the guest, then if Providence was smiling Helen followed me and made out all the necessary forms while I went on to the next house. At the first three houses everything in the garden was lovely, they'd taken to each other and both sides were willing to try and settle down. I said to Helen it was too good to last, and sure enough we came then to Mrs Amps, the sexton's wife. She, while proclaiming her willingness (with splutters) explained that she was out doing field work all day, they only had a fire at night and this would be too cold in a few weeks time for the mother and baby. This seemed reasonable and I only wished she'd said so sooner instead of saying she could take a pair if we were very pushed.

'The Hannan boys were blissfully happy with old papa Chambers and mama raised no difficulty anyway for the immediate future, and we advanced on Mrs Stannard. That old warhorse was coping more than gallantly, I only hope to heaven that Jana, who looks a minx, won't set the whole village by the ears. On enquiry we discovered that Jana had been in England for 5 years, but Mrs Z. is a "stateless" Russian who escaped from Russia into Germany and there married a Pole, they both managed somehow to escape to England lately. The Pole is now in London and wants to join his wife and earn his living by repairing boots, Jana wants work as a milliner. They had some card which was supposed to have been stamped by the police, but this had not been done – I said I'd tell our local bobby and see what he said.

'Then we met Mrs Larnotz and the inevitable Kitty just outside

our front gate with tales of woe that Mrs Peck was only feeding them
on bread and butter, so I said rather sternly that Mrs Peck was not
responsible for feeding them anything at all, it was pure kindness of
heart that she gave them anything, and Mrs Lz. and I agreed (at least
I suspect we did) that we were going to dislike each other a lot before
we'd finished. Mrs Lz. snuffled and said poor Kitty was under a
psychologist for her nerves and who was going to give her a tonic?
Upon which Helen chipped in with exactly the right cheery manner
"Oh, the lovely country air will do you a world of good Kitty, you
won't need a tonic!" Mrs Lz. could cheerfully have bitten her.

'The two others proving happy with Mrs Cooper and Mrs Howes
we made very hungrily for home only to meet Mrs Lz. who stopped
me to exclaim that Mrs Zr. had a lovely billet, there was a nice clean
table cloth and they were going to have roast pork and Mrs. Zr. would
eat it tho' she was a Jew, while Mrs Lz. would only get an apple
dumpling! The poor billeting officer fled lest she should disgrace
herself with hysterics.'

A fleeting visit was planned to see Clare in Newquay and Doff
and George in Marlborough. On the whole Marlborough had
had a quiet war as far as enemy action was concerned but the
running of the two schools, together with all the accompanying
problems of entertaining, staff shortages, rationing, and even
ten evacuees in the Master's Lodge, created great pressure and
strain. Despite the value of the work he was doing George felt
that he was somehow and in some ways missing out:

'How terribly remote and pampered your letters make me feel! It
really is rather curious that anyone should feel even slightly
distressed, not to say jealous and resentful, because he hasn't been
bombed. I suppose it is an indication of something or other that our
present tranquillity makes us feel a little awkward and bogus. You
might say that it points to high morale, but we have no criterion for
measuring height of that sort. All I can do is to sweep off my
mortar-board to those of you who appear to live in a hail of HE and
AA fragments and wish you all good luck and enough respite to
maintain some comfort.

'Well, my personal contribution to the war-effort lately has been
some work in a forestry camp by the River Exe on the
Devon–Somerset border. We worked under Forestry Commission
supervision, but were almost entirely left to arrange ourselves, which
we did. We were clearing felled plantations and burning the rubbish;

measuring up and sawing trees; stacking, carting, and unloading the props eventually into railway trucks at the station 3 miles away. We rose at 6.45 a.m., breakfasted at 7.15, worked from 8.30 to 12.00, ate again at 12.30, worked again from 2–5.30, gorged at 6.30 and went to bed or to sleep on the good earth about 9.15. The river provided excellent cold baths as the weather was abnormally hot; we sweated like – I don't know what really – and got filthy as we worked in dust and ashes from the fires. It was good fun and I feel prodigiously fit; I'm also pretty learned about "big four and a halfs", and "eight footers" and so on.'

In his rather unstructured naval life David was moving from boat to boat. At one time

'They asked for volunteers for "fast motor boats"; we all assumed – i.e. the skippers of the slow motorboats – that they meant MTBs and the response was not overwhelming as MTB men have the reputation of getting covered in medals in about 3 weeks, nearly all awarded posthumously. But I hear now it is for Coastal Motor Boats. I don't know exactly what CMBs do or are, but it sounds rather like the same thing that we are doing now, but with boats built for the purpose instead of for moonlight nights with female company on the quieter reaches of the Thames. I shall try to find out more about it tomorrow and if it looks promising I might have a go at it.

'I think I must tell you a story of a series of signals which came in at night from two armed trawlers. They went like this: –

HM Trawler "A"   "Sighted suspicious craft"
                          "Have challenged craft and received no reply"
                          "Am opening fire"
                          "Believe have scored direct hit"
                          "Am being fired upon."

HM Trawler "B"   "Have to report hot engagement proceeding
                          between HM Trawler 'A' and the North East
                          Bar Buoy."'

Early in October David took over a crash boat – an American power boat of 32 feet and 18 knots called *Quicksilver*.

'Needless to say it wasn't built for its present job but it is quite reasonably seaworthy and we have had its cockpit decked in to make it more so.'

It was with this boat that David had to cope with a mine which came drifting ashore and

'we had to take out one of those he-men who "render them safe". It was bouncing about in the breakers when we found it, looking very large and explosive to my inexperienced eyes. However he put out in our dinghy to grapple with it and managed to tie a rope on to it and then to bring the other end out to us. We towed it out to sea and then set about trying to let it off with our fowling-pieces. No success whatever. He made us shoot at 200 yards and though it was six feet in diameter, both it and we were bobbing about in the swell so much that neither rifles nor machine guns had the slightest effect on the creature. It was exciting though because with every shot one expected a colossal bang which never came. So then he decided to beach it – which could only be done inside the harbour. We signalled the lookout "Am bringing mine into harbour for beaching". As we closed the piers we could see a lot of running around in circles going on inside. It felt like being a classic case of b.o. to see people quietly vanishing as we approached and peering at us from behind the most solid object they could find. And of course no one could have resisted the temptation to look blasé about it – indeed, having been set an example by the he-man, we were feeling quite fond of our mine by then, particularly as he had told us the thing we'd been shooting at was worth £600. Well, it goes without saying that we beached it safely and that after fetching his bag of tools (for all the world like the traditional plumber, although he was a Lt Commander) he "rendered it safe" and had it taken away in a lorry.'

On another occasion

'we did our first real lifeboat turn-out. A small trawler was bombed about 10 miles away, quite close to the shore, and was reported sinking. We made full speed to the place and found the crew rowing away in their boat, and the ship badly down by the head. Just as we had their boat tied up alongside us, someone shouted "she's going". She dipped her head even further, a wave broke over it, and she rolled on her side. Her skipper said "Hats off, boys" and the survivors took off their hats – tin hats, balaclavas, sou'westers, and watched silently – so silently that the sigh of the ship as the decks went under was quite clear, and horribly like an animal. The funnel went under, and then the masts, foot by foot, and great bubbles came up, and all the loose gear that had been lying about the decks. I had never watched a ship go down before; it is a moving sight – I don't know why. But as soon as she was gone we had to get busy. Some of the men in the boat were slightly injured, and two had been blown overboard by the explosions and not seen again. A fishing boat was coming out from the shore so we left them to tow the ship's boat in and beach it, and we went to look for the two missing men. But it was a hopeless search. We followed the gulls which were feeding on the fish killed by the bombs, and cruised about among broken planks and spars, but found nothing more than an empty lifebuoy. After taking bearings to fix the position of the wreck, there was nothing more that we could do, so we set off back to the port.'

David's work as a crash-boat commander brought forth challenging comments from Paul who claimed to consider it

'a complete waste of time; it is a well-known fact among all RAF pilots that

1) No crash boat is ever within 100 miles of where it is wanted.
2) If there's more than a Round Pond ripple they say it's too rough.
3) Every member of the crew is purblind.
4) They have an instinctive flair, when seeing two pilots drowning to pick up the German and leave the Briton to the Roll of Honour.'

David of course had to reply to this:

1) No crash boat within 100 miles of where it is wanted. Well, that's a matter of relativity. You might equally well say that no aeroplane ever crashed within 100 miles of a crash boat, which is unwise of the aeroplane.
2) If there's more than a ripple it's too rough. H'm, slightly touché. There's more than a ripple today; and I doubt if we would get more than a boat's length outside before it began to fill up our scow which was built for the richer and more ostentatious kind of American to show off to the girls in, and which has an open cockpit, excellent for languorous moonlit nights in California, but apt to take in a large dollop in a breaking following sea. However I assure you that we should try if one of your colleagues was down in the sea. We have an ulterior motive for wanting to go out in a really rough sea. A certain Admiralty Surveyor has refused to have our cockpit decked in, in spite of our opinion that

it is the only unseaworthy thing about the boat. So unpleasant is this Surveyor that it would be worth taking in a large wave and sinking just for the pleasure of proving him wrong and haunting him. So if anyone crashes today, we shall sink merrily, discussing ingenious haunts. Not that that will be much comfort to the chap who has crashed.

3) Crew purblind eh? Needles in haystacks and black cats which aren't in dark cellars make good proverbs but you could make a better one out of these ingredients: dark sea, eyes full of salt water, waves higher than eye level, an airman submerged except for his head within a radius of 5 miles or so, and a feeling of prudence that you shouldn't keep a searchlight on long enough at a time for anyone to draw a bead on it. It's better in daylight, of course, but we are too low in the water to see properly at the best of times. So why don't we ever get cooperation from spotting aircraft? And why don't pilots ever manage to get flares or smoke signals going?

4) Well, yes, it would be more exciting to pick up a German pilot than an English one. I should like to see what he had to say for himself and I could brandish my revolver at him. But if the choice ever arises I will bear your letter in mind and forego the pleasure.

'You may wonder why I don't resent, on behalf of the Senior Service, these allegations from that mere stripling the RAF. Well, it is because (look out for my trump card) almost all crash boats are now run by the RAF who, in spite of their merits as birdmen, make lousy seamen.

'But in spite of all this argument, which is only for saving face, I am rather inclined to agree that it is all a waste of time. Because, in spite of all our preparations, your colleagues refuse to crash here. If they only knew that we had every possible comfort for damp birdmen, do you think they would choose our bit of sea? Blankets, stretchers, fire extinguishers, chocolate and 2 (two) gallons of Navy rum. We can put them out if they are on fire, or drown their sorrows in drink, or give them dry socks. But in spite of it all, no customers.'

But, as David reported, life became increasingly tedious:

'the reason is that there have been no crashed planes, or bombed ships, or other disasters to take us to sea for goodness knows how long – and I have been bored to tears for nearly a fortnight. In a fit of the blues I filled up a Request Form with the words "To apply for a Commission" and handed it in at the base. This started a most comic series of interviews. The first was with the Commander who is our immediate CO. He summoned me to his office and I found him giggling over a form which he had to fill in about me. I couldn't see it of course but it seemed to me just the sort of thing one would expect. One is evidently still judged for a Commission in the Navy upon a) prowess in ball games b) education – type not extent c) eyesight – in that order. In reply to "Proficiency in Sport" I volunteered that I sometimes climbed mountains or sailed boats, thinking that the latter might be of some use, but he said "I know the Admiralty. Didn't you play cricket for your College or anything like that?" Thinking back a long way I remembered rowing up and down that horrible river in Cambridge in a race of some kind – would it have been Lents? – so I said "I rowed". "For your College?" he asked. "Yes" said I, because I couldn't think of any other organization one could row for. "Ah" says he and wrote it down.

'The next thing on the form was "Appearance". He took a good look at me, with one eyebrow raised and a broad grin – I was wearing sea-boots, old flannel trousers, and one of those polo sweaters you are always trying to give to the poor. "The temptation to rag this is almost too much" he said, and wrote something down. Then the next one. "For God's sake" he said "what does this mean? It says 'Is the candidate moderate?' Are you moderate? I should hope not."

'Well so it went on. A good time was had. The next interview was with the Base Commander. The first thing he said was "Ah Howarth, so you were up at Cambridge and rowed for your College." Having delved most amiably into my past he asked how the hell I came to be in the patrol service, and said the way we wasted our manpower was appalling and that I was just the sort of feller they needed as an officer, so I came away from him feeling very important.

'So there it all is; I shall be given about five minutes notice to pack everything up and go up to London. The only thing that worries me is whether some painstaking clerk at the Admiralty will look up the Trinity College records for 1931 and find that I didn't row for my College, because I really cannot remember what that race was all about, and I have a guilty fear that it may only have been a trial and that I shall become an officer entirely on false pretences. But unless I am found out I have no doubt it will all go through sooner or later, and in the end the last of the family to remain an Other Rank will be able to speak to his cousins again.'

The relative calm and inactivity of Lowestoft was particularly unacceptable to David because he knew of the difficulties and dangers of living in Downe.

'Are you still determined to stay put? I really don't see how it can be a question of duty to stay there much longer – in fact I should have thought the contrary was generally considered to be the case nowadays, for those who simply haven't got to stay in hot spots. But it's not for me to say, except that I still can't get used to the idea of you bearing the brunt of the blitz while I sit here in brass buttons and almost perfect peace. For my amour-propre and peace of mind I wish you anywhere else in the wide world, except perhaps Hamm. I should think having a pain in the tum and your teeth out as well would put the tin lid on it.'

Uncle wrote his own account to the Budget about his 'pain in the tum':

With greetings to all Budgeteers.

Ode to a Home Guard.
On the occasion of his (own) Birthday.

What the devil the use is he,
This so-called soldier of 63?
He's lived through one big war already
And wasn't exactly a chicken when
That happened (except in heart maybe)
And they found him a job in an office then.
So what sort of use can he possibly be,
This first-time soldier of 63?

He finds his rifle deucedly heavy –
He might just possibly point it straight
If the bird sat perfectly still while he did so,
But is it likely the bird would wait?
Not it, so whatever use could he be,
This tremulous soldier of 63?

They thought he'd collected a duode-
nal ulcer, and sent him the other day,
To a fellow who did what he could to see
Through the poor old tum, with a strong X-ray.
(A not unusual thing to see
In soldiers, or others, of 63)

> The duodenum was quite OK
> But nevertheless they've got him in hand,
> And feed him on milk and slops and such,
> And cosset him up to beat the band.
> And very nice too, for such as he,
> But hardly for soldiers of 63.

And – (there was more of this, and it was very beautiful, but perhaps not quite appropriate for the fast-approaching festive season, for which all good wishes to everybody.

And so to the next, and, perhaps mercifully, last canticle).

> So if, by any subsequent mail,
> You hear that he's passed in his dinner-pail,
> And wonder how bravely he met the foe,
> You may bet your boots that it wasn't so.
> For the war won't be won by such as he,
> A Pop-eyed, knock-kneed, half-toothless, hairless, and generally
> incognizable* soldier of 63.

> *Yes: see Dictionary.

A PS in one of Chris's letters read:

> A hundred Nazis wouldn't dare
> To face that old but trusty pair
> They're worth an Army Corps between 'em
> – Uncle and his duodenum.

Christopher had almost completed his OCTU course in Aldershot and had reached the stage of

'being lectured on how to be a decorous and conventional officer (e.g. do not talk "shop" in the mess; and avoid reference to women, politics, or religion; and don't say "bloody" too often. In fact, brush up your horticulture and meteorology. Ridiculous. Those who don't talk "shop" talk politics and religion; and those who don't talk shop, politics or religion all talk women. And for these last, "bloody" pronounced in different ways practically constitutes a language in itself).

'The ban on politics is lamentable and thought-provoking. Nowadays, as our astute enemy has long realized, war is politics, and vice versa. Slogans, leaflets, fifth-columns, Haw-Haw and all the rest of it are just as much part of the German war-machine as the army itself. Our reply to this political offensive is, as far as the Army goes, to pretend it doesn't exist. We never deny to our soldiers the German lies about Churchill's vices and Mosley's virtues, or teach them some home truths about the Nazis; we simply take the line that soldiers must do what they are told and not worry their heads about such things.'

His Intelligence Corps training took place at Smedley's Hydro at Matlock. After Aldershot it

'is pure paradise – excellent food, no air raids, grand country, masses of interesting work, someone to clean my buttons and a couple of score of very friendly and unmilitary companions. I am going flat out at the work which suits me down to the ground.

'Later. A bit of news has just arrived in the form of a letter from Dalton. He ticks me off gently for not having been to see him and says "Since you haven't come without being sent for, I've asked that you should be ordered to parade at my Ministry on an early day – I hope this week. I should like to talk to you about the possibility of work for which you would be specially qualified."

'He seems determined to make up my mind for me. I shall probably accept his offer, though the job has one great disadvantage, – it is spectacularly unheroic.'-

There was some delay before Chris was released by the War Office and he was able to spend a few days at Felthorpe.

'Last night there was a meeting of the village to arrange something extra in the way of war-effort. After a strong lead from the Lord of the Manor, the village spontaneously elected me Chairman. The whole thing was apparently a ruse to keep the Vicar out – I was a mere pawn in a crafty game of "haute politique". Anyway, the vicar lost, as he scarcely got a word in edgeways, and the village determined to organize socials and whist drives and a house-to-house collection for Norfolk War Charities, and to form a Savings Group, which was all very satisfactory, especially as there wasn't too much feudal pressure from the Hall, and quite a few spontaneous suggestions.'

By November he had moved – officially – to the Ministry of Economic Warfare. He wrote about 'blockade work' but in fact his appointment involved him in liaison work with Special Operations Executive (SOE), and about this he wrote nothing. SOE was under Dalton's overall control and was concerned with sabotage and the resistance movement throughout Europe. With its headquarters at 64 Baker St it was Dalton's 'black life' and for over a year Christopher was not only working for and accompanying Dalton as a private secretary, but was also his courier and liaison to 64 Baker St.

As far as the family knew

'It seems that the Army has "released" me – that is to say I retain my commission and can be called back to service, but otherwise I am a civilian. I wear civilian clothes, get civilian pay (£350), and become plain Mr.

'My job is a really fascinating one – just couldn't be better in my view. Technically I'm the Assistant of the Minister's Economic Adviser, and I'm supposed to help with questions of general blockade policy. There are opportunities in all directions and all the work is interesting. I only hope I can hold the job down.

'What pangs of conscience I had about leaving the Army have disappeared. True, young men shouldn't leave the Army in the middle of a war; but I'm certain I shall be more use where I am now, and it's literally true to say that Londoners will be facing more dangers than soldiers for the next two or three years at least. In fact I am in more danger this second than (with one trivial exception) at any time in my 14 months service. The fact that I am sharing this danger with my landlady, now happily taking a bath next door, is humbling but irrelevant!

'I asked Dalton whether, in the event of the invasion taking place it would be possible for me to be released temporarily for a more active job and he agreed quite cordially.

'The thing that does rather annoy me is having bought £35 of Officer's kit and then not using it. What offers, Brother Pat?'

Christopher had been disputing – through the Budget – with Stephen about the re-arrangement of Europe once victory had been achieved, and Stephen explained:

'For the benefit of those who were following with eager attention the controversy between Christopher and myself which threatened to develop – I have had lunch with Christopher and we fixed up Europe quite nicely, all things considered.

'Ah well, there's 41 soldiers in the house now, not to mention us, the Home Guard, the First Aid, the Robinsons, the Rumbles and the Clements, and I begin to realize the true meaning of the phrase "you can't call your home your own". They are incredibly quiet and anxious to please, but of course you can't stir without falling over them, and to anyone who is rather shy and conscious of an absence of uniform (other than Home Guard) it is practically a matter of being immured in one room and running the gauntlet as seldom as possible to another one when unavoidable – e.g.: bedtime. Also they have most of the hot water, which it seems brutal to refuse them, and inconvenient and chilly to allow them. Poor things. I hope someone builds them an absolute palace of a barracks soon, but I'm afraid they won't.'

At the end of his OCTU training Pat also was able to have

'a very pleasant dinner with Chris at the Great Eastern and I really thought he looked very well; he seems to have a very great deal of work to do, but it seems to be the sort of work which is so much what he wants to do that it almost amounts to a hobby.

'I fear that I have let my brother (elder) take a stage higher than I, for I passed out as a "B". Of course I cannot query the honesty of his officers or the truth of his grading (?) but here at least the standard seems to have been high. Only 2 men in our platoon got an A and only 30% of the Company got either A or B so although I deeply regret having to bow to my superior brother, I have no shame of my grading.'

Pat had been commissioned as a 2nd-Lieutenant in the Royal Norfolk Regiment which had its headquarters and barracks in Norwich; he was due to report there but first had a few days at Felthorpe.

'I have been trying to convince myself that I am now an officer and to remember not to salute the "wrong" people, to go to the most expensive seats in a cinema, and to keep out of fish and chip saloons. I think I have nearly got myself in tow now though there are still occasional moments of embarrassment, not always my own fault. For example, this morning I had to go into N. to get my battle-dress cleaned, my hair cut etc. and as I wished to get used to the idea of being an officer before I have to report to the Unit, I decided to go there in uniform. Picture then the young, good-looking 2nd Lieut. stepping smartly through the streets of the city of his regimental depot; everything went perfectly and I was really beginning to stand up straight, to return the salutes of the admiring Other Ranks, when I met my Lady-Mother. She plays up well and I still feel the honourable bearer of HM's commission for I have just been saluted by the Air Force (and for those who don't know, the RAF ground staff rate themselves above any ordinary army general) and then came the whole pitiful collapse. B. decides to take some parcels to a depot or something and when she is met at the door by some fair person who offered to help carry them she disdains the kindness with the appalling remark "It's all right thank you, the CHILDREN will carry them" – collapse of Pat who was really feeling a little grown-up until then; these Parents!'

After five days at Felthorpe Pat

'reported to the Depot at Norwich. I called on the Adjutant and saluted him bravely, explaining who I was, but in all honesty he did not seem in the least bit interested. I then came down the hill to Nelson barracks and wandered into the Officers' mess – an awe-inspiring moment; just outside on the square were about 100 recruits still in mufti, and I could not help wondering which of us was feeling the more uncomfortable and unnatural. I decided to stay in and see what it was really all about and my gosh! Dinner! Don't get me wrong, the food was excellent but the conversation – it just didn't exist; most of the officers were out and there were only about 7 or 8 of us, and between us we spoke about 200 words throughout dinner. I'm told that it's always that way inclined, but it'll tax my trappist tendencies to conform.'

Three days later he was posted to the 9th Battalion, the Royal Norfolk Regiment, stationed on the Norfolk coast. He was delighted because it was intended to be a fighting battalion, but 'sorry because it makes Felthorpe tantalizingly inaccessible – no snipe now alas'.

He found that he was Platoon Commander of No. 15 Platoon

– 'rather nice lads, all Norfolk save for about 10 who are London; the Sergeant (most important) is a cheery optimist and very easy to work with'. The role of the battalion was coast defence, opposing any German sea-borne invasion, and at that time the possibility of an invasion was still very real.

David started at HMS *King Alfred* on 12 December.

'I hardly know where to start in describing *King Alfred – Alfie*, I find, to its inmates. Perhaps the inmates themselves should be the beginning. After coming to associate a seaman's uniform with trawler hands it is somewhat staggering to be among outwardly similar people who read Penguin Specials, and do *The Times'* crossword puzzle, and speak pure Oxford. The first thing that happened when we arrived was lunch, and most of us nearly burst into tears at being served by real waitresses with a meal of roast pork and two veg, blackberry and apple pie, cheese and biscuits, and beer and coffee.

'I've not had much more than a look at the syllabus so far, but I think I know most of it. I shall have to speed up my signalling a lot, but on the other hand I know more navigation than is required. Torpedoes and gunnery are pretty much sealed books but I've picked up something about minesweeping and submarine detection. The course lasts eight weeks, followed by a week's leave for buying uniforms, and then another fortnight back here as an officer.

'It seems to me that the Navy never misses its step in matters of psychology. At lunch our eyes stood out on stalks when real officers' food was put before us and we gasped when everyone was helpful and told us and showed us all the things we wanted to know before it had occurred to us to ask. Then the CO, addressing us as "Gentlemen", hinted that we would now carry out orders, not because we might be punished if we didn't but because we would know there was good sense behind them. This was followed by the rather elaborate dinner with its implicit assumption that we were gentlemen and knew what to do with the knives and forks. The result was that everyone was making good resolutions and brushing their trousers and finding out where the nearest dry-cleaner is, and remembering not to swear and spit. I wonder if the Army OCTUs played this successful trick on their new cadets?'

*　　*　　*

As the second Christmas of the war approached, Dad was able to get over to Eire to see Paul. He flew from Barton aerodrome, outside Manchester, and stayed in Dublin with Sir John and Lady Maffey. The Air Ministry had authorized Paul to give his parole and it was therefore possible for him to go with Dad to Dublin University where, after meetings with the Registrar and the Provost, it was agreed that he could study externally for an Honours Degree. 'On the strength of the interview we went off and bought a heap of books, the very sight of which would have led me to commit suicide. However, Paul was thrilled and keen.'

Dad thought that

'On the whole Paul looked fairly well. He tells me that he has days when he feels full of energy but there are other days when he gets terrible fits of depression and misery. One can well understand how at times the loneliness of it all – and particularly the long evenings – must be most depressing.

'The Anglo-Irish are very sympathetic to him, and as individuals I have no doubt that the Irish themselves are sympathetic.'

Paul had a rather dreary Christmas which included

'an excessively drunken party which bored me so much that I refuse to describe it. Otherwise nothing has excited me out of my rut. But the rut has become a little less clearly marked as the result of a sudden influx of Air Force on my privacy. For a few days chaos reigned supreme and through it all I pursued one objective and one only – a bedroom to myself. Luckily (or by some other influence) I succeeded and have converted it into a bedroom-cum-study, so that I can continue to work in quiet, disturbed only by the noises essential to a fairly full hut, and the blare of Henry Hall through three doors. For the last two or three days I've more or less got down to a routine again, at the cost of a great deal of unsociability, and now I can merely hope for the best.

'My newest and most welcome distraction is expected any minute – a young lady companion for my consolation. She's apparently very pretty though black, and most loving – a 4½ month old cocker-spaniel bitch. Lady Maffey, who to an internee bears a marked functional resemblance to a cornucopia, induced a friend to present me with his last remaining cocker puppy, in spite of its having a pedigree that needs a library to hold it; and she herself "threw in as

a Christmas present" all its accessories, basket, rug, brush, lead etc! I
can't help admitting that I'm most excited at the prospect of being a
dog-owner, in spite of the fact that I shall be a very ignorant one. I
shall call her "Julie" for reasons known to any novel-reader though I
admit the comparison is in some ways inappropriate.* Originally, of
course, she was meant to keep me company, before human
companions arrived. But I've no doubt she will be far more
glamorous, and probably far more comforting, than my colleagues.'

The Felthorpe Christmas was scarcely more exciting. As Beryl
explained:

'the difficulty about celebrating Christmas with only three is that we
can't all three decide to be "happy" at the same time. I started much
too early and had been soundly damped by the others three times by
Church, so that when, driving home, Helen started to vamp a carol
rhythm on the horn while passing two cyclists and brushed the car
along the hedge, I was very cross, and her defence of "feeling
Christmassy" didn't go down at all well! After his ration of sausage
Dad suddenly brightened up and announced it was Christmas Day
and he wanted "Presents". That was a bit awkward 'cos Helen and I
had opened Paul's and Kiff's presents days ago and played them to
him several times, while the parents' own presents to each other had
been planted out in November. Thank goodness Helen came to the
rescue and bestowed a very handsome nailbrush on him and a superb
toothbrush on me (both by special request) and a lovely stand of
"spills" each. Then the phone rang and a telegram came through
from Kiff and things were positively festive for nearly five minutes.
   'At tea, alas, the family unity was split once more when Helen flung
the cake and its plate to the ground and parental grunts of
disapproval were countered by the cry "Oh, do be HAPPY". The
Howarths rang up this evening which was very nice of them, tho' I
did think it was a bit thick of Dad to pitch them a sad story of "No
Turkey" when he had one with Pat last week.'

But this mood was soon changed.

'We never really believed it would happen, but Helen and I spent
Saturday morning setting out Christmas cards on the mantelpiece,

* See *The Fountain* by Charles Morgan.

putting fir branches in the downstairs rooms and bits and scraps of heather, jasmine, 7 violets, 2 stylosa, and 6 anemones between ALL the bedrooms. Then she took the trailer to Thorpe and brought it back laden to the brim with Doff, George, Clare, Susan and all their luggage. Pat rang up and said he would take a taxi out and be along in time for tea, which he was, and final triumph, Kiff arrived with Dad about seven o'clock. YOU SHOULD have heard the yells when they both walked in and the party was complete.'

Christopher wrote of the reunion:

'I couldn't believe my ears when I arrived in Norwich and Dad told me Doff, George, Pat, Helen and Clare were all at FH. But there they were all right and the result was one of the best weekends ever. For Paul's benefit let me say we were all looking very fit and cheerful, except possibly Clare who had gastro-whatnot and was sent firmly to bed, which was rotten luck. Doff is really quite grown-up these days and oozes with mother-love in the most disgusting way if Susan is anywhere around. George seems to be growing serious-minded under the strain of headmastership but from time to time he relaxes and talks nonsense and acts looney in the way he used to when I was a boy, and sometimes he comes out with a most improper remark all of a sudden. Pat is fast developing into the Conscientious Young Officer (he will be conscientious won't he, either doing something vigorously, or vigorously objecting to doing it, – one of the two. It all comes of deeply worrying about the Right, and the Good, and Duty and Whatnot, instead of just muddling through like the rest of us, relying on instinct) and I forecast a couple of pips for him before long, together with a keen eye for the slacker. Except on the tennis court brother Pat was on his very best form. Sister Helen's state of mind and body I have already commented on in these columns – the transatlantic touch is wearing off a shade, I think, and one begins to appreciate the good points of travel in general, and US in particular, which the lipstick and lingo had temporarily tended to conceal. As for Christopher himself, I'm afraid he's growing rather comfortable and conventional these days, but he clearly enjoyed his weekend and had a good appetite. Felthorpe Hall itself and its two headgardeners, Lady Beryl and Sir Basil, were what they always were, which is good enough for me.'

And so, in January 1941, with the sad exception of Paul, the family was reunited for the first time since the start of the war.

Fourteen days after the first family reunion since the beginning of the war Paul made his first attempt to escape from the Curragh camp. He had just been promoted to the rank of Flight-Lieutenant which

'somehow seems very humiliating being promoted while interned, even "with effect from" an earlier date; but it's really very welcome and reassures me that I'm far from officially forgotten. For some reason it makes me more than ever keen to return and win the war; after many days of internment one starts to fossilize and then when something suddenly reminds you of the days that were, you abruptly come to life and long for a Hurricane. Particularly is this true when the news is all of the offensive, and actually of massed daylight raids over France, 100 escort fighters is taking a leaf out of Goering's book with a vengeance! How I wish I had been one of them!'

On 20 January there were two other RAF officers and three sergeants, apart from Paul, interned in the camp and

'it snowed a really bad blizzard all morning and left snow perhaps three or four feet deep in the drifts. More to the point, it didn't do the electricity system any good, and the lights kept going out for fair periods. This naturally enough gave rise to thoughts of escape if it should happen in the evening, as the defences depend largely on the flood-lighting.

'Night came, rain replaced the snow, and the lights functioned perfectly without a flicker. Thereupon I and another officer advised very strongly against any attempt. We had a scheme for a "break" up our sleeves, but it seemed idiotic to use it with no outside preparations whatever, no plans, and the most b—y awful weather since last January in England. I went on protesting but was hopelessly outvoted because my companions are still in the first psychological stage of internment, when one merely wants to get out without any thought of the consequences.

'So we went. Naturally enough we went in civilian clothes and the Irish press has virtually accused us of breaking international law for possessing and wearing them. The fact is we were compelled to buy civilian clothes by the Irish Army itself because they would not allow us out on parole in uniform as we wanted; and even for the Irish press to suggest that it's against international law to use mufti if you can get hold of it seems insane.

'The escape itself is divided into the break and the freedom.

'The break took place beautifully at 9.20 p.m. – so beautifully indeed that our guardians refuse to believe we had no outside help in spite of our protestations. I don't know if Father has given you much idea of our "compound" but the great point was (it's being considerably strengthened) two parallel 10 foot barbed wire fences flood-lit. We had an excessively ingenious plan to get the lights out with a home-made device of a poker and large quantities of parachute cord. It worked beautifully, without being even discovered and then bedlam was let loose. One of the sergeants found himself (not by arrangement) with an excellent opportunity of distracting our immediate guard and did so effectively. The rest of us ran out to the fence through the windows, tossed over a bundle of coats and started to climb.

'We had only been able to put out one side of the lights, and so the fence was still fairly illuminated by the lights on the other side of the compound; and I confess that I was somewhat nervous of the trigger-conscious sentries. But they didn't fire, and apart from that it was much easier than I expected. Ten feet of barbed wire is no fun, certainly, and I tore my trousers and myself a good deal; but it's possible and I reckon I got over both fences in about 30–45 seconds: over my hands I wore boxing gloves backwards so that I could grasp the barbed wire, and flying boots for my ankles. I got a deepish scratch on my right calf and lots of them on my right thigh. But I got over with the others, picked up my mackintosh, ran to the other barbed-wire fence, 5 foot high and unlit, clambered over that and found myself free on the golf course. I tried to run and found the backs of my knees hopelessly weak with excitement. So I just walked.

'The freedom for me was exactly twelve hours. We had arranged to break up singly as the hue and cry was sure to be started quickly, and we didn't want to be caught in a body on the plain. So I found myself alone, naturally slightly bewildered and surprised, on a cold dark night with masses of snow on the ground, and a fairly heavy rain shower turning it into slush. I had on flying boots, grey trousers, sports jacket, two pullovers, a mackintosh and gloves. My cap had been dropped in the excitement as also my gold pencil (which a guard, bless his heart, recovered later) but that was a blessing very much in disguise as my description was later circulated by short-wave police wireless (the two sergeants who couldn't get out heard it) mentioning not only the cap but even my minute scars on my left hand and the mole on the back of my neck! Otherwise I had a flask full of whisky, £1-18-0, tobacco and cigarettes and four apples. Has anybody ever escaped with less preparation or in such impossible weather? It was simply ridiculous as I realized even then, and we had wasted everything even by trying. My only real chance seemed to be to walk 100 miles cross-country to Ulster, and that without maps or food in the bitterest weather.

'However, I set out. I knew the country as far as Dublin fairly well, and acting on a hunch I circled round still on the plain so that I could strike off in a fairly unlikely direction. I met no patrol so they hadn't got out yet, and broke off the plain in a NW direction. Then I set out cross-country and prayed. The night was dark and clouded, though the snow reflected what light there was, and my ability to spot the pole star was useless. But I steered about NE by feel of the wind on my face and simply hoped that it wouldn't change. I threw the boxing gloves into a gorse-bush and wore ordinary RAF gloves. The going was dreadful; where there wasn't snow there was water or slush and one tended to walk into drifts which didn't improve matters. I soon realized that I must be leaving horribly conspicuous tracks and tried to avoid snow, but I imagine my footprints showed up everywhere.

'At that stage of the proceeding my morale was excellent, I had little hope of seeing the border but I hoped to give everyone a good run for their money, and anyway it was pleasant to be free. The rain stopped and I tramped on over plough, roots and fallow and through the hedges. Irish hedges are sometimes full of holes but they can be the very devil; the farmers are incredibly lavish with barbed wire.

'Just this side of Newbridge I crossed the main Cork–Dublin road after doing some Richard Hannay stuff of lying behind a hedge listening to a patrol going by. Then for the first time I slightly lost my bearings and in order to get them clear and also as a test for a plan I was being driven to, I went into Newbridge and walked down the main street, without arousing any interest. Newbridge is about 3 miles away and I arrived at about 11.00 p.m. I had already decided the cross-country to the Border was simply hopeless, and was now forced to two possible alternatives – to lie up somewhere for a week or so until the alarm began to subside, or to try and bluff my way by road. Quite apart from the weather I had virtually no food to lie up, so I decided on side-roads; an English accent isn't terribly conspicuous in this country.

'The Liffey river was guarded at Newbridge and I knew nowhere else to get across it, which wasn't helpful, but I went down a lane which followed it to the left (i.e. N–NW) and hoped to get across it later. I went for miles and miles down this road between river and railway, mostly through slush which added to the icy water which I already had in my boots from falling into a ditch some miles back. Eventually, about 1.00 a.m. I sat down and gave myself a cigarette and apple and some whisky and tried to get to sleep. It was far too cold, even out of the wind, as I couldn't find a barn or anything, so after half-an-hour I went on.

'I was beginning to feel pretty unhappy now as my feet were almost numb with cold and I was getting blisters, but it was still further increased by coming to a lane with drifts about 4 ft deep for some ½ mile. This really exhausted me properly, and I realized that even side-roads were no good. Eventually I came back on the Cork–Dublin road and decided to stick on it, though the chances of my getting through were infinitesimal.

'So, after another rest, I set out along the road where dozens of cars and lorries were drifted-up. I was by now really tired of unending and slippery slush and my morale wasn't too good. Finally I found a stranded bus and swopped cigarettes with the driver and conductor on the step, while convoys of searchers on motorbikes went past without worrying about me. Those convoys made me think. It was now getting light (about 8.30 a.m.) and lonely, tired and dirty pedestrians might be regarded with suspicion, while here on my bus they took no notice of me. Why not combine comfort with comparative safety by taking a bus? I had walked 16 miles and I think 22 or 23 in my own devious way.

'So I got on a Dublin bus which was at any rate a luxurious way of escaping. But it didn't work. We got through one barrier beautifully with a sergeant staring at me and saying "Well that's OK" and we all wondered, me loudest of all, what they were looking for. But a quarter of a mile later – 9 miles short of Dublin – we were again stopped and I suppose I gave myself away for the NCO started to ask me questions and requested me to show my papers which was the end of me. The rest was dull, for I was arrested, taken to Dublin, held there in a guardroom for hours until I was brought back here in the evening.

'I was actually arrested at 9.30 a.m., later than the others, but I'm not proud of it. The whole thing was a catastrophe, for we had a good scheme and wasted it. The weather forced us on to the main road and there we knew we were cold meat. However, in some ways it was amusing, though physically horrible. I seem to have no constitutional ill-effects but my feet are indescribably tender and I'm scratched all over with barbed wire and hedges. As a matter of fact I'm fairly proud of my stamina; without training or food (except 2 apples) I walked 22 or 23 miles by night through indescribable snow and slush and partly cross-country. Moreover I did 39 hours without sleep, an easy record for me, and on my return was told I couldn't have walked that far because I looked so fresh!

'Finally, we won a lot of experience. The biggest surprise to me was the trouble the Irish Army went to to recapture us. I thought they would just throw a cordon round the Curragh, but including the Border patrols they must have turned out some thousands of men, I should think, including convoys of despatch-riders, and light lorries. The worst result of the whole thing has been that our tunnel has been discovered, as I prophesied, in the subsequent search of the hut. This was a far more promising effort as we only need go about 30 yards and might get away unseen.

'Now I am peculiarly barren of escape ideas. I think I shall have to do some work.'

Christopher was living in London, at the Chelsea Cloisters in Sloane Avenue, and continuing to work for SOE.

In the winter and early spring of 1941 there were frequent and heavy air raids on London. He wrote of one:

'If this keeps up it will be London's biggest "blitz" to date. I have just returned rather breathless from putting out some incendiary bombs which fell with loud metallic "plop-clatter" in the street outside my window. I careered downstairs and managed to get a bomb to myself, which I put out with much gusto and waste of sand. Soon dozens of enthusiastic cloisterers were pouring into Sloane Avenue and the little streets running off it, some frightfully efficient, carrying sand-buckets, others just enthusiastic, and all most unsuitably dressed – in pansy suits or smart frocks or bedroom slippers. It was a queer scene – little groups of men and women running about like that with buckets of sand in the erratic orange glow of the incendiaries.

'I was in the cinema when the blitz began. Rather a close one came down and the building swayed unpleasantly. The audience let out a momentary, collective, giggled "phew", then was suddenly quite silent, waiting to see if it was a singleton or one of a stick, then said to itself "quite near enough for me, thank you" and began to prepare to leave with much feeling for hats and clicking of handbags and banging of seats tipping up, and then, just as though it was one person it changed its mind, sat down again and saw the film through. Only two people left.'

In one of his letters Christopher spoke of 'fourteen bombless days', but raids were nevertheless frequent and damaging:

'We've had a very large blitz indeed. From dusk on Wednesday to dawn on Thursday the beastly planes were overhead doing their stuff, and the bombs came down one after another, all the time.

'The climax camc for the Cloisters at 3.00 when a land mine came down just off one of our corners blowing in numberless windows and several doors and making a horrible mess of our neighbouring block of flats. Three of my windows spread themselves over my flat (and over my week's butter ration incidentally) and my curtains and accompanying oddments were blown down. I climbed gingerly out of bed, put some clothes on and went downstairs into the street.

'Outside everything was lit up by the fires in the adjoining block. There was a fire in the middle of the wreckage and flames were steadily consuming what flats still stood.

'When I arrived on the scene an admirable middle-aged lady, slightly injured, was leaning out of the skeleton of her second-floor flat giving instructions to would-be rescuers. She made some suggestions in a perfectly level voice, as to the best place to rest the ladder against. For all the emotion she showed she might have been hanging Christmas decorations in a village hall.'

His first visit to Oxford for two years was altogether different:

'I'm really sentimental about Oxford, though I keep on telling myself that I can't have enjoyed it as much as I now think I did, but I don't really convince myself when I do. Anyhow, revisiting the place was tremendous fun. I did all the things I'd wanted to – an undergraduate sherry party, a party to the Playhouse, the "George" afterwards, a visit to the Union and Christ Church. Sunday tea in N. Oxford and all the rest of it. Frank Pakenham stood me some drinks – he's an RC now and spoke earnestly to me about my religion (lack of), leaving me with a book all about whether the stone did or did not roll away from the grave after the second (or was it the third?) day; which I am reading patiently because I am so fond of Frank. He's also written a play, all about the Russo-German pact in which the hero is me. Fortunately it is not expected, by those who have read it, to be put on anywhere; so that is all right.

'So Oxford, as you see, has not changed much in the war, thank God. The undergraduates drill twice a week and are younger and fewer; the Union dining room is closed; the Clarendon is

requisitioned, dismantled and empty; the grass in Tom Quad has
deteriorated; the streets are more crowded; less butter is eaten with
crumpets; inferior brands of sherry are drunk. But fundamentally
Oxford is just the same.'

But generally he was doing very little outside his job which

'as a matter of fact leaves me most days with very little energy for any
outside occupation. The work is becoming progressively harder and
more amusing. As a result of gradual changes I now find myself
rather risen in the world with a room and a secretary to myself and
earning bigger money. But it is all rather ephemeral, I feel.

'Dalton took me to greet the Premier at Paddington, which was
quite fun. It was a distinctly upstage gathering. A small bomb
dropped on Platform 13 would have extinguished practically the
entire War Cabinet and Diplomatic Corps. Incidentally the
Diplomats looked ever so much more distinguished than the Cabinet
Ministers. Don't ask me why.'

He was able on one occasion to spend a blissfully idle
weekend with the Howarths at Downe and 'couldn't even
summon the energy to go and watch Stephen in HG uniform
pretending to be a bush (£3 for the winner) which shows how
idle I was'.

As Aunt Ellie explained,

'the united brains of the family were directed on the problem of
rendering Stephen's tin hat invisible, for a HG camouflage
competition. My tasteful concoction composed of two veils and part
of Sally's last year coat was turned down in favour of a baby
camouflage net such as Christopher used to put over his lorry in
France. Stephen came home very pleased with himself because he
was "runner-up" for the Company, which wasn't too inglorious, but
let him off having to do it all over again for the battalion in the
afternoon on Sunday, so that he was able to hear a wireless concert
he was determined to hear.

'We feel very pleased about David's exam because there were
55 candidates in his group, so we feel that having come out third
ought to enable him to get what he wants in the way of a job. I
had hopes that he would be on one of those large affairs, like the
King George VIth, which always appeal to me as being safer than those

horrid little MTBs etc. But he tells me that you have to be more or less born and bred in the Navy to be on a battleship.'

David's passing out third in his group meant that he avoided 'the jobs reserved for the dregs of each division' and he became Flag-Officer to an Admiral, based on Scapa Flow.

'It's a curiously nebulous job. I'm not sure whether I work from breakfast to bedtime every day, or whether I don't do any work at all but live the life of a country gentleman. The only thing that is clear is that nobody cares in the least how much work I do or how I do it; it is judged entirely by results, and the criterion is that the results should be unobtrusive. So long as the Admiral doesn't suddenly discover that some naval operation that interests him has been going on without him knowing it, and so long as the domestic wheels are so well oiled that nobody notices the way they move, I have done my stuff.

'I hope I shan't ever make a great deal of money. I don't really like being waited on, however efficiently, though when one is not it seems pleasant in anticipation and in retrospect. Of course, there are some things I rather like having done for me, but they are all the things I shouldn't do at all if it was left to me, such as brushing my clothes and cleaning my shoes. But to have cars you never see the works of and a garden which grows perfectly adequately whether you do anything about it yourself or not is very unsatisfactory. A garden gate fell off its hinges and disintegrated the other day, so I rang up the civil engineers and this morning saw a new garden gate there, all spick and span, but I wasn't interested in it as I should have been if I had sawn it all up and nailed it together myself.

'The Admiral and I went over to the mainland the other day. It was a very exhausting day – at least I thought so; at the age of 58 he didn't show any signs of thinking so at all. I often feel like the Young Man in *Alice in Wonderland* – "Do you think at your age it is right?" But we did nine separate journeys in various cars, two in speedboats, and three in aeroplanes during the day, and between whiles he gave two lectures and inspected five different establishments, including a flock of Wrens in their Wrennery. I still don't like aeroplanes much. It was a very small and unreliable looking machine that we were going in, and not the sort of day I prefer for flying; but as he said, we can't let the RAF know we're frightened. I said the main thing I was frightened of was the prospect of stepping out of the thing on an RAF

aerodrome, looking bright green and being sick in front of the guard
of honour. However we set bravely off and to cut a distressing story as
short as possible, I was sick, but I did it so discreetly that nobody
knew. I told him afterwards and he thought it a first class joke. But I'd
rather be in a ship whatever it did.

'We have had quite a lot of interesting visitors here lately.
Christopher's chief was one of them, bringing with him a young
secretary who was Christ Church and the Foreign Office to
perfection. The Minister seemed a nice fellow and very much on the
spot, and he surprised the Naval Authorities who had been expecting
"one of those Labour chaps" to arrive in a brown suit, a red tie, and a
bowler hat without any h's. He didn't stay long enough to go on any
of the marathon walks which Christopher suffers unfortunately; I
should have gone with him for the sake of the opportunity to talk to
him alone. Of course my stock soared when I told him I was C's
cousin. Anything even slightly related to C. is OK by the Minister.'

Almost as soon as he joined his battalion Pat was sent on a series
of courses – on motor mechanics, pay, weapon training – which
at the time he resented because he wanted to have time to train
with his platoon. One of the advantages of the courses was that
it was usually possible to get time off in transit and over the
weekends. Pat got up to London on two occasions; and on one of
these

'I went to see my ex-bosses at the Home Office, just to show that I
was still alive and interested, and went down fairly well. I got some
interesting details; the magistrates are still very sober and have got
the various types of looting pretty well worked into the various classes
of severity; there has not been any serious increase in crime per head
of population but the offences have changed considerably. Far more
larceny and an almost complete absence of the most interesting cases
of indecency. On the other hand there is a huge increase in the
number of girls brought before the courts for care and protection on
the grounds of their suffering from VD. Inevitable I suppose and no
doubt the public will blame the drunken and licentious soldiery.
There was a considerable difference of opinion on the question of
shelter morality; all agree to the fact that all is not well, but no one
can agree as to how serious the situation may be.'

But there was no doubt that Pat was becoming bored and restless; happy with his platoon he nevertheless found the endless wiring of the beaches and the 'stand-to, there may be an invasion' tedious. His mood was not improved by receiving the Military Medal from the King at Buckingham Palace – he recognized this as a great honour but he found it difficult to stand alongside the immensely brave and heroic sailors of the *Jervis Bay*.

His restlessness increased and he responded to an army circular encouraging officers to transfer to the Army Co-op (RAF); he was not accepted because he had not held his commission for a year but his letters created a small storm in the Budget. He wrote:

'I feel that I ought, and want, to be one of the volunteers. I do feel at the moment the Budgeteers of fighting age are doing rather little – not in any way their own fault. Chris in London – very unpleasant but civilian; Paul in Ireland; George at Marlborough; Stephen in the City; David giving parties; myself sitting safely away from a town – maybe I'm over-sensitive, but I don't like it.

'Dad is obviously of the opinion that to have run fast and successfully at Dunkirk entitles one to sit back in peace for the rest of the war; I disagree most profoundly and feel that one should have at least one major campaign a year.'

David was supportive when he wrote:

'Pat's remark, by the way, rang the bell with a loud and discordant clang. In general we don't seem to be doing so much to discomfort the enemy now as we did, and though I suspect we are putting in some pretty dirty work behind the scenes, I still don't feel I am doing much towards it.'

All of this brought many criticisms. Doff wrote that Pat was 'convinced that George is delighted to stand by and watch his friends in the thick of it'; Stephen wrote asking whether it wasn't 'a bit hard on me and Christopher and David to say that we are on your conscience, when I suspect this may not be your conscience at all, but a natural urge for danger which I share'. Christopher accused him

'of holding old-fashioned ideas about the war in some respects. This
is not a soldier's war, nor a sailor's, nor even an airman's war.
Physical courage, especially the physical courage of the Armed
Forces, is becoming of less and less importance; and moral courage
and faith in victory, especially that of civilians, is becoming more and
more important. I think you pay too much regard to physical courage
in relation to the present war. Very few people have needed it so far,
and those who have have not been in the forces at all.

Pat had to backtrack and to try to explain himself more fully.

'Please don't take it personally because I know you are all doing the
job for which you are chosen and for which, in the opinion of the
country, you are most suitable.
'Nonetheless the Budget is entirely non-combatant at a time of
war.
'In regard to my personal inclination; in 1935 George said I had a
"suicide-complex" – by that there was no intention of suggesting
heroism or do-or-die spirit, merely that I feel uncomfortable when I
know other people to be in a worse condition than I. I cannot accept
that the 20 year olds of St Pancras can in any way be classed with
Paul, CP, and I for the responsibility of the war. I do not mean to say
that Dad started the war! but merely that Dad's class (and mine) must
bear the responsibility for our share in involving the world in war. I
therefore feel that it is definitely unfair to expect the boys of St
Pancras to fight – in the literal sense – our war.'

The criticisms and the controversy died down and Pat continued to guard the coast, rather reluctantly.

'On Tuesday I did a very silly thing; for months we have been
putting up hundreds of miles of wire round our positions. There are
two main types of wiring – the first consists of barbed wire run from
high pickets to low pickets, forming a series of Vs, and across these
Vs you run 3 or 4 horizontal strands all windlassed to the diagonals;
these Vs are on either side of the taller pickets. The second type pulls
out like a concertina; there are two rolls on the ground and a third on
top of them. In my position there is a hedge and then a double apron
fence, then the triple coils, then another double apron, all in contact
with each other. I decided to see what sort of an obstacle it really was,
so I got myself timed over it – 4 secs! This unfortunately got to the

ears of the CO who made us weave wire between the different types
of wire so that they were bound together in a mass of wire about 4 ft
high. I got so annoyed at this that I waited until it was complete then I
got 7 men and we charged it; I was through in 6 seconds and the
whole lot were through in about 12–15 seconds. It would have taken
us 2 or 3 seconds to walk the distance, so I suppose we can say that
we gain a second for every month's work, which is rather a depressing
thought.'

A rather malicious enjoyment was derived at that time from
the *Daily Mirror* which was running an 'anti-army nonsense'
campaign.

'We are forbidden by all sorts of commands to "polish our brasses"
on equipment – very reasonable and elementary camouflage – but
COs think "my men will be smart" and defy the laws, thereby
causing a lot of work to the men, and slightly endangering their lives.
The *DM* thought "to hell with this", so they invited their readers to
send in the lists of Regt.s where this order was being disobeyed. Sure
enough, two days later a large space was devoted to saying "The
Royal West Kents are polishing their brasses" and next day "The
Sussex Regt are –"; next day we got an order from the CO. "Brasses
will NOT, repeat NOT, be polished." Bless you *DM*.
'Again, they are now including stupid orders such as "The
Brigadier notices with disapproval that his car is not being saluted by
soldiers; attention is drawn – disciplinary action", or "when men are
without jackets, the shirt sleeves will be folded so as to leave a 2″ fold
above the elbow"; or again, "when men are in shirtsleeves, braces
will be worn; these braces will be blancoed." We really have got a
good weapon here.'

And so Pat settled down temporarily to more wiring, to being
the defending officer at courts martial, to Home Guard exercises and training, and to a life generally of 'no change'.

Since the beginning of the year Beryl's letters had contained
news of the conversion of Felthorpe into a hospital.

'The workmen have got a hole thro' from the study into the boys' room, another from the back passage into the cloakroom and the new partition across the cloakroom.

'Rumour has it that the study will be finished this week. The architect has been over with the carpenter to measure the windows for the blackout, and the matron has written to say she is "waiting to come as soon as we can do with her." Meanwhile the yellow crocuses are up in the ha-ha and lots of snowdrops down the drive.

'So home to electricians, plumbers, black-out men, and the last of the movers –

'On Saturday a "Regional" Big Wig wired from Cambridge that he would "inspect" us on Monday. He came, saw, and approved! For tonight someone has rung us (again from Cambridge) to tell us to expect 8 PATIENTS TOMORROW.'

It was not long before Beryl found herself involved in the universal problem of supply of food:

'I have only this moment got back from Norwich after a daily struggle to procure enough food for the patients to eat. It really is a bit of a battle these days, and though we are registered as an "Institution" that only means that we draw the ordinary civilian rations of 1/- worth of meat, 4 oz butter, etc. For the rest I just have to scrounge 1 lb of slab cake in one shop, if I'm lucky, a 9d ginger one in another, 3 lbs of sausages here and a hope of a little tripe on Wednesday if I get in early! Those of you who have housekeeping to do, even for a small family, can just begin to imagine what it's like. I hope to be able to get a variety of shops to promise me at least 1 lb a week of something and hold it for me, but it is all very difficult at the moment.'

Doff was finding the same problem.

'The food situation down here is just purely comic these days. It's all very well for the Ministry of Food to say eat oats – there aren't any; they say eat cheese – we're allowed three-quarters of an ounce to last for a fortnight. There aren't any eggs, suet, dripping, currants, marmalade, etc. etc. so housekeeping is a bit of an effort.'

Aunt Ellie found a useful 6d book called *Listeners' Recipes* which was 'up-to-date and doesn't suggest using things that have been unprocurable for months. Several of the dishes, such as "Savoury Batter" and "Vegetable Mince" have been well received by the family.'

By the summer of 1941 rationing had been introduced for many foodstuffs. The quantity allowed to each person varied from time to time, depending upon the seasons and supply, but the housewives had to work on the assumption that each adult person could receive, weekly,

> 4 ounces bacon or ham
> 12 ounces sugar
> 1/10d worth of meat
> 2 ounces tea
> 2 ounces cooking fat
> 4 ounces margarine
> 4(2) ounces butter
> 1(2) ounces cheese
> 1 egg per fortnight
> Jam on coupons
> Marmalade on coupons
> Syrup
> Mincemeat seasonal, from 8 oz–2 lb
> Lemon Curd per month
> Honey

Fish was unrationed but very difficult to obtain, as was all offal. Tins of food virtually disappeared until in December 1941 they were put on 'points', each adult receiving 16 points a month – which would buy one large tin of American sausage meat.

In June clothes rationing was introduced and Doff started a second-hand clothes shop at Marlborough; she was kept very busy because the demand for these off-ration clothes was tremendous.

But all rationing problems were put into the background as Beryl prepared to kill a fatted calf.

'Felthorpe calling the family after an uneventful week (except for one terrific excitement which is so hush-hush that I can't tell you about it till the news is generally released!).

'On Sunday June 29 the *Daily Express* rang up and said there had been an escape from the Camp and was Paul home? HOME! I ask you! We said no, we had heard nothing of him for weeks and they could not tell us anything more, but made us promise to ring them up in Birmingham when we had any news to release.

'Then we thought we might ring up the Air Ministry to ask if they could tell us anything but they were very cross indeed at anybody knowing anything, and said it was still utterly hush-hush until it was announced that all who had got out of the camp had succeeded in getting out of Eire or had been recaptured, so we had to shut up very tight.

'Late on Monday came a telegram from Belfast –

"Stop all letters of all kind till further notice. Tell Monica. Very important. Flourishing. Paul."

So we told Monica but could not release it further.

'On Thursday we rang up the AM again to see if something could not go out in the Budget, but the reply was still hush-hush, so it was not until Paul phoned to say he'd be in London on Saturday and home on Sunday that we dared to send you the great news.

'On Sunday he and Monica arrived in time for lunch. Unluckily Dad had a big Home Guard meeting in Norwich so it was not till we got back to a late tea that Paul made the polite and filial gesture of asking what the parents would think of his getting married pretty soon? We made the traditional noises about careers and incomes (present and prospective) but discovered after some twenty minutes pleasant theorizing that the afternoon had been spent making all the necessary arrangements and that at the cost of hours of telephoning and 35/- worth of calls "A wedding had been arranged" and was to take place on Thursday!

'So the next three days were a whirl of wedding plans, honeymoon plans, and a minimum of hospital business if it could not be postponed. Pat came home on Tuesday and we raked up a bachelor dinner which we all agreed lacked no peacetime touch except cream for the strawberries.

'On Wednesday we dug up a little peacetime hoard buried about July 1939, poured it into the Humber and blued it in this good cause. Just as well we did as the car was invaluable. It was great fun to be driving across England once more, but OH how one misses the signposts and nameplates.'

On his honeymoon, after a very successful and happy wedding, Paul eventually wrote an account of his escape for the Budget:

'Imagine me sitting in the Curragh with 10 other unfortunates, of all of whom I am heartily bored (and they are heartily bored with me). Naturally enough one's thoughts turn to escape for, in internment, even the war looks quite fun from a distance. Escape needs organization, and organization needs a leader, and to his great astonishment and secret pride, Mayhew is chosen for the task. From then on, of course, Mayhew turns from Algy Longworth into Bulldog Drummond, and things go swimmingly. First, we fixed our objective; six seemed a modest but satisfactory total to aim at; so I chose six whom I regarded as "nationally important" (though not alas the most pleasant or the most deserving). There then remained the difficulty of getting out of the compound. We have our huts surrounded by about 5 ft of barbed wire except for a gap of about six yards wide to permit ingress and egress; and round the compound proper we have two 10 ft barbed wire fences simply festooned with concertina-coils of barbed wire. Finally, round the main gate is another 5 ft barbed wire fence with a bolted (and a very easily unbolted) wicket gate in it. Outside the compound there is yet another 5 ft barbed wire fence, about 20 yards outside. As the great day approached (June 25th, the first day of the race-meeting) they started to put another diagonal fence inside and up to the top of this one and fixed a nice coil on the top to discourage climbing; so it was apparent that we weren't attempting our break-out any too soon.

'Well, bearing in mind that Anglo-Irish relations are in a delicate state, and that therefore violence is to be avoided what would you do chums? There are five guards inside the compound and a sentry box on each corner; there is one sentry outside the gate between the inner and outer fences, and in the guardroom about 100 yards away there are some 20 guards waiting for the call. In those circumstances and being a pacifist by nature, we decided on subtlety rather than brawn. The plan was, I regret, not initially mine, I merely made what suggestions occurred to me and had the final dictatorial word – oh yes, and chose the cast, so to speak; anyway, the plan went without a hitch as follows:

'On Weds. June 25th two sergeants are despatched to Dublin on their monthly trip with late parole until 12.30 a.m. that night. During the day we all behave normally. Most of us go to the Races (I won the Tote Double and finished 13/- up, a good test of steady nerves) and

in the evening we settle down to a noisy and apparently drunken
poker-drive. Much display is made of empty bottles and when the
guard makes his routine call at midnight, he probably thinks we're
safely drunk for the night.

'At exactly 12.14.25 a.m. however, drunkenness gives way to
sobriety. Everybody knows their part so I merely throw down my
cards and say "OK boys, I think it's my bedtime". The Officers
thereupon move to action stations in the passage by the door, but
concealed from view. I thereupon summon the Sergeants by calling
for Julie (safely locked in her room) and they take up positions the
other side of the door. Finally (12.14.30 a.m.) I look out of the door
and whistle for Julie, noting that everything is normal. Then we swing
into action, and two officers go out of the door and through the
wicket-gate to a small hut by the gate where we always ask questions,
send telegrams, sign parole etc. In this hut are two guards, and by the
gate is another one, while the other two in the compound are away up
at the top and out of danger. The officers start to write a long and
involved telegram to a mutual pal to be sent in the morning. Then, by
curious coincidence, at exactly 12.15 a.m. the two sergeants return
from Dublin, most convincingly the worse for wear. Here Fuhrer
Mayhew got bad jitters; but the officers and the sergeants admirably
took no notice of each other, and one of the guards in the hut left his
hut and went to open the gate. I then despatched three more
sergeants out of our hut as though they were going to bed in their hut.
The gate was opened. Dublin sergeants came straight through and
then started a little drunken insubordination toward the officers.
Naturally they left the hut and moved toward them to argue, and then
with admirable precision attacked the guards from behind and
pinioned their arms to their sides. At the same moment the "Blitz"
began and the three sergeants ostensibly going to bed changed course
and went to the gate. There they incapacitated the guard left in the
hut by pulling the door to, slipping a noose of rope over the handle
and tying the other end to a tree.

'They then went to the officers' assistance. At this moment there
were only 3 cares, the guard outside the gate (frequently he wasn't
there) and the sentries on the corner; and these we had already
decided to risk. So I led my six escapers and we stampeded through
the wicket gate and through the still open side gate. Rifles were fired
off everywhere, as expected, but all, I think, were most agreeably
blank. I threw myself down under the outer fence in a little gully that
gave some protection and cut through the diagonal and vertical
fences underneath the coil with the most perfect pair of wire cutters

imaginable. (How did I get them? Shush). All this time poppings were everywhere, but we were in the gully out of the floodlighting and I felt pretty safe. Some of my co-escapers claim to have heard the whines of live bullets, and if it's true they must have come from the revolver of the officer on duty leaving his hut; but I think it was probably the result of imagination helped by the twang of cut barbed wire. Anyway, we went through that wire like a piece of cake, and soon I found myself on the golf course with my five chickens in good order around me. It takes a long time to tell but I think we took under a minute from the word go (probably nearer 30 seconds) to the golf course; and needless to say the guards were left almost literally standing.

'Here I regret a discreet veil must be drawn in view of the 14 other wretches left inside. But I cannot refrain from relating how I spent 20 hours consecutively up an oak tree, a performance that as well as being hideously uncomfortable must leave King Charles behind. Anyway four of our six got to Belfast (the two recaptured have only themselves to thank) and two out of the three "private efforts" succeeded – a most gratifying total, six out of nine. But the really gratifying item was the cooperation and unselfishness of the people left behind.'

And so to marriage, a honeymoon, and a telegram telling him to report back to his squadron.

Life at Downe was changing; with David able to spend only a very occasional leave at home it was Stephen who was next to move – to Romsey in Hampshire. He resigned from Hoare's Bank and immediately found himself being groomed to become Finance Officer in Saunders-Roe, aeroplane manu-facturers.

'The odd thing about the job is that though I suppose that it's all very vital and so on, none the less I personally seem to spend a large proportion of my time fighting Contracts Dept. of the Ministry of Aircraft Production tooth and nail in order to try and make the war cost a bit more and collar the extra bit for ourselves. It's the way the Government wants it done, so we do it, though there doesn't seem much enthusiasm in the industry for excessive profits; why should there be when, if by gigantic efforts you succeed in putting one across the Director of Contracts, the fruits of your special pleading, innuendoes and your lies disappear straight into the maw of the Inland Revenue in the shape of 100% Excess Profits Tax? The chat about capitalism's excessive profits is completely beside the point at present so far as firms doing Government work are concerned; because of the extremely stringent control of and enquiry into profits and costs. If profits are made they are made by individuals hopping into black markets and out again, and that sort of thing, not by legitimately trading businesses.

'The Government's interest in costs stops short, of course, of labour costs. These must be accepted without question. Labour in this racket is really in an incredibly strong position. As it is well organized, with the Minister of Labour behind it, managements climb down in most disputes; and the result is very high wages and a very high standard of amenities such as canteens, supply of special transport and so on. Labour, I fancy, views the whole thing as a splendid and unexpected tactical advantage in that century-old struggle with capitalism which really conditions the outlook of industrialists on both sides of the fence just as much as, if not more than, the reason for this abrupt change in the two sides' fortunes. Some of the aspects of the whole business are a bit unsavoury; for instance, those of our men who belong to a certain union not long ago went slow in order to justify very high piecework prices. Having got their prices they worked hard for a bit and earned such terrific bonuses that they feared that prices would be cut; so they just went slow again. I don't think it's any good blaming them; it's just the inevitable outcome of the long battle of the Industrial Revolution, which now conditions the minds of shop stewards and works managers far more fundamentally than the temporary excitement of the war. Well, it's the way the Government are running the war. It involves an enormous amount of bargaining, accounting, estimating, which you would have thought might have been bypassed; but the Conservatives cling to their individual interests and Labour fights the war it really knows how to fight, and there you are.'

It really could not be expected that Stephen would get away with these remarks without provoking Christopher into a spirited reply:

'The lamentable situation Stephen describes is merely a demonstration in the world of labour of the principles on which our employing class has run our economic life for the last two centuries – the principle of selling what you have to sell (in this case labour) at the best price you can get, making the most of the market, forming combinations to strengthen your position and so on – in fact, doing the best for yourself and the devil take the community. This is only what the employing class would be doing now (as it did in the last war) if it was not prevented by law. Even as it is, it makes the best of what opportunities remain, profiteering in every trade the law has not yet reached, speculating in stocks and shares, agricultural land and real estate, tax-dodging, black-marketing, agitating against the new controls, campaigning against the Excess Profits Tax. After that it sits back and delivers pious lectures to much-envied labour on the need for Disinterested Duty to the Community.

'The reason why the profit motive looks so ugly when seen in Labour rather than Capital is that Labour has no spokesman to sanctify its selfishness by creating it into an Economic Theory. In the last century the employing class, having a monopoly of press, pulpit, publishing and politics, worked up a complete philosophy to prove that Private Enterprise, Individual Initiative, Business-is-Business, and all the other euphemisms for Me-First were not merely the only practical way of running things, but were actually the principles underlying the Sermon on the Mount.

'Stephen can indict a certain attitude of mind, but he cannot indict the working class rather than the employing class. It was the latter who started the ball rolling; and the harm that Labour is now doing to the community is merely a fraction of what Capital has done in the past, would do now if it was allowed to, and will do in future if it gets the chance.'

Stephen answered this letter:

'Christopher is dead right about my being a reactionary employer of labour, except that I'm not an employer but an observer. I don't think I'm excessively susceptible to capitalist propaganda, and anyway, though I admit I see it all here from the management side, there isn't a single person in this company, not even the managing director, who holds any shares – they're all salaried and not paid commissions, or profits, or anything. And so I doubt whether I am getting a very distorted view – no more distorted, for example, than Pat's view of the army because he's an officer. And with all that, I stick to it that labour is showing up badly – not cooperating, and with only one idea and that is to get as much money out of it as possible, by fair means or foul. It's a miserable picture. I expect there are enthusiasts, but as a whole I can only conclude that the men get the leaders they choose, and as they always choose cantankerous, class-conscious windbags, I suppose they like them. Either that, or they're completely indifferent which isn't much better.'

A letter from Christopher reported that

'Walking across Piccadilly Circus on Sunday afternoon, who should I bump into but Brother Pat. I had just emerged from a concert and I pushed him into a taxi and carted him back to tea. He seemed in good form and had lots of good military gossip.'

Pat was on his way from one of his many courses and he was still becoming increasingly bored with the inactivity associated with being a coastal defence battalion. He wrote that since he joined the battalion ten months earlier

'No. 15 platoon has dug 54 weapon pits and has put up over 20,000 yards of wire, and if you multiply that by three – you get 60,000 yards for the three platoons of the Company, and about 275,000 yards for the Bn. If my arithmetic is correct this must be about 158 miles. I suppose I can't tell you how long our Bn Front is, but I expect you'll have a pretty good idea.'

Although Pat very much enjoyed the responsibility of being a platoon commander, he also found it difficult to settle down to 'stagnant warfare' and it was no great surprise when he announced:

'I have "done the dirty" and have been accepted by the RAF proper. I applied after one more plea for pilots, and I decided not to tell Dad or the rest of the family because I was fully prepared to expect nothing more, and the news would have worried Dad and caused pitying cries of "that idiot again – ridiculous" from the rest of the family.
'I was extremely surprised to get a summons to Cranwell within 3 weeks.'

He had no particular difficulty in passing the various interviews and medicals and was told that he would be called up in two or three weeks, but before any transfer could take place the Army stepped in and any further transfers were stopped. In the few weeks when he had been expecting to join the RAF Pat had been becoming increasingly excited at the prospect and had been in close touch with Paul.

The chance to meet Paul and talk about all this came at Felthorpe. Beryl wrote:

'Doff, George, Susan and Michael had been in the cottage for some time, Helen and Clare were here, Pat had been home for a night the previous weekend and promised to come for at least Saturday night, and Kiff had seven whole days due to him starting that Saturday too. We wrote and wired to Paul and he replied that he was not due for any leave at all yet, but under the circumstances he'd been promised a plane and 24-hours if, if, it was fine enough to fly.

'Sunday dawned bright and clear at Felthorpe. The Home Guard had a church parade and the Red Cross turned out in force to watch, so that occupied our morning. We started lunch and had got to the plum tart and a most peculiar yellow custard when there was the roar of a low-flying plane overhead. "PAUL" we yelled and scrambled round the piano to get out onto the lawn. Paul it was, he shot over the copper beech, soared over the lake and came back up the ride as if he was going to take the chimneys. He assured us he did nothing in the least dangerous, but I for one had my heart in my mouth the whole blooming time. So far as my recollection goes Kiff was shouting and Doff dancing, Dad waving his napkin and making shooing noises as for hornets; finally the parents decided they could not stand the strain and dragged the family back into the house as a gesture to the pilot to remove his plane. (Pat had left for St Faith's at the first roar.) The family sat down again and looked at the yellow custard; from excitement or fright no one had any appetite left at all, so cigarettes were lit and we adjourned to the front door to wait for the car. In a very few minutes it arrived, so Paul was added to the bosom of his family – complete for the first time since Christmas 1938!'

It had been an eventful autumn at Felthorpe, including a bad night when a returning Blenheim bomber crashed in Mill Hill wood, bursting into flames and killing all the crew. There was absolutely nothing that Dad or Beryl could do to save them but there were interesting repercussions.

'Some RAF officer rang up to say that he was considering recommending two of his men for their gallant conduct on the night the plane crashed in our woods and had Dad got to the scene in time to see anything? Dad replied cautiously that no one else was there when we arrived and it did not seem possible that anyone had had time to come and go away again, so the Officer said he had not yet got the men's statements in writing but he would ring up again and read it to Dad when it came. We had a talk with the patients who had run with us and were all positive that none of the RAF had arrived until some minutes after all three bodies had been found by our party and it had been ascertained that nothing could be done for any of them. But when the RAF rang up again and said their two men had burnt their hands in "extricating the bodies from the wreckage" Dad told them (rather too mildly I thought) that he was afraid the account was rather too highly coloured and explained exactly what had happened. He said that one of the two had certainly been very knowledgeable and helpful when he did come, but if he burnt his hands it was not in extricating the bodies and that the ammunition had stopped popping off before they got there.'

The hospital had steadily developed and before the end of the year there were twenty-four patients.

'They seem a nice lot of men but it is a bit of a squash in the Recreation Room of an evening.
'The food situation seems pretty smooth except for breakfasts; eggs once a week if we're lucky, and the nimble herring proving peculiarly elusive in any of its forms makes it difficult to provide any alternative to bacon, and that is stretched pretty thin if it has to do 5 mornings out of 7.'

There was a new Quartermaster for the hospital because Helen had decided to join the FANYs.

'The new girl is feeling quite incredibly new [she wrote]. At the moment I'm sitting on a long bench writing on a trestle-table – what price the Army! To add to the comfort and the joy of life I might add that we ate our scones and margarine off enamel plates and drank stewed tea out of enamel tooth-mugs. Heavens! How like school this is!'

'I am a driver in the employ of the Inter-Services Research Bureau and am simply thrilled with the job. The company is excellent and the atmosphere very friendly and informal. I started off the job with a swing by driving some Colonel round London, waiting at least half an hour at each stop, and arriving back at 6.00 p.m. just in time to clean the car!'

Just before joining the FANYs Helen had written from Felthorpe: 'We had a grand weekend with the Paul Mayhews. Shooting all Saturday with Dick and on Sunday playing tennis with him.'

But five days later Paul wrote:

'The only event that registers at all on my brain at present is the death of Dick by an OTU accident, I imagine. I saw it in *The Times* on Friday and since then I've been miserably depressed and defeatist. Dick was just about the best friend I had and the one of whom I was the most proud to be a friend. I never saw him angry, and he always, with that permanent smile, made one feel one was always welcome.

'Really it is the most useless tragedy of the war. If a man is killed in action I suppose nice comforting arguments can be put forward that "he died for his country" and that mankind benefited by his death; but that the best youth I ever met should be killed in some bloody sordid little training accident is simply a tragedy unrelieved even by the most jingoist theories.'

Paul's promotion to Flight-Lieutenant had given him additional responsibilities both on land and in the air; he even 'found himself acting-CO for two days! Luckily, we have an efficient Adjutant and nothing very sensational occurred, so I coped fairly adequately, but I seem to have moved somewhat fast upwards recently.'

'Did you read of a very heavy daylight attack on Brest in the course of which we lost 5 bombers and a fighter? *Ipse aderam* – as Caesar would have said – my first offensive operation of the war. Our part was all very dull but I might as well give you some idea (confidential please) of a "sweep".

'We knew, or suspected, that something was in the air on Monday when we were officially asked what we thought of long-range Hurricanes as potential escort fighters. Our reply was unprintable but had no effect and on Wednesday morning we were told to stand by for the biggest offensive operation ever carried out by this Group, and this was followed by the news that Thursday was the day.

'Picture our position. A new CO unused to modern tactics or single-seater fighters, a squadron untrained for even the simplest defensive interception, one flight-lieutenant non-existent and the other out of date: and with all this, equipped with aeroplanes that in speed and even in manoeuvrability fell far short of the 109E, to say nothing of the 109F. I think all of us were considerably scared, though we didn't admit it. I know I was rather more scared than in the Battle of Britain.

'We picked our 12 best pilots and planes and flew down to an aerodrome only about 10 miles from Clare's school as a jumping-off place on Wednesday afternoon, and consequently guessed that Brest was the target.

'Thursday dawned fine but with a welcome layer of cloud at about 3000 ft, and after a short "briefing" we took off rather nervously at 11.30 a.m. As usual my nerves vanished as I took off, but as a result of being in these awful planes we were all rather on the defensive psychologically. The attitude was rather "If I get back from this I shall be pleased" whereas had we been in Spits or short-range Hurricanes it would have been "If I don't get a 109 I shall be furious." On the English coast we picked up two squadrons of Spits and flew off as a wing.

'The scheme was roughly that three successive waves of bombers should knock hell out of Brest. They would have no "close escort" but each wave would synchronize its arrival with a wing of fighters which would keep clear of the "flak" but escort the bombers in and out. We were the first wing over, and our wave of bombers was composed of Stirlings; we were to sweep up and down the French coast at Brest and attack any Germans to be seen.

'After leaving England we climbed steadily until about 10 miles from France. We were at 17,000 ft and identified Brest by a vast cloud of the most intense "flak" you can imagine, far exceeding anything I've seen in England.

'We were a little late or the Stirlings were a little early, and we found them already going imperturbably into the middle of it. We were flying straight into the sun which was very unpleasant and my doubts were not allayed by the Spits doing the dirty on us. They were, of course, immensely faster than us, but had promised to stick by us. However, on sighting Brest, they opened up to full throttle and turned fairly sharp left. Since we were on the right of the formation we were thrown into considerable confusion. I was on the right of our squadron and was consequently in the worst possible position. So I gave up the unequal struggle and separated my flight from the rest of the formation to keep it together. It was a nasty moment, particularly as our precious cloud cover had dispersed, but I soon realized that the Germans had either been caught napping or else didn't fancy the odds. Anyway, there seemed to be about 100 British planes and no Germans – rather a change from the B of B. It was really incredible; I only saw 1 Me. and that had 3 Spits on its tail, so there was little room for my flight. Some of the squadron saw a formation of 6 Me.s but could do nothing in LP Hurricanes and only one fired his guns (unsuccessfully). I milled around with my flight for some time, and then the bombers came out again; there was a good deal of smoke over Brest, but I could see nothing of the results of our bombing. I found a lonely-looking Stirling and escorted it back to England making rude gestures to the crew and generally enjoying myself.

'The whole thing was a piece of cake for us though I believe the Germans put up rather more fighters for the later waves. If we had Spits I wouldn't mind doing sweeps regularly – it's not much fun in these things. The one fighter lost was unfortunately one of our sergeant-pilots; he got separated from his colleagues and nobody saw him again – the old, old story. But we bought some very valuable experience cheaply and the squadron's a lot the better for it, even though action was lacking. Incidentally I had to lead the squadron back for the first time, as the CO was summoned to a "post-mortem".'

By Christmas it seemed probable that the whole of Paul's squadron would be posted overseas, but

'it doesn't look like being in the immediate future and a "semi-official spokesman" has even said there's a 50–50 chance of its being cancelled altogether. This would be the most frightful anti-climax and paradoxically enough rather a disappointment for yours truly. I've got so worked up to going and I'm so convinced that for the first time since I returned we have a really good selection of pilots, that I quite look forward to going, provided that there's a chance of getting back again fairly soon.

'God knows how long we are going to be here now. Our original draft, on which for various reasons we were very keen to go, has now fallen through definitely; but we are still certain to go sooner or later, and the middle of next month is mentioned as a likely date, though nobody of course has the slightest idea where we are going now.'

Embarkation was virtually certain by early February, and embarkation leave was granted.

'I went on leave on the 3rd and had a very good time spending the first five days at Belton and the last two in town. At Belton I spent many hours in bed and armchair, an hour or two being very domestic with dirty things like coal, wood-cum-saws, and the breakfast plates, and about five minutes a day pretending to be energetic and walking. It was a most admirable existence.

'On the 8th, Mon and I went to town and proceeded to hit the big city an appalling and most exhausting crack, on the theory that our last leave was very cheap and there probably wouldn't be any more. We did the thing in style, and had a potent 48 hours. With the Savoy as our obsequious headquarters and purveyors of all black-market food, we devoted one morning to shopping wherein Mon viewed the entire stock of John Lewis and Co, and the rest of the time to "entertainment". We lunched with Chris very exotically at his expense, and with Helen (in between the claims of Churchill and Sir John Dill) at our own expense; and we danced at the Savoy as long as Caroll Gibbons could take it – our dancing was simply brilliant, needless to say. Altogether it was expensive, but a Good Thing.'

From Dad:

'Paul was killed on Thursday 19 February. He took up his flight on
operational duties about 5.00 p.m. on that day and ordered it down
shortly after 6.00 p.m. He however remained in the air for a short
time longer. On coming down he flew across the aerodrome, and on
turning, his engine stalled, and I understand he had not sufficient
height to recover. The medical evidence, confirmed by two doctors,
is that he was rendered immediately unconscious, and that he died
five minutes after reaching the Hospital, never having regained
consciousness. In these circumstances he would not have suffered
from the subsequent fire.

'It is thought that there was an error of judgment. We know that
light was failing and we know that he was flying a new plane which he
had only had for two days. Maybe the new machine failed to respond
as he expected. There has been an enquiry by the Air Ministry, but I
have not been advised of the findings.

'That is all.'

3

SLOWLY TO PEACE
February 1942 – May 1945

By the middle of 1942 the war, and the attitude to the war, was changing. Peace still seemed to be far away and people were becoming war-weary, as were the writers to the Budget. During the first two and a half years of war they had experienced the excitement and challenge of the original upheaval; they had come to know what it was like to be in danger; and there was no longer any novelty left in rationing or in shortages or in the misery of the blackout.

All this was reflected in their letters which nevertheless continued to reach Felthorpe throughout the remaining three years of war, telling of difficulties and dangers, and of hopes for the future.

David was brought into the Special Operations Executive (SOE) after a talk with Christopher who saw David's obvious value and qualifications for working, from the Shetland Isles, in the Scandinavian arm of the service – he knew about boats, he loved Scandinavia, and he could speak Norwegian. David was attracted by the idea, joined SOE in the summer of 1941, and for the rest of the war was involved in work which he was not able to mention or describe in any detail until the war ended.

While on leave at home in March 1942 Christopher wrote a full account of his work with SOE during the previous year. This 'Letter to a post-war Budget' was sealed and put away in great security 'to be opened in January 1945 or at the end of the war, whichever is the earlier'. In the event, it was opened in November 1983, and this is a summary of its contents:

'It all began for me in November 1940 when Dalton, whom I then thought to be an ordinary respectable Minister of Economic Warfare summoned me to go to see him in London. He explained to me in

general terms about his "black" life and offered me a job. I had little
hesitation in accepting – I was pretty fed up with the Army, and the
outlook for British soldiers over the next year or two seemed dreary. I
abandoned khaki for civvies, announced to the world that I was
joining MEW and started on my duties.

'The first thing I discovered about my job was that there was
nothing to do, so I "read myself in" – browsing in the office files
which were gathered together from the most secret State papers,
Foreign Office telegrams, Secret Service reports and goodness
knows what else besides. Every scheme put up by SOE for fostering
subversion was filed away here – a whole library of plans of varying
importance and practicability, concerned with bribing this man and
assassinating that man, blowing up this power-station, sinking that
ship, flooding aerodromes – nothing was ruled out, nothing too
fantastic to be considered.

'In January I was transferred to 64, Baker St, the HQ of the SOE
and given a job in the new Intelligence and Planning Dept.

'My job here was quite a busy one, I was responsible for the
distribution of all information papers through the organization. In
addition I had to publish daily a digest of all these papers for the
convenience of people who could not wade through them all.

'Eventually I began to feel that my job was not full enough and at
my request I was transferred from the Intelligence to the Planning
side of the section. The planners were responsible for working up
ideas, which had been provisionally approved, into workable projects.
For example someone thought that raiding the railways in the toe of
Italy from submarines based on Malta would be a good idea and I was
told to look into it. I spent a great deal of time looking up the most
important stretches of railway line, the most vulnerable points on
those stretches – bridges, tunnels, embankments etc. – and then
wondering how best to deal with them. At the end, I emerged with a
booklet listing bridges (with photographs) and tunnels, with large
scale maps showing the best route from the landing point, currents,
likely disposition of sentries and so on, together with
recommendations as to the best time for the raid, the amount of
explosives needed to bring down each bridge (and where they should
be applied) and many other similar things. This particular booklet
was approved and was flown out to Malta where it prompted, I
believe, more than one successful raid.

'Towards the end of the summer I had another shift of job – a
particularly hush-hush intelligence job. The documents I dealt with
would tell us, among other things, how much the Germans knew
about us and the movement of our agents abroad. My job was to

follow closely the movements of our agents and our own operations, and to pick up any evidence that the Germans had got wind of them from the marvellous intelligence papers which were fed to me. [These were the famous Ultra intercepts.] I then rushed the evidence to the country section concerned and a message would be sent to the agent that the Germans were after him and he would be given appropriate instructions. It seems almost incredible, but it's perfectly true.

'My last move inside SOE was to be Dalton's Private Secretary on the SOE side. One of the first things I had to do was to accompany him round the "country stations" – various requisitioned country houses and estates where SOE trained its agents, experimented on new devices, produced and packed arms and stores and so on. There were no less than 40 or 50 of these stations, covering hundreds of agents and staff.'

Like both Christopher and David, Helen was unable to write freely of her work in the FANYs because she also had been posted to No. 64 Baker Street, and was a driver in SOE. So closely was everyone observing the security regulations that when she went into the office canteen in Baker Street and saw Christopher and David sitting there she was as astonished as they were.

Most of the information about her work was made known to the family after the war. Initially her duties were simply to be on call and to carry out whatever driving jobs arose, but occasionally, when the moon was right, she would take a carload of officers and an agent down to one of the holding stations and then on to Tempsford aerodrome in Bedfordshire

'where we would all drink quantities of hot coffee laced with rum while the agents were dressed up in their flying kit and parachutes. Sometime in the middle of the night or early morning they would take off in Halifax bombers or sometimes in a tiny Lysander, and all those of us left on the ground would wave frantically, then climb into our cars and drive rather fast and rather silently back to London.

'I got the opportunity of meeting and driving a lot of very interesting people. My passengers included people like Hugh Dalton [Minister of Economic Warfare], Lord Mountbatten [Chief of Combined Operations], General Sikorski, General de Gaulle and many others.'

Helen might be driving Lord Mountbatten but Marlborough could more than match that; as George wrote:

'On Thursday, Sept. 11th, (I think) the CO and a major came to see me and said that the Queen was coming on the 17th to inspect them, as she was their Colonel-in-Chief; could they use part of our playing fields for the inspection? I said they could and told them the best place and its obvious convenience: they were duly grateful and then asked whether the Queen could come to our house before the parade for a wash and brush-up and sherry. I thought immediately, "No housemaid, no nursemaid, two infants, one anti-monarchist wife, garden full of weeds!" So I asked when she'd come, for how long, with how many people and what would be required: the CO replied about noon, for no longer than 20 minutes, with one lady-in-waiting and there would be a General (Hon. Colonel), an orderly officer and a senior wife, Mrs B.; a bottle of the Queen's favourite sherry would be sent down to us and if we'd provide a biscuit and slice of cake, a lavatory and facilities for washing etc., we would earn endless gratitude from the regiment. So I consulted Doff who said "Lord! I suppose we must – won't the staff be thrilled? – I haven't got a hat – Must I curtsey? – we haven't got a fitted basin except in your dressing room – thank God she isn't coming to lunch – I must tell the Potters" – etc. and so on and so forth. Whereupon it was decided that the CO and the General and the orderly officer and Mrs B. should come in for sherry on the evening of the 16th to make final arrangements and confer about procedure. The staff simply seethed with excitement: Doff wired for Helen's hat and we borrowed some silver-backed brushes and Turkish cigarettes; Doff borrowed a fur, and pearl necklace and some long gloves; Mrs Potter made 2 cakes with real eggs and butter; our one tin of cocktail biscuits was produced from the store cupboard; College workmen began tidying up paths and grass in front of the house; our gardener and I assaulted all grass, paths and flower beds within easy view of the drawing-room; furious cleaning, dusting, sweeping and polishing began in the downstairs reception area and in our bedroom and spare room and the lavatory; immense tidying up and putting away of oddments went on; silver objects were burnished and placed in suitable positions; several thousand flowers were cut and arranged in almost overpowering masses in the halls, drawing-room, bedrooms but not in the lavatory which was cleared for action; and really by 6.30 p.m. on the 16th the house looked like a party of some importance. Then the conference began; the General was a cheerful little Irishman (retired in 1934) and Mrs B. was young and pleasant and as agitated as we were. HM was driving over from Windsor with one lady-in-waiting, ("She's charming: we've often had her before – the Queen calls her Katie") and would be escorted by 2 dispatch riders and a staff car; she'd arrive at the house at 12.05 and be met at the door by the General and Mrs B., who would bring her into the hall, introduce us and leave us to carry on: we'd give her a drink etc. and she could go upstairs afterwards when the orderly officer coughed or indicated somehow that it was time: then we'd see her out and off, leap with Susan into our car (ready in the Yard) and dash in pursuit up to the cricket field. Police and sentries would be told to let us through: the inspection would be private but I could give passes to Marlborough masters and their wives. After the inspection HM would go to the Ailesbury Arms for lunch with the officers and then home to Windsor and the little princesses! After verification of points about dress, curtseys, bowings, modes of address, sitting down or standing up, walking backwards, posting of sentries round the house and so on, the party broke up in very good humour.

'Sept. 17th dawned clear and bright, while wind-up increased with consciousness in Mr and Mrs F. M. Heywood: by 11.15 a.m. the house was ready and picketed with armed soldiers and police, while a crowd began to thicken in the road outside. The Royal sherry gleamed in a decanter, the Royal cakes stood to attention beside the quivering cocktail biscuits, silver winked wherever it could between the mounds of flowers: upstairs all was prepared for the washing of Royal hands, the arrangement of Royal hair, the powdering of the Royal nose, the brushing of the Royal coat and anything else that the Royal nature might find necessary. Ditto ditto for Katie and flowers as before in both cases. The staff were disposed at points of vantage, save for Potter, glorious in tails, and Mary, dribbling with excitement, – who mounted guard in the drawing room: Susan suitably apparelled was placed in a tactical position suitable for a quick getaway at the end and a good view at the beginning: Michael blew bubbles indifferently in the garden. Enter down the grand staircase Doff, looking like a society wedding and Ascot with a dash of incipient bilious attack: enter also F.M.H., in a stiff collar and gents' natty s.b. lounge suiting, nervously counterattacking his forelock. A large camouflaged car swishes up to the door and decants the General, all shiny boots on bandy legs and ribbons across bosom; Mrs B. (see Doff above), and an exquisite young Etonian 2/Lieutenant in attendance. Some shrill chatter and high pitched laughter betrays the tension of the moment; Doff and Mrs B.

announce their intention of vomiting; the General bangs his boots
with his cane; the Etonian subaltern stands at ease or to attention or
sags or hops in and out to talk to the sentries. At 12.04 the sentries
suddenly become intense, the General puts his cap on and Mrs B.
adjusts her smile before walking out as if to the rack and thumbscrew:
frenzied activity on the part of the Etonian: Doff says "My God, I am
going to be sick": F.M.H. abandons his hair and concentrates on his
tie. Two dispatch riders roar up to the gate and halt on either side:
the crowd cranes its collective head: a staff car crunches in and a vast
Daimler sweeps after it: a police car pauses outside. The Daimler
calculates nicely and stops opposite the door: a man holding a bowler
hat pops out and opens the car door while the chauffeur raises his cap
as if a funeral was passing. Over a pile of rugs, bags and spare shoes,
Royal Lizzie, in powder blue, clambers down followed by Katie: the
General and Mrs B. do their stuff while Doff and I lick our dry lips.
Then Doff is dropping a curtsey and taking the outstretched hand:
then I (saying to myself "Bend from the Adam's apple, not the
waist") have clutched the Royal glove. "What a charming old house!
Your flowers are lovely! It's so kind of you to let me come in like this"
and we're in the drawing-room. More murmurs about flowers and
nice, light rooms and the view from the window draws her to a
powerful defensive position with her bottom wedged between a
radiator and the radiogram, her flanks protected by the window and a
little table and flowers forming adequate camouflage all round except
in front where Doff and I close in with Potter (and sherry) and Mary
(and cake and biscuits). Sherry is accepted ("How very nice and
refreshing!" uttered with superbly assumed surprise) and a biscuit,
the cakes are untouched and I think of all the teas for the next week!
We talk about gardens, school, evacuation with great gusto until an
officer begins to hover and the General indicates zero hour. "Is it
time?" she says. Doff then asks, as woman to woman, about
ascending the stairs, but the Royal needs are not pressing and
anyhow she has gloves on and her hair is disciplined: so out to the
Hall and more chat and gracious gratitude and further handshakes
accompanied by a quite abandoned curtsey and a 90° bend from us
respectively. After a bit of sorting the right people get into the right
cars and with a smile and a wave the contents of the Daimler are
removed. Doff then sprints for Susan and I for the car and we career
up a side road and get onto the ground just behind the procession.
The inspection and march past look very well and by 1.15 we are
back at lunch, feeling very relieved: the house and garden are very
spick and span, we have lots of flowers and 2 excellent cakes. Our

prestige in the town has increased by about 4 packets of cigarettes a
week!

'So that's that. Just now and then we don't mind having Royalty in,
but really we're plain people, you know, and quite content without
fuss!'

Very welcome visitors to Marlborough were Dad and Beryl
who reported that 'A great sense of relief pervaded the school
(and town) as the news had just been made public that the Air
Ministry's greedy hands had been persuaded to grab Malvern
instead of Marlborough and that an imminent upheaval had
been averted by a hair's breadth'.

Another welcome visitor was Stephen who

'was passing through Marlborough and was lucky enough to find
them in. First time I've seen them in heaven knows how long.

'I have acquired a title in this firm now, being known as Financial
Manager (pause for hearty laughter). The financial situation of the
Company is practically out of control, of course, so I devote my time
to hoping for the best and endeavouring to avoid minor disasters. If a
major disaster occurs, as the Managing Director likes to tell me, the
firm will be in Carey Street and I in the Old Bailey. In the meantime
if the wages are in the kitty on Friday morning I feel that I have done
my stuff.

'I must say how the *Sunday Pictorial* occasionally helps the aircraft
industry. One of our people was called to Southampton to await a
ship – he was in the Merchant Navy – and was told that it might be 10
weeks. We told him to say that he had been instructed by his
employers to notify them weekly of the time wasted on the quayside
so that they could tell the *Pictorial* – and a white and shaking official
bundled him back on the next bus.'

By 1942 the war had become 'static' for Pat who was still
guarding the beaches of Norfolk against an increasingly improbable invasion. Most of his time was taken up with training
exercises and going on courses.

Among the various courses on which he went – Junior
Leadership, Vehicle Maintenance, Anti-Tank-Gun, Pay – by
far the most stimulating and challenging was the 'Battle School'.
He wrote:

'After a three-quarter mile run across fields, we spent a peaceful hour "locating" fire. We then re-collected and walked down a valley. I thought it odd at the time, and was therefore not unduly surprised when four Brens opened up on us. The idea was to give us a "Battle Inoculation", you go flat on your face and crawl along while tracer bullets are fired all around you. Bullets hit the ground 18 inches in front of your head, 6 inches behind your heel, and fly 4 inches above your back, and only the last figure is a slight exaggeration. You don't believe me? Well, one officer was hit in the thigh by a ricochet, and one Sergeant got a tracer bullet through his pack which he was wearing on his back.

'This afternoon we went out on the obstacle course, which is a series of manmade inhumanities. You start off on the beach, cross a triple-dannert wire fence, climb over heavily wired scaffolding, run up high sand dunes, jump into the local sewer – literally – walk 80 yards along this, up to your thighs, and then go under a home-made culvert, the space between the sewerage and the ceiling of the culvert is 18 inches, wade through a pond thigh-high, drop 18 foot into a pool at the bottom of a shell-hole; three more shell-holes and filthy mud, then a 14 foot wall with a rope but no footfold, over the wall and a 14 foot drop into a lake, crawl under wire 18 inches off the ground, through a deep pit full of the most sick-making smoke, up a steep hill, and fire five rounds from your rifle. Throughout the instructors throw bombs, crackers, gelignite, etc. at you. We lost one officer who did something to his stomach and is in hospital. We have been here three days and have lost three officers.'

In a second letter he wrote:

'Last week was not a very dangerous week – no blood, merely toil and sweat. We had quite an amusing time running through a wood and suddenly being confronted by a disappearing target – the idea was that you fired at it from the hip; I did this for the first two, hitting one and missing one, but then I decided that after several years of rabbiting in Mill Hill I ought to be quick enough, so I used a ram-rod left arm and shot from the shoulder. The Instructors didn't like it but I hit 9 out of 10 and came equal 1st so they really couldn't complain.

'On Friday we had an interesting experience. We were put into slit trenches and were run over by Churchill tanks. You feel as if you are going to be buried alive, but in fact you are extremely safe and it certainly gives you confidence.'

Christopher thought Battle Schools were an excellent idea –

'I gather Pat has written an enormous letter this week on his Battle
School. This means he must have survived, which is a good thing.
One of our boys has just come back from a course where seven out of
fifteen trainees finished in hospital, with broken ankles, bullet
wounds and bits of bakelite bombs in them. This new idea of war –
that each side should kill off its own soldiers – is a most attractive
one. You get the same results in the end, without the disastrous
international ill-feeling which accompanied the old, cruder forms of
conflict.'

Life at Felthorpe was largely unchanged – hospital, garden,
Home Guard, Red Cross, Carrow works.

'The CHSS [Convalescent Hospital Supplies Stores], bless its
blithering ways, has chosen the moment the frost went when every
hand is urgently needed in the garden, to produce 2000 odd little
face towels to be cut in half, hemmed, marked, counted (that was
much the worst bit) and sent off as men's face cloths. They've
followed this with wool for 288 pairs of gloves: half my workers don't
knit, and a lot of the knitters who can knit gloves, say they are
"fiddly" things. The gloves of course are required for Russia before
Easter, they will presumably be sent off in April, arrive in – June? and
be put into store until October, but they must be finished before
Easter.'

On many occasions bombs were dropped on Norwich and in
June the city suffered very heavily as a result of a 'reprisal' raid.

'So to bed before 11 to wake about 1.30 and find the sky full of
flares again. Rolled out of bed and into our siren suits and trotted
round the house. It did not seem to be a bad raid from here, then, two
bombs dropped just before I got out and shook the house a bit and I
fancy the raider who'd dropped them came hurtling for home just
over my head as I came out of the front door, with searchlights
chasing about much too high; if the HG could have a gun here – but
there you are.
'Horrid pink glows lit up the sky over Norwich and it looked like at
least two really bad fires, but no more big bombs dropped, just flares

some of which were probably our own, so we had a cup of tea with the nurses and lay down to wait for Carrow to report. I was nearly asleep again when the bell went, and the man said lots of departments were alight, so up we got again. The usual brief argument about the woman's place being the home, but having sat here for three raids and been sent absolutely nothing to help with, I was determined I'd lend a hand somewhere with this one and in we came together.

'I don't know what time we got to Carrow, getting on for three I should think, left the car by the Abbey and ran down to the entrance by the fire station. Heavens, it was a sight, sheets of flame seemed to be searing up everywhere.

'I joined a rather spasmodic trickle of salvage work that was going on, collecting anything loose from the Fire Station by the gate that was not yet ablaze, and some tea chests that were being dragged out in handcarts. Dad had vanished into the inferno and one hoped fervently he was not charred to a cinder, but there didn't seem to be anything to be done about it.

'Then the head of the Canteen Dept appeared and we got into the kitchen and found water and gas functioning, but not electricity. We took down some blackout which made it light enough to see what we were doing, and got to work boiling water for tea and cutting bread and butter and cheese for sandwiches.

'On looking back I must have spent from 4 a.m. till nearly nine boiling kettles, making tea and cutting sandwiches, men appeared at the counter and we sent jugs and trays down the yard, but we never stopped.

'Well, breakfast was most welcome, and then I got a message that from the Depot room someone had salvaged a lot of stuff, so we borrowed a room down at the end of the Close and I prevailed on passers by to carry the furniture and stack it there. Then a Fire Service man said cheerfully "There's a lot of your stuff in a cupboard on the 2nd floor", so I organized a chain across a young river that was pouring along the ground floor from the hose pipes playing on the rest of the house, and up some rather rickety stairs to a large cupboard where we'd stored large quantities of cotton wool for swabs and we started passing it out. When we were in full swing more firemen arrived and said "Hi! What are you doing up there, that wall's dangerous!" However, we thought as we were there we'd finish – so we did.

'And so, eventually, to a sad peregrination of what was left of the works, paddling thro' swamps of mustard seed, past burst bags of rice, and all the sad remains of burnt out buildings.'

For the housewife and the family there were many articles – rationed or unrationed – which lay on the margin between the ordinary market and the 'black' market and which tested one's consciences. Aunt Ellie explained.

'I am never tempted to scrounge extra bits of butter, or to buy stockings without giving up clothing coupons, but oh dear! I feel I should fall for a black market in petrol if I knew where there was one. It is, I feel, rather particularly hard to be cut off completely from one's urban centre headquarters of all local activities, short of walking four miles. But the Divisional Headquarters are adamant.'

Food was always difficult, particularly in the quantity needed for the patients in the hospital. From time to time Beryl wrote about it:

'Fish has taken this week to be unobtainable (I suppose it's the gales) and the supplies of cake to be tiresomely short.
'I got to the sausage shop and found it shut but thank heavens, I got in the back alright.'

Food was not the only problem; Doff's main worry was the children's clothes.

'They neither of them have a single thing to wear this summer. Susan having outgrown everything and Mike never having had any. Let's pray for a hot summer so they can run about in vests! So if any Budget readers have any old clothes that would cut up into coats, trousers, frocks, blouses, knickers or any other article of clothing, it would be most welcome.'

This situation was relieved by Dad's gift of twenty of his clothing coupons which brought Susan two frocks, but there were many other unexpected shortages. Helen was triumphant when she found a sponge for Dad's Christmas present, and Christopher was prevailed upon by Doff to 'try to negotiate a revision with the President of the Board of Trade of the teat, rubber, utility, BoT allocation, Swindon Area, – who would be an Uncle!' Occasionally an opportunity arose for mutually welcome exchanges; when fourteen Canadian despatch riders were temporarily billeted in the Master's Lodge at Marlborough they carried out with Doff a lively exchange of tins of army meat for fresh eggs and vegetables. Clare found eggs and vegetables were an acceptable exchange in Reading University for twelve table-tennis balls for the hospital, and Stephen reported, 'I have just sold an old suit for twelve golf balls.'

Meantime Christopher had begun to feel that his job at SOE, however interesting, was unduly sedentary, and he accepted an invitation to transfer to 'Phantom' (GHQ Liaison Regiment), a 'private army' equipped with armoured cars with the role of reporting direct from the battle area to the army commander, by-passing slower official channels. However, while waiting for his posting he decided he would try to get adopted as a Labour candidate at a Parliamentary by-election 'Soldiering would still come first of course and I should go abroad with my unit when it moved'.

Nothing came of this idea but he had the opportunity to discuss it with Attlee (Deputy Prime Minister and Leader of the Labour Party) and Dalton, and he wrote of the differences between the two men.

'Attlee was kindly and helpful and evidently wished me well. But, my word, he is also very dull. In conversation he is the exact opposite of Dalton. Get Dalton started and he roars away delightedly for hours. Attlee doesn't enjoy talking, is often at a loss for something to say, and manages to make any subject sound boring. The two men are strongly contrasted in other ways. Dalton is nothing if not full-blooded; Attlee is really the epitome of desiccation. Dalton has obviously fought his way to the top; Attlee gives the impression of having been stranded there, Noah-like, by a receding tide. On the other hand he's a nice man with hardly an enemy in the world.'

After joining Phantom, Christopher was assigned to its Assault Detachment which specialized in amphibious operations. He wrote that the Detachment

'includes all the regiment's "toughs" (i.e. anyone who has taken any exercise since leaving school), and is supposed to go on Commando

raids. It hasn't been on one yet and no one would be more surprised
and horrified than me if it ever did go on one. But we are issued with
sinister-looking knives with black blades and cultivate a silent, dark,
tough look, said to attract fair ladies at parties. If we ever do go on a
raid (the very thought makes me turn pale) we shall deal with
intelligence and communications rather than with the enemy himself,
so if a Commando job can be called "cushy", this is certainly it.
There is no prospect of action for me personally for at least a couple
of months.

'Apparently I'm allowed to tell you where we are. It's rather a joke
– we're at that notorious hide-out of wealthy anti-Bolsheviks, the
seed-bed of pro-Nazi conservative intrigue, that forcing-house of
dark plots against the people, etc. (see Cassandra, *New Statesman*,
News Chronicle, etc. passim) – famous Cliveden.

'Cliveden belongs to the Astor family, and Jakie Astor is our
Squadron Commander; so the rest follows, our regiment being what
it is.

'Architecturally Cliveden is splendid, politically not so good. Is the
"Cliveden Set" just a joke? I'm not sure. I think it was a serious
business in Munich days, when Geoffrey Dawson belonged to it and
The Times was pro-appeasement. But it is hard to take Lady Astor
seriously these days. If she was as influential as she is vigorous, she
would simply have to be locked up. But I can't believe that the stream
of public figures who visit Cliveden and hear her tirades against
Churchill and Russia depart with any intention of doing anything
about it.

'We're billeted in the servants' quarters – luxurious by military
standards – and occasionally we go up to the house for a talk and a
meal. In this way I found myself dining the other night with George
Bernard Shaw and wife, and General Cunningham.

'Shaw is charming. I expected him to be conceited and very much
the lion of the party. But he is the soul of gentleness and good
manners, and I completely fell for him. I also took a good view of
General Cunningham. He was in "civvies" and very much on the
defensive, poor man, but he described his campaigns
good-humouredly and with due sense of proportion and you couldn't
help admiring him as a person.

'But life at Cliveden is not all a matter of dining with Bernard
Shaw. The wretched war will come seeping in through the cracks.
For instance, on Wednesday afternoon we carried 40 lb packs for a
sharp three-mile walk, with an excruciating assault cliff in the middle.
I carried an entire transmitting set on my back, the bottom edge of

which exactly coincided with my kidneys. At 0100 hrs tomorrow we're going to be chucked into the Thames and made to race up a cliff and establish a w/t station at the top. I think I shall just quietly sink, and leave it at that.

'My fellow soldiers are exceptionally keen and good at their jobs, and unlike the rest of the regiment, there is a distinct and unpleasant aroma of war about this squadron – much more than I bargained for. But I find I'm becoming quite keen myself so it may not be quite so distressing in time.'

Soon afterwards Christopher was faced with the threatened exercise and

'jumped into the Thames in full battle-dress, equipment, and with two accumulators weighing 20 lb each on my back. I swam for fifty yards. But it rather spoils the story to have to add that the accumulators kept me up, being made that way.'

This demonstration/exercise was carried out in front of General Sir Bernard Paget, as Commander-in-Chief, Home Forces, who failed to recognize Christopher at the inspection. This led later to

'the event of the week – lunch with Bernard yesterday. He invited me as handsome compensation for not recognizing me on that inspection, and I took Pat along. The talk was mostly military, with bits of family thrown in. The General's morale was high and he had plenty of cheerful news about the war.'

Pat wrote about that lunch:

'Bernard was most interesting and knew far too much! All my carefully-stored tales of "no officers", "Drafts" etc. fell very flat because he was very well aware of our difficulties – which was excellent for morale. I thought he looked tired, as he has a right to be, but he was wholly delightful and amusing company.'

There had been no highlights for Pat for many months; he had been promoted and was a Captain and a Company Commander and this kept him very busy, particularly as the battalion

was short of officers. It was however difficult for him to settle
down to the inactivity and to be satisfied with 'schemes' and
'administration', and playing rugger for the Division.

In September he

'felt it was time to get a move on; I feel about 42 years of age but I'm
only 25 and it is over two years since I was in the remotest danger, so
I thought I would look around for a good second-front post.'

This was not possible at the time but by the middle of
November he had once again

'made another effort to change my job. The question was "what was
it to be?" Glider pilot and Paratroops? Commandos? – another
Regiment? Christopher's lot? Well, that at least was a complete
change. So Friday morning appeared and saw me in the office of
Phantom for an interview with the Colonel. He was at the War Office
so I saw the Adjutant with whom I conversed at some length. I rang
up again at 13.45 to be told that the Colonel was out again but in view
of my "qualifications", the "adjutant's opinion of me", and "on the
strength of my brother" (this I consider a military insult!) the Colonel
was prepared to accept me. This is the first hedge cleared, now there
is only my own Colonel – I've tried so often that I expect there'll be a
snag somewhere.'

He actually got as far in this application as being ordered to
report 'on Wednesday or Thursday' but this time the decision to
withdraw was his own. This was achieved quite amicably and
with understanding because

'We are on the move, all by ourselves to a place where we join an
entirely new lot. Get made up to a higher establishment, get
hundreds of men and officers, and eventually go into battle. That, at
any rate, is what we hope will happen. The Colonel immediately
asked me to stay, I immediately agreed, and now we sit and pray for
everything to work out right.'

Before moving off to a camp and on to Winchester barracks,
Pat was able to take three of the battalion officers over to Crown
Point for a day's rough shooting; it was, as Beryl said, 'a grand
day'.

In her letter to the Budget that week Beryl thought

'we may have made history in our own small way. There are five
Roman Catholics among the patients, so I told Quartermaster to ring
up their chaplain and invite him to come over whenever he liked and
to hold any services he wished. He came on Saturday and said he
would return at 8.00 a.m. on Sunday, so we got the end ward
(Helen's old room) ready with the three beds along the wall and a
table all correct along the east wall. Martha produced two little
bronze candlesticks and luckily there were several chrysanthemum
plants left in the greenhouse, so a big bowl each side helped to
mitigate the bareness of the ward. The chaplain is reported to have
said to one of the patients that it was the first time Mass had been
celebrated in the parish of Felthorpe for 400 years, but I don't know
whether any record is kept in Norwich or if he was just guessing.'

Stephen shared with Dad the problems that were created by
air raid damage because

'A fairly considerable section of our works caught a packet in an air
raid not so long ago, so life has been a bit hectic on the technical side.
I was very sorry to read of the Colman enemy action. I suppose by the
end of the war industry will be in tents and deneholes and so forth,
everywhere except in industrial centres. What will be the effect, I
wonder, on our production efficiency in comparison with America,
where they can concentrate to the limit on modern methods, with
aircraft factories three miles long by one mile wide and so on? If we
live up to our cooperation ideals, I suppose it won't matter much; but
if we don't we shall get rather a jolt.'

Helen was still in London but was not finding the work very
satisfying because there was not a sufficient demand for her
driving. It was not surprising when she wrote:

'This is just to let you know I'm changing my job. I'm rather fed up
with this London work; there's not enough to do and I'm getting in a
fearful rut. I and a friend have been accepted as orderly-drivers in the
country and I'm rather pleased that at last I've got down to driving.
This hanging about is getting on our nerves and to run around
dressed in khaki looking as if we were saving the British Empire by
our hard work just isn't good enough.'

In November she was transferred to Pollards Park, in Chalfont St Giles.

While Christopher, Pat and Helen were all on the move, David was firmly tied to the Shetlands, exceedingly busy but unable to tell anyone what he was doing. All that he could say was:

'After all this time there is nothing in my head which can be put on paper. Heaven knows that is not to say that nothing happens. But on the contrary, I live in a whirl of great but unmentionable events, and during the last six weeks in particular I have been occupied with my biggest job of all. Perhaps you will hear of it one day, in fact you certainly will, but I don't know when the day will be.'

In fact, David was then engaged in fitting out a Norwegian fishing boat which, despite having a double bulkhead to conceal six English divers, had to be able to penetrate the German defences at Trondheim harbour without raising suspicion. It was towing, submerged, two 'chariots' (two-men torpedoes) with which to attack the German battleship, the *Tirpitz*. The boat successfully passed through every control and got right into the German anchorage, but then it was hit by a head-on storm and the chariots broke loose. There was no alternative but to sink the fishing boat and to take to the land; of the ten men, crew and divers, nine managed to get to Sweden.

In February Pat, Helen and Christopher all managed to get home for a few days' leave, but unfortunately not together. This was particularly sad because Christopher was soon to go overseas with the Assault Detachment of Phantom.

Before finally embarking, Christopher had lunch with

'Teddy (*Picture Post*) Hulton who has a mania for "getting key people together and starting a new nation-wide political movement" – a mania shared, it seems to me, by every male adult in the City of London. The only trouble about these people is they all insist on the other man joining their movement, and never dream of joining anyone else's themselves. One day, I suspect, one of them will catch on and do really well; but not yet, and anyway not until one of them falls under the control of a really first-class man, and becomes a temptation to the Independents in Parliament and the more restive Labour MPs. I see no serious signs of this at present.'

On 14 March 1943 Christopher was aboard 'a fine ship', sailing from Scotland 'where those exquisitely tedious songs and dances come from'. He had got forty books with him, had been promoted and was now a Captain, been lucky enough to get a cabin to himself, and after a fortnight was able to write that so far the trip had been a complete pleasure cruise.

'The past fortnight has changed my views about life in the Navy. Hearing so much about its "Eternal Vigilance" I'd imagined gaunt exhausted men peering into the darkness through storm and tempest. But if this ship is any criterion, the average naval officer does himself very well. His food and drink are well above average civilian or Army standards, and his hours of work are shorter. But I like the sailors very much – they're friendly, polite, and efficient and attractively proud.

'They have most amusing stories to tell. A Lieutenant who was on one of the Murmansk convoys has described to me how he watched a Russian tanker go up in flames after a torpedo hit. They gave her up as lost, and so did some of the Russian crew who jumped overboard. The skipper of the tanker was a woman; she got the crew back on board with the aid of a machine gun, got the fire under control and got the ship into port. Pretty good going for a female. In the whole of Britain there's only one woman who could have done the same, and that, of course, is Beryl. And she would probably have shot the crew and put out the fire by herself.'

On 6 May the family received a telegram from him – 'ARRIVED SAFELY STOP MUCH HEAT MANY FLIES'. He had landed in North Africa, just before the fall of Tunis and Bizerta, in order to take part in the invasion of Sicily.

He reported that there was 'a lot of work about these days and I'm travelling all over the place on odd jobs', but he celebrated his twenty-eighth birthday

'stranded in the middle of nowhere with 9 men and a broken down 3-tonner. The lorry is a captured German one, and when the carburettor works the radiator leaks, and when you've mended that she blows a gasket. She's broken down four times in two days on what's meant to be a 400 mile trip.

'[Later] We camped on a delightful solitary hill-top, miles from anywhere, and went to bed after watching a splendid sunset.

'When we woke up the following items of kit were missing – 5 pairs boots, 3 pairs trousers, 3 pairs shorts, 4 shirts, 2 toothbrushes, 3 razors, 2 overcoats, 2 gascapes and a groundsheet. Our Arab Allies had had a night out. We'd taken the normal precautions – slept well together with the trucks back to back – but their technique was too good for us.

'When the dreadful truth slowly dawned on my men, a punitive expedition spontaneously organized itself (I was still in bed) and sallied forth with pistols and tommy-guns against the Arab race in general. Unfortunately – or fortunately perhaps – the only target available was an old, old, wrinkled Arab tending his flock on a distant hillside. The poor old thing must have had the shock of his life, fiercely accosted by an armed band of angry, unshaven, unintelligible men at five o'clock in the morning. I hurried up in time to reassure him and dismiss the punitive expedition for breakfast.

'I had a busy time yesterday getting replacements out of the local Ordnance. Luckily none of my own kit was touched. They must have looked it over and contemptuously rejected it.'

Three days later they learnt that their embarkation date for Sicily was 6 July. The role of Christopher's Phantom patrol was to go in with the first wave and to report straight back to Montgomery's HQ, bypassing the slower Army Signals, with the first news of the landing. For the next month he was only able to send one letter, but he kept a diary which was circulated as soon as considerations of security allowed; the following are excerpts from it.

5 July
    In to Tac. Div. early. Tie up a few final points. Feel completely set now. Know everything except H. hr and enemy order of battle. Have every paper except the map. Feel tremendously confident that the plan will work – especially if we only meet Itis. Wish I had a more important and exciting part to play.

6 July
    Embark on Landing Ship Tanks. Embarkation arrangements

efficient. My little patrol is complete and on good form and all our kit
is tested and retested. I clutch my precious mapcase, inside which is a
précis of the entire Corps plan with all the innumerable codes.

The LST is absolutely crowded, 300 men and 30 vehicles. We've
got some Lt A.A. as passengers – very welcome – they've set up their
Bofors on the top deck, that'll surprise the enemy. A shower and a
change of clothes and I feel fine.

8 July

Still off Sfax but ready at any time now. At five, Staff Officer tells
the officers D. day (Saturday) and H. hour (0245) and the point of
attack. I tell my patrol everything I know, they seem very pleased and
cheerful. The bad news is a message from yesterday's Army
Commander's conference – air superiority not yet achieved over
Sicily. We are told to expect bombs on and round the beaches. It will
be no fun lying off Amber beach during D. day.

At six o'clock we sail. The whole convoy consists of LSTs – about
25 of them. Escort is a light cruiser ahead and destroyers and small
protecting craft round about. A good sight. Here we are – the Second
Front at last. I wonder if we shall be spotted tonight?

10 July

Wake at 0100 after rotten night. Blowing a gale and extremely
rough. Much distressed over prospects of operations. How can a
LCA [Landing Craft Assault], launched from LST, possibly be
launched, let alone land in a sea like this. My LST is now hours late.

Depression deepens when H. hour comes. No news for two hours.
Force broadcast at five states incredible fact that HQ ship has
received no news yet. A blow to our hopes. Everyone fears worst.

Just after 5 everyone electrified by message from SNOL [Senior
Naval Officer, Landing] ship 'Red and Amber beaches captured'. We
all pretend not to believe it – impossible that an objective – Amber
beach – for which a two-brigade 24-hour attack was planned should
fall to an initial assault of a handful of men in a gale. But suddenly a
stream of incredibly good news starts coming in, and the whole
atmosphere of the ship changes. It is almost too good to be true.

Our three patrols are all coming through now and Largs (HQ) is
getting their stuff well. Unfortunately they are very faint for us.

At 11.30 Sicily sighted, hours behind time. As we draw near,
splendid and peaceful sight greets us. Scores of ships of all shapes
and sizes. Shining white beach (Amber) and blue sea now calm. No
sign of planes of any nationality despite frequent alerts. No wreck, no
fires even. It might be just an exercise. I think I have been cheated of

a battle once again. Unless we can get MTs our Phantom party will never keep up with the advance. Keep the ship fairly well informed about the battle but the Phantom link is not working as well as on the exercises.

About 1500 we attempt to land and fail. Back off shore again and wait.

Message from Squadron HQ states 5 Div. are only a couple of miles from Syracuse! The Itis are evidently not trying. Large numbers of Spitfires over us now. I hope we get ashore before dark.

Very little news coming in from patrols. The Spitfires are going home. A mine suddenly goes off in the water very close to the ship. Everyone startled and lie flat on their faces for a bit. No harm done, but very mysterious.

Now dark. Sure enough the first enemy planes are over the beach to the right of us. Streams of red tracers from our Bofors guns make a pretty firework display. Four bombs fall. Now the planes are attacking to the left of us. But we are going in now to unload at a pontoon, so we should soon be ashore. Our way in is lighted up for us by big flares dropped from enemy planes. We come in just right for the pontoon and our doors open and our ramp goes down and our vehicles stream out. We feel our way in the dark over the beaches towards the vineyards and fields selected for the site of Div. HQ. Our party walks – and gets there first. Morale not very high as it is midnight. Get through to Largs but not to patrols. The battle has really gone splendidly with the unfortunate result that our patrols are unable on their flat feet, to keep pace with their formation HQs on vehicles. Consequently their news is out of date and is scanty as they spend their whole time moving.

11 July

Battle has slowed down now. Enemy shows no sign of serious resistance. Pozallo falls. Little news from patrols. Feel am little use at Div. HQ so ask for roving commission of whole battlefield in my jeep. An armoured column of ours will strike far inland tomorrow. This is obviously the Force for me to accompany. Ask Squadron HQ for OK.

12 July

Paul's birthday.

HQ says B.G.S. does not want us to accompany the Armoured Force; we are to stay put ready to move when wanted. A little later HQ says we are to get a ship to Malta. So it's all over for us – just when it began to look amusing.

LSTs are leaving for Malta at 1.30. After terrific rush we get most of party on. I catch a late LST by myself. Am only passenger. Extremely well treated. After dinner we reach Malta just as *Illustrious* and 2 Battleships leave for Palermo. Anchor off shore. Phantom has done only fairly well. Circumstances against us.

14 July

Scribbled message from Alastair states we are ordered back to Sicily tonight! Someone has blundered somewhere.

15 July

Wake as we enter Syracuse harbour. Attractive looking town, fairly badly blitzed. A funnel marked with a Red Cross sticks out above the water – an Italian Hospital ship sunk. Many LSIs, LCTs and LSTs in harbour. On a quayside Pioneer Corps are cutting away parts of jetty to facilitate LSTs disgorging of vehicles, Iti prisoners roll barrels of water from LCTs – pouncing on old tins of bully beef and odd biscuits they find hidden away. Iti civilians swarm in the dock area cadging cigarettes or trying to sell lemons and tomatoes.

17 July

Over come the planes at 0415 hrs. There is a pompom exactly above my cabin and sleep is out of the question. Mercifully the raid is short and no bombs drop close. Spend morning writing report on the operation. Our old Sherborne commando friends want us to provide a patrol to raid Catania with them tonight. I volunteer and Alastair readily agrees.

Feel positively keen about the operation although it bears all the signs of a hasty improvisation and is probably quite suicidal. Write a note to the Family 'in case'. Great anti-climax when we reach Corps and learn that the show is 'off'. Apparently our ground troops on the left have been doing better and a new landing is unnecessary. How often has this happened to me!

The question of looting is becoming acute. MPs searched our truck as we left Augusta. The attitude of the non-commissioned towards the Itis is one of supreme contempt and arrogance. On the other hand they do behave rather contemptibly; how many Englishmen if the Germans landed at Dover, would go round cadging cigarettes? Twenty years of Fascist pride-of-race propaganda has evidently made not the slightest impression on the Itis.

29 July

We are to return to Phantom HQ in N. Africa, at Bugeaud, near

Bone, pending decision of AFHQ. Board LCT 1700, and establish excellent relations with the skipper who gives me some filthy Sicilian wine which I pour overboard, and a massive rum.

Sleep on Alastair's camp bed on deck. Deliciously cool and no flies.

1 August

At 06.00 wake and find we are aground in the midst of sandbanks, two miles off shore and 15 miles S. of Sousse. Another LCT is aground near us. The others are delicately picking their way seaward. Decide to row off in our dinghy to one of the free LCTs and go on to Sousse in it to organize the rescuing of the men and our move from Sousse to Bone. A long strange row is followed by a warm welcome from the free LCT and a slap up breakfast. They are very caustic about the navigation of the grounded LCT's skipper.

In three hours, reach Sousse and get Naval Ops. to send a rescue ship. Then agitate for MT to Bone at Movement Control. Much pressure needed. Eventually agree to go in road convoy starting tomorrow. Fix up rations, blankets and cooking facilities for the journey.

4 August

Uneventful journey up to Bone, where we start the enormous 10 km climb up to Bugeaud. The 3-tonner groans upwards in first gear, taking nearly an hour. We arrive about 1730, welcomed by Julian. The camp is in a cork forest on the mountain top – extremely cool and pleasant.

5 August

Inspection in the afternoon – we look even scruffier than usual. Decide to send the men on leave for five days. Expect we shall stay in North Africa for a bit – perhaps an operation in a month or two.

The news that Christopher was going abroad had not been welcome to Pat, who wrote:

'I had hoped that somehow or other I would be the only Mayhew ever to get abroad again – not because I suffer from any undue bravery, but purely from a sense of selfish restlessness. You beat me to France by four months Chris – I hope it won't be so long this time.'

Pat was bored and he was becoming easily irritated. He wrote:

'Lost – one Mayhew in search of an interest; any interest you like, but just something to get me excited again. I feel horribly stale – one day is essentially similar to those preceding and following.'

His mood was not improved by having to listen to

'one of those horribly sincere Christians who are so Christian that they have lost all sense of humour and have become ridiculous. A sermon, duly calculated to destroy the last vestige of incipient Christianity in the fluttering breast of a soldier – conscripted to a Church Parade. Here it is in brief:
'A lady social worker called at an East End mission and was so impressed that she wanted to give all the working women something to brighten their lives, so she bought each one a flowering plant. The lovely white hyacinth made the woman's table look dirty, so she cleaned the table, and then the floor, dresser, grate, poker, knife, fork and spoon." – Lesson to be learned: "how like the white hyacinth is the love of God". This was followed by a story about the foul-minded soldier who decorated his billet with pictures of Hedy Lamarr, Dorothy Lamour, Veronice Lake etc. all in scanties. One day, however, our hero put up a picture of the Babe in a cradle with all the shepherds and for very shame the villain took down Dorothy Lamour. Lesson to be learned – etc.
'Unmitigated, blushmaking, ridiculous nonsense. The padre in question would be far better off if he joined the ranks and learned just a little about the men to whom he is trying to represent Christ. That there still exist people who see a grand revival of Christianity based upon the Lamb, or white robes, or old women and hyacinths, is the most depressing news. There will be no real Christian influence in this country until the churches are full of men as well as women, and to talk to the Army about "Jesus, meek and gentle" is a farce.'

Like the rest of the family he greatly enjoyed George's account of the invasion of Marlborough College by the Army.

'By the early evening Court was full of military vehicles; camp beds were all round the ambulatory of the Memorial Hall and the stage had become an officers' mess with field kitchens set outside; classrooms were littered with recumbent figures on or in sleeping bags; the pavilions on the playing fields had been occupied and various other buildings too. The Bursar, armed with a note-board, was plodding round to record any damage to College property which he could detect.

'The night passed quietly, but the morning brought strange moments. It so happened that the morning was of that day in the week on which we had a congregational hymn practice in the Memorial Hall instead of a Chapel service. I went to the Memorial Hall at 9.00. Behind the rows of blatantly expectant Marlburians, there were in the ambulatory still a few officers in their camp-beds, and one or two drowsily getting up, rubbing their eyes and registering various emotions when they focussed on some 700 boys between them and their breakfast; for on stage, sitting at trestle-tables, were earlier risers dealing silently and methodically with what orderlies brought in and set before them. I went onto the stage and told them that we were about to have prayers and practise hymns, but it was not to disturb or interrupt their breakfast. I was told later by some of those who could watch what went on behind me, that, as I said prayers, knives and forks were motionless and mastication ceased, but that during the ten minutes or so of fortissimo hymn-singing that followed, the breakfasters ate and drank with wonderful aplomb and detachment.

'We then went into school for the first morning period; most of the classrooms were still occupied by soldiers who were still asleep (but not for long), shaving, dressing, or brewing up on portable stoves. They had to put up with instruction on a variety of subjects as long as they stayed, but by the end of the period they were gone. By the middle of the morning Court was clear of jeeps, personnel carriers and other forms of transport, and all was over.'

By the early summer it had become clear that Pat's battalion was not going to be made up to strength and would not become a fighting unit. He therefore volunteered for overseas service, and in May Beryl wrote:

'The only important news is that Pat has sent me a line to say that I may tell you in this letter that he decided to make a change; his battalion remains where it is, but I expect we shall not have more than possibly one or two letters from him in the next few weeks.'

Pat left England almost immediately having

'loathed leaving the Bn even more than I had expected; but I feel that
I've sent so many people to the war that it's time that I went myself.

'For some inscrutable reason I found myself OC a Special Train;
this rather shook me and I foresaw myself running all round
England/Scotland/Wales in search of absconding soldiers. However,
they behaved extremely well and were no trouble at all, all arriving
with everything they started with. My job earned me a 1st Class
carriage to myself and an enormous sign on the door, so it was worth
it. I got to the first destination to find that I was supposed to be a
Major, not a Captain, (hence OC train). This was an excellent bit of
luck as I am now in a 4 cabin with a lavatory and bath attached. Not
many of the officers have arrived yet – two padres are going to my
eventual destination – wherever that may be – so my spiritual welfare
will be well guarded; I like one of them a lot, a fat, cheery Scot who
ought really to have been a friar.'

He landed in North Africa and spent a fortnight in an Infantry
Transit Depot where his only complaint was that he had had his

'first attack of the local dysentery – this really has to be known to be
believed. I've never met anything quite so exhausting, you are
absolutely powerless – it makes not the least difference whether you
eat or not (in fact you can't), you are absolutely at the mercy of your
stomach, which is quite merciless. At breakfast this morning I ate my
first meal for four days and am now practically cured.

'Will you include Chris's address in about three different letters so
that I am sure to get it – if he's in this continent then there might
come a time when I can find him.'

At the end of the fortnight

'We left the IRTD just for a place on the map, with no posting
orders. The journey was almost funny – a train which went very
slowly indeed and stopped at every tiny station. At these stations you
could buy lemons and hard-boiled eggs from the Arabs, or a drink
from a nearby pub, or wash and shave under a local tap. When it was
time to go, the engine whistled and started off – you finished your
drink or shave in comfort and then by a brisk walk you caught it up! I
spent most of the time sitting in a Jeep on an open truck in really
perfect conditions looking at superb scenery. One of my breakfasts
was unique – eggs, bacon, tomatoes and beans, all cooked on a

Tommy-cooker in a 1st Class compartment, with tea made over an open fire in a cattle-truck (shades of the Great Eastern Railway!).

'On arrival we found that no one knew where we were supposed to be going, so after a very quick "appreciation of the situation" I plunged and created mythical orders given me to join the Northamptons! Not a bad choice because they are very closely linked to the Norfolk and share the same Infantry Training Centre. I like the look of the battalion a lot.

'I jumped at the chance of becoming the Bn Intelligence Officer. You have a very small section of men under you, and have interesting jobs, from guiding the Bn in a night march, to handling prisoners of war. You have the most independent job in the Bn and I think it suits me.'

He left for Sicily on 22 July and there was no news of him until the end of August. It was impossible for him to send letters home but he kept and wrote up a diary of his time on the island. It began:

1 July

Tremendous ceremonial parade at 10.00 – Montgomery arrived very punctually; he was dressed as usual in black beret and battle-dress and was standing up in his car playing with his little horse-hair fly-switch. The senior officers are introduced to him and then he finishes with formality, calling the Bn to close in around the car. For a quarter of an hour he swaps wise-cracks with the troops and ends with a five-minute talk on how pleased he is to get 78th Division and 5th Northamptons in particular into 'my' Eighth Army. If he had had the 78th Division, he could have taken Tunis and Bizerta by himself. Altogether he sold himself to us very brilliantly.

20 July

8th Army getting bogged down in front of Catania. Move to a concentration area 7 miles north of Sousse; Bn brought down to 2-hours notice to move.

22 July

At midday we get the orders to move. Get called for at 01.00 and start a convoy drive down to Sousse Harbour; very dark night, and my m/c has got no lights and the road is full of sand-patches and badly filled craters; Colonel, leading in the Jeep, is going much too fast for a night convoy. Arrive at Sousse and drive straight into the cavernous,

ill-lit, mouth of an LST – rather fun, like the Lex garage in
Piccadilly. My bike is too low on the ground and gets bellied on the
ramp.

Last troops on board and all bunks taken; however we find 2 hot
and cold showers and have our first bath for 4 weeks; also a flush
lavatory – one of the most welcome creations of civilization.

25 July

At 05.30 this morning we saw Mt Etna rising high and forbidding
over the horizon. Troops in fine form, making jokes about '5th
Northampton WILL capture Mt Etna' – a very accurate prophecy.
By 06.30 we are milling around off-shore; huge cloud of smoke over
Syracuse after last night's air raid.

Drive ashore at 07.30 (having bellied my m/c again!) and go
forward to find Bn concentration area; eventually collect everybody in
an almond grove about 2 miles inland. We were prepared to be
sniped and shot at, but our reception was ridiculous, like Belgium in
1940 – streets lined by cheering crowds, flowers and fruit thrown into
the trucks; only hostile atmosphere was from a crowd of about 150
men outside the Fascist HQ in Vizzini. Buy eggs (odd, rather thought
we might just take them).

27 July

Our first German prisoner. Hermann Goering Div: and to all
intents and purposes a deserter: he was found sitting down by a well
about ½ mile to our front, having got 'lost' on patrol. Italian deserters
and civilians pouring through our lines – they sometimes give useful
information i.e. there is a minefield by the station – pass it on to the
Canadians who have got to attack the place.

29 July

Sporadic shelling throughout the day. We move again at night; dull
and tiring march with the permanent noise and dust of Priest guns
moving up. Get into new area about midnight and then try to sleep –
difficult because a tremendous artillery barrage is passing overhead.

30 July

Orders received at 07.30 that the Bn is to come under command of
the Canadian Bde. Go to their HQ with the Colonel and gather that
we are to take part in a night attack with them that night. Canadians
are definitely good fighters, but their staff work is deplorable – we
spent hours that day trying to discover our orders; succeed eventually
and make a recce. Colonel far too 'brave' – standing up on skylines –
driving along and suddenly asking 'do you think we're on a

minefield?' – as there is a huge crater and an overturned carrier I say
Yes, but have great difficulty in making him go a different way.

Moved up at 20.30 and rested there until midnight.

31 July

Bn moved forward to the start-line at about 00.30; led by the
Intelligence Sec. Crossed a bit late, and the Canadian barrage was
going well on our left before we finally moved. Tremendous
anti-climax; Germans had moved out and all we had to do was march
over appalling rough and steep country. All Coys in position by
04.30.

1 August

At 00.30 orders came through for the Colonel to go to Bde, he
couldn't be found, so I went up and received orders from the Brig
that we were to move forward at 05.30, pass through the other two
Bns and carry on down the Centuripe road. Got back and gave the
orders to the Colonel at 01.15; Bn order group at 03.00 and ready to
move by 05.00. Tired and wanting a cup of tea and rest – no chance
of either. Cross over bridge about two miles out of the town and find
it all prepared for demolition; Tom vaguely cuts some wires and we
carry on, informing Bde.

After getting some four or five miles along the road, C. Coy are
fired upon by 2 M/guns from a hill to the right, about 1000 yards
away. Our position is miserable – we are on a plain and in front of us
are the foot-hills of Centuripe, above us; every movement we make is
spotted, and our only hope is artillery. We therefore go to ground and
wait for the 25-pders. There are obviously 3 or 4 M/guns and a troop
of 88 mm guns.

Artillery support arrives, a battery concentration, and we move
forward in extended line right across the plain. Troops look grand.
Germans decide to quit. Leading Coys are on to the position and
start digging in.

A. Coy go too far forward, on to the exposed side of the hill, and
run full into the fire from the 88 mm guns. Shells falling all over the
Bn area; went up to the gunner's OP – very unsafe – in a pig-sty at
the top of the hill.

Get hold of the Colonel who sends me down to Bn HQ to contact
the Brig and find out the next move. I do so, enjoying a cigarette in
the comparative safety of Bn HQ's gully; the shelling has slackened
considerably.

For the rest of the day the Bn was at 'rest', collecting and
evacuating the wounded, burying the dead.

Bn had a quiet, and wonderfully restful night. We had been on the move for the 3 previous nights and were tired.

2 August

Centuripe is a perfect 'Ruritanian' romance – the town is perched up on top of immensely steep hills; the official height of the town is 2300 ft, but its main peculiarity is the steepness of the climb. The only road to it zig-zags endlessly up the inside of the Southern spur and it has been cratered by the Germans. I met the Colonel at the top; he tells me 'We've got to get ammunition and food up here, so go back and get mules or build a road'! I stumbled down, back to Bn HQ. Recced for our road construction with Spud and John. We found the best route and turned the Pioneers and Carrier Pls. on to clearing and building; they worked magnificently and in 4 hours we were able to get fully-laden jeeps fully ¾ of the way up. The Bn then rested.

4 August

Monty visits us, 'nobody but the 78th Division could have taken this place, a wonderful job' – very clever. 51st Div. send their congratulations which was good of them.

6 August

Very lucky day; we are concentrated as a division in a huge orange-grove below Aderno. Germans shelling us vaguely throughout the day, but cause us no casualties at all. At 15.00 hrs are Bde orders: Aderno is to be taken that night – we are to have over 100 guns in support; we are the reserve Bn and are unlikely to be required.

7 August

Aderno is a fantastic sight as for two days the RAF has bombed it incessantly, and we have completed the process with a 2 hour barrage from 100 guns. The town was not 'flat', but there was not a house with all four walls, far less a roof. I have never seen such damage; as a final gesture the Germans had blown craters as much as 20 yards wide. The town was a chaotic shambles. The civilian casualties were very light since they had evacuated themselves; as we passed through, they were returning, and greeted us with tremendous clapping and cheering.

We received orders to pass through the leading Bn during the night, and carry on to Bronte. We were to be supported throughout by artillery – it was to fire on points about every ¼ mile, and we were to call for it by wireless. It was my unenviable job to call for it, reading a map – in the dark, aided by a dim green torch – on a road of which I had no prior knowledge. I was very scared of moving too far up and of calling down artillery fire on to ourselves! We started at 21.00 and had a nightmare march with Teller and S mines in the road, and this pernicious artillery support which slowed us up seriously.

8 August

At 06.30 we were still a mile short of Bronte and were moving down the road when 2 M/gunners fired on us from high ground to our front. Ernest and I dived for shelter behind a hugh block of masonry on the left of the road; it was dead safe, but unfortunately it didn't lead anywhere, and it was not until some bright fellow engaged the M/guns with a Bren that we were able to rush across the road and behind the houses on the other side. The artillery were too far back, their wireless had broken down and we had to do the tedious job of winkling out without artillery support. It was a very slow job, and took us to long past midday. We collected a lot of prisoners. At 18.00 hours that evening we received orders to occupy Bronte. Our first three Coys were in the town without difficulty, but D. Coy and Bn HQ came under heavy fire from German 6-barrelled mortars. D. Coy lost heavily and there were one or two casualties in Bn HQ. I got permission to move Bn HQ to a 'safer' spot to which the Colonel agreed – my efforts were well-intentioned but futile. One mortar bomb hit 3 of us and we retired hurt.'

Pat subsequently and rather hesitantly, wrote of his experience of being wounded:

'If you can imagine a sound made by a cow with croup, then you will be able to tell when you are being fired on by a "Nebelwurfer" six-barrelled mortar, for the noise is similar, though it needs to be magnified a thousand times. It may be childish to be frightened by a noise, but then we know that it is not an innocent noise. The bomb is of very great power and it bursts on impact, so that it has a considerable danger area from shrapnel, which keeps very close to the ground.

'Few things could have been closer to the ground than I was when I heard three of these bombs coming from the hills overlooking the Sicilian town of Bronte; even while they were in the air, I realised that they would fall very close to me. The first burst short, the second closer, and the third too close. My first recorded sensation was that on an extraordinarily heavy blow on the outside of my left arm, about two inches below the shoulder, and this was followed by the usual legacies of the near miss – ringing ears, a mouthful of earth, and a shortage of breath. For perhaps two seconds my mind ceased to function, but then came a period of very vivid and rapid thought. The exact order of my thoughts remains intensely clear to me, and I put them down here solely because I think they are what most people think immediately after they are hit, and they may therefore be interesting: "Well, I'm not dead. Odd, I would have betted against my ever being hit. What's wrong with my arm? I can't feel it at all. Is it still there? (I felt with my right hand.) Thank heaven, it moves around when I push it. I don't think I've even broken a bone; a flesh wound and something wrong with the nerve. I'm bound to get 48 hours' rest for this – 48 hours of wonderful sleep."

'I got rather shakily to my feet, cradling my injured arm in my sound one. Blood dripped from my elbow, and I thought for a moment of pressure-points, but decided that it was merely normal bleeding. The signal officer saw me, volunteered to take over my job, and told me to go back to the Regimental Aid Post and get my arm dressed.

'With considerable difficulty I climbed back over the hill with a signaller who had been hit in the neck. He was weak, and I was one-armed, and we had to throw ourselves flat as further mortar bombs came over, and had to overcome the perpendicular terrace walls. Once back on the road, however, I met one of our stretcher-bearers, who had just brought back a casualty. He bundled me into the back of one of the artillery carriers.

'The rear medical point was on the road's verge, and there my stretcher-bearer got me out of the carrier, cut off the sleeve of my shirt, lit me a cigarette, and started to dress my arm. I felt ridiculously well and cheerful, for I was still numbed and in no pain, so I talked at great length, thoroughly enjoyed a cup of tea which the gunners provided, and gave all the latest battalion news to the brigade intelligence officer who came over to see me.

'I passed through a field ambulance – more tea – and continued my evacuation to a casualty clearing station (CCS) at Paterno, arriving at about midnight, some 4½ hours after I had first been hit. I was thankful to be placed among those for an early operation, for the numbness was leaving my arm and it was becoming painful. I was given another cup of tea and was taken almost immediately into the operating tent.

'They gave me pentathol as an anæsthetic, though I was so tired that it was almost unnecessary. It was now 1.30 in the morning, but the surgeons were still cheerful and talked me into oblivion. "Do you know where you are? . . . Yes at Paterno. What's the map reference? . . . Oh, hell, I ought to know but I've forgotten. There are two injections; one . . . can you feel anything? . . . Yes, but I can't feel my spine or move my legs. And two . . ." but that put me right out. I came back to consciousness in bed in a tent; it was daylight and I went to sleep again.

'At 8 o'clock that evening I was again evacuated by ambulance, this time to another CCS at Catania, where I stayed two days in comparative comfort; my arm was continually uncomfortable, and for some reason my fingers had become very sore, but I was never in any real pain, and it was eased by a redressing. My evacuation continued – to Lentini, where I spent a hideously uncomfortable night in a crowded hospital in an air raid – and from there I was flown to Syracuse and then on to Malta, easily the most comfortable part of the journey.

'I arrived at my ward in Malta at about 5.30 in the evening; it was a wonderful place, cool and clean, with a wireless, and bookshelves, and flowers on the tables.

'My experience is of course very limited but I talked with all the other patients in the ward while I was in Malta, and I found the following to be two very general opinions. First, that unless the wound is very serious, it is almost painless in the initial stages; the shock of the bullet or the shrapnel tends to numb the area that is hit, and it is not until later that the feeling returns, and with it the pain; but by then you are usually in the hands of the medical authorities, and they can help you.

'The second general opinion that I found was a universal admiration for the medical staff. Wherever you go, as a battle casualty you find first-class technical and team work from the medical officers and stretcher-bearers; in the immediate splinting and bandaging of the Field Ambulance, in the early surgery of the Field Surgical Units, in the Blood-transfusion Units, or, further back, in the nursing and the treatment of the CCS and the general hospital. They all give you immense confidence.

Pat soon accepted that he might not be fully fit until the beginning of October. The 'wound' itself was healing very rapidly.

'The only snag is the futility still of my 3rd and little fingers which are very weak and feel permanently like a painful pins-and-needles!

The movement in them is increasing very considerably but I can't hold even a cigarette between either of them and my thumb. The nerve obviously got badly shaken, but not severed. It ought to have happened in England! My only medical treatment is a dressing a day and I'd have been a superb guinea-pig for B.'

By the middle of September Pat was beginning to face reality.

'I am not hurrying back to the Bn because I cannot

1) Lie on my back and work with hands above my chest – my elbow collapses. This means a handicap in crawling through obstacles
2) I couldn't get over a 5 ft wall by myself (essential if there's an enemy machine-gun on your side!)
3) I cannot use my arm while lying on my chest (i.e. crawl) and I'm not battling without being able to crawl.

On top of which the MO wouldn't let me go!'

On 5 October he wrote that he had had a medical board:

'You can now devote all your anxieties and cares to Chris. I was placed in Category D for a period of 3 months, so I won't be seeing any battle until January 3rd 1944 at the earliest.'

On 10 November Pat was able to write:

'Here I am once more in England, and thoroughly enjoying it. The grass is green, the trees are both tall and of a wonderful colour, and it's early closing in Swindon.

'I had a delightful, dull, and interesting journey back. Delightful because the plane behaved in a most gentlemanly manner and only made me feel sick for 5 minutes; dull, because it's a very long way and the plane was pretty uncomfortable; interesting because I saw Malta from the air, spent half a day in Gibraltar, and finally saw a glorious dawn over Land's End from about 7000 ft.

'And here I am in an EMS hospital near Swindon. I am the only officer, and "Middle East hero!", having toast made for my tea, and all sorts of other kindnesses showered on me. The future? I expect now to be sent to some special centre – there are only 3 and I'm playing hard for Oxford.

'And now, a final word to thank all the Budgeteers who so nobly maintained the service – the attack was just going in on Centuripe and the German mortars were beastly hostile, but I lay in a slit trench and read all about Felthorpe and Marlborough and Downe, and believe me it made all the difference.'

In many of his early letters from Malta Pat was asking for news of Chris. ('I must know if Chris is all right') and he was immensely relieved to hear, when his mail caught up with him, 'the great and glorious news that Chris is OK. I hope he doesn't have any more of these "landing" jobs – beastly unhealthy.' 'Delighted to hear C.P. was in Africa on the 5th – should let him out of Italy. I was spending anxious moments thinking he might have gone to Salerno.'

Christopher greeted Pat's news with:

'So Pat has been wounded. It must have hurt a lot so I can't say "splendid"! But how nice it is to have the crazy fellow locked up in hospital for a bit, out of harm's way. But what a terribly respectable wound – just the kind of thing that Sapper's heroes got in encounters with the wily Petersen. ("Top-hole little scrap, Algy old boy" said Drummond "but do you mind pouring it out for me?" he added apologetically. Algy looked grimly at the neat white sling, and wondered as he shook the Dry Martini . . .).

'Being his left arm I suppose it can't hurt his tennis, and as for Pat's golf-swing – show me the wound that could worsen that. So really it's all very well arranged.'

After Sicily the Phantom Assault Detachment was left with little to do and Christopher found life at Bugeaud tedious and anticlimatic. ('There is an air of "fin de siècle" about, intensified by the war news. The outlook for the Assault Detachment is very uncertain. Frankly, I don't think there's much of the war left for us. Thoughts are turning homewards.') The fact that for a number of reasons – especially the delays caused by the storm – 'our boys didn't have a very successful time' was a great disappointment. At the same time it was becoming tempting to look forward to peace, and that was disturbing.

'We're now stooging around in North Africa, waiting for another job. Military life is seeming more and more intolerable as the prospects of peace brighten. Dear me, how much I should like it to end. I should then gather all my familiar dirty, travel-stained kit into a pile and burn the whole lot. How I hate it all – the canvas bucket with the greasy bottom, the stained Bren pouches, the cardigan with the torn sleeve, the battered suitcase with its stubborn locks choked with sand, the bent books with melted butter and bits of bully-beef between the pages. Loathsome, loathsome, all of it. I want to be static for a bit, with a room to live in, and a chest of drawers to keep my clothes in, and bookshelves. Then I'd like all my teeth overhauled, and a brand-new pair of spectacles, and new civilian clothes.

'Some marvellous Sunday afternoon's music is coming over on the radio, but dreadfully badly reproduced and not worth listening to. Perhaps if I moved almost out of earshot, and shut my eyes, and let the distant strains remind me of what it ought to sound like, I might squeeze some pleasure out of it. But I expect it would only make me feel how nice it would be to be home; and I get that feeling often enough already.

'Music-starvation produces some queer sensations sometimes. I remember an Aircraft Recognition film – there was a cartoon sequence with a soldier frantically flipping over the pages of an Aircraft Recognition book, while a Stuka dived on him. "Too Late" bawled the merciless talkie and you saw the bomb drop and the poor soldier re-appearing on a cloud with a harp. All very ordinary, though funnier than usual, and I dozed peacefully on. But then suddenly, though relevantly, I suppose, in a perverted kind of way, the talkie burst out into those three tremendous bars "Ye Choirs of Angels and Archangels" from the *Dream of Gerontius*.

'The healthy man's reaction would have been to smile gently and let it pass. But wait until you've been a month or so without any music. It's wonderful how unbalanced you become. I sat glued to my seat, paralysed with excitement, repeating the few bars over and over again to myself, until gradually the roaring engines of Spit 1xs and FW 190s brought me to earth again.'

It was decided that all Phantom should return home, and Chris planned to try for a transfer back to MEW, or Combined Operations proper, or the Intelligence Corps, in that order.

While waiting movement orders he found himself

'presiding over a Court of Inquiry into a bomb accident in which one of our men was killed, and two others permanently blinded. It was the fault of the man who was killed. He found a grenade by the roadside, picked it up, and took it to the two others. It then went off in his hands. If we find that he was "negligent", his wife and children may not be eligible for a pension. Why, I can't think. Presumably so as to dissuade others from accidentally blowing themselves to bits. Very stupid. And why single out wives and children for punishment? What have they done to deserve it? And anyway, let a man's sins be buried with him, say I.

'So the Court of Inquiry is hard at work perverting the law and the evidence for all they're worth for the sake of an unknown widow and two small children.'

Chris finally landed back in England late in November, some three weeks after Pat.

While they were in Africa, Chris and Pat had been very worried by the news that Beryl had had to go into hospital for a major operation. She was kept in for over a month and was then allowed home, very much a convalescent patient, to be carefully nursed by the Felthorpe matron and nurses. She fully recovered but it was several weeks before she could involve herself again in all her Norwich and Red Cross responsibilities. Meantime there were delightful moments when she and Dad got right away from the war, even if only in the grounds of Felthorpe.

'After lunch Dad and I went to look for the Pintail's new nest but failed to find it (she lost the whole of her first family in that cold spell in April). One Pochard/Tufted (I think they've crossed) is nesting in the tangle near the gorse at the end of the lake, another right on the edge of the lake about halfway between the boathouse and the gate, a third we are pretty sure is on the island. After tea we armed ourselves with a hammer, tacks, and a tin beaten out flat to nail across the hole the rats have chewed in the boathouse door. We thought we'd be very cunning, and while I spread the food for the ducks and whistled, Dad went on round the edge and hid behind a tree near the gate to see if he could spot Mrs Pintail leaving her well-hidden nest. Cock Pintail came and inspected the food and sailed off to call his lady, but he's no fool; he saw Dad at once and swam off again. So we gave it up and started work on the door; that took us 5 minutes perhaps, then we looked over the edge and there were those cunning Pintails as pleased as punch with themselves, having chosen that precise moment when our backs were turned, to emerge.'

On another day

'You'll never guess what Dad and I have done, not if I gave you three hundred guesses; I can only just believe it myself – we rowed down the river for a picnic! It was entirely Dad's bright idea, he hired a boat from a man at Thorpe and this morning we set out with a picnic lunch and rowed for about an hour and a half, landed under a hill where the grass was short, ate our lunch, slept a bit and rowed back again; it WAS fun. The last time I took a picnic on the river must have been the summer of 1939, but then of course it was a sailing boat. The last time I took a picnic in a rowing boat – goodness me, I don't think it can have been later than 1914; and probably earlier.'

But Beryl's letters to the Budget soon had a familiar ring:

'I had a Nursing Committee on Saturday afternoon. Then on Sunday I took Mr Christie to the 9.30 train and went on to the Norfolk and Norwich Hospital at 10.15 to meet Dame Beryl Oliver and other big noises of the Red Cross. She inspected the blood transfusion work – about 20 cubicles, each with 2 VADs in attendance. We moved on to St Peter Mancroft and found the Norwich Detachment in far greater strength than I had dared to hope, filling more than half the church; there we had quite a nice service, but alas a very dull sermon. After the service the Detachments lined up opposite the City Hall for an Inspection, and then marched past the Dame on the Hall steps.'

Between September and November most of the family got to Felthorpe at one time or other, Helen having demanded (and got) 'compassionate' leave to see Pat, her 'long-lost and wounded brother'.

When Helen transferred to Pollards Park, and later to Stevenage, she worked in two of the Special Operations Executive's holding stations for Polish agents who had completed their training and were waiting for the right weather conditions to be dropped back into Poland. Her duties were to help run the house, keep the cars in working order, give what help she could to the agents and to be ready at any time to take them to London, or to Tempsford aerodrome.

'It was at Stevenage that I met S—, an absolute stunner of a young man who was anxious that the people of Warsaw should hear the *Warsaw Concerto*, so we made a trip to HMV in Oxford St to see if we could buy an unbreakable disc. I can't imagine what that assistant thought, but he hadn't got one, so we bought an ordinary record and had it specially packed by the packers at the aerodrome when S— finally left, and the *Warsaw Concerto* was successfully parachuted into Poland on S—'s back and played over a secret radio.'

(Helen later met up again with S— and his wife, 'spent a lovely day with them in Kew Gardens', and saw them on their way to Scotland.)

During the second week of 1944 Helen was on leave in London and

'went up to the Masonic Hospital every day to see Chris and thought he looked very much better.'

Chris had developed pleurisy.

David was another member of the family who had been troubled by illness during the year, being firmly kept in bed for a fortnight after a dose of pneumonia. This was his second bout in six months and he found it intensely irritating. But these were only the briefest intervals in a very full and demanding life, which brought both great success and sad failure.

'This is a pretty awful job. All three officers of this unit, plus one "other rank" completely vanished from human ken on a nice sunny afternoon in a sailing dinghy in enclosed water. So I have been busy, what with collecting evidence, arranging searches, tracking down all the verbal arrangements they had made, and reading past files. It seems to have been a thoroughly unseaworthy boat, and all the evidence there is (not much) suggests that it just broke up and sank. One or two small items have been washed up, but no bodies as yet, which in most ways makes it all the more difficult.'

By the end of the year he had

'got everyone working overtime, and that means I have to work overtime myself. I come straight home in the evening and go to bed, and get up and go straight to work in the morning, and that's that. I sleep well as usual, but not so well as a chap whose story I can now tell you as part of it has been in the papers.

'Two small ships loaded with petrol, ammunition and explosives caught fire in Lerwick harbour about 9.00 one morning. They were a mass of flames in a few seconds and soon the ammunition started going up and damaging houses for several hundred yards. It was obvious there was going to be an even larger bang at any minute so they decided to try to sink them by gunfire, although it was known that some of the crew were missing. They filled them full of HE shells without managing to sink them at all, so that part of the town was evacuated. Then a furious little man emerged from one of the ship's forecastles whence all but he had fled half an hour before, demanding to know what the hell was up, and dressed in green pyjamas.'

David was rather amused when

'the Admiralty sent me the 1939–43 Star with a note to explain that it may all be a mistake and if so, I shall have to send it back. I suppose I am technically entitled to it, as all you have to do is to serve "afloat" for six months, which makes it a farce as a decoration. There must be some ticklish, border-line cases, such as the crew of the old *Iron Duke* which has been afloat at high water and on the beach at low water for three years in Scapa, but if your keel remains clear of the empty bottles you are as much a hero as if you were on a perpetual Murmansk convoy.

'Just to show you that I am living a sensible life unpestered by superior officers, I will tell you that I ordered a new uniform when I was last in Scotland, and I have had it two months now and never worn it. As a matter of fact I have been visited by two Admirals in that time, but with the cooperation of our office staff, whose job it is to look after potentates, I have got a routine worked out which gives me a minimum of trouble. The office receives the distinguished visitor, and when the tour of inspection gets near my end of the village somebody says "Sir, I'd like you to meet an ex-Flag-Lieutenant of Scapa." This is my cue to pop up from inside an engine or under a ship in dock, wiping my face with a bit of cotton waste. A good laugh is had by all, and the magnate usually congratulates me on the busy scene, and says he wouldn't dream of interrupting the good work. So I shall still have the uniform in all its new glory next time I come south, barring moths and mildew.'

The family had to wait until the end of the war before David explained what he had been doing during the previous four years, and why he had been able to write so little about it.

'I am now allowed to spill the beans to some extent about what I've been doing for the last four years. After being so extremely secretive and even deceitful for so long, it makes me feel guilty to tell the truth; but if the Budget has not ceased publication I owe it a letter which I hope will be an explanation of why I have not written anything to it worth reading.

'Ever since I came here in June 1941 I have been second-in-command of a small independent "naval" base set up to maintain contact with and supply the Norwegian underground. Although the base is run by the British, most of our men are Norwegian fishermen; we started with about 40 and finished with 100 odd Norwegians and 25 British. We have been all along in the fortunate position of owing no allegiance to anyone nearer than London. It was less fortunate for me, as the technician of the party, that even in London our authority was not a naval one – I have no sailor to appeal to for help or support in any of many troubles.

'When we started in '41 we hired a large derelict house in the wilds of Shetland, with a snug little anchorage below it in which we kept about a dozen Norwegian fishing boats. They were wooden ships of about 65 feet overall length and a displacement of 80 to 100 tons, and with them our crews operated successfully all over the Norwegian coast from well in the Arctic down to the Skagerak. In those days one of my most amusing duties was to design and make various kinds of "Q-ship" armament and armour for the boats, and in the course of time I got them fitted out with a fairly formidable armament which popped up from unexpected places. I was also – and still am – responsible for the upkeep of the ships; and as it is daylight all night long in the summer and we could therefore only operate in the winter, when the North Sea and Atlantic between here and Norway

are one of the wildest bits of ocean in the world, I have learnt to know
by the bitterest experience what is a seaworthy boat and what is not.

'I am supposed by higher authority to be writing the history of the
base, which I am well fitted to do because my own part in it has been
entirely unheroic, but it will be in such obviously bad taste to add to
the spate of war books which will try to rival *All Quiet* and/or *The
Seven Pillars*, that I doubt if the history will see print. However, I
think it would be no exaggeration to say that a sea story exists in our
unit to which it would be hard to find an equal since Elizabethan
times. Piracy and gun-running have had a vogue on all fronts in this
war, and produce good adventures in themselves; but the sea element
has not been so prominent on other fronts, whereas here the truly
horrible inhumanity of the Arctic winter has pervaded all our
voyages. I can fill the history with examples of shipwreck, incredible
escapes and brilliant bluff, hurricanes, sea-fights, man-hunts through
blizzards in the Arctic twilight, and plenty of coarsish humour and
pure courage.

'It's difficult to pick out incidents to compress into a letter which
anyone will be bothered to read, but we had, for instance, a 55-foot
boat hove to for seven days in the great storm of Nov. '41 when the
wind reached a speed of 120 m.p.h. The crew who survived that were
wrecked on an island on the northern coast of Norway, made their
way 150 miles down the coast in uniform and stole another ship under
cover of an RAF raid which caused the Gestapo, then 100 yards
behind them, to dive for cover. Another crew had occasion to steal a
100 foot ship in Lofoten but could only steal fuel for 50 miles, so they
rigged the hatch covers on the mast and sailed her the remaining 500
miles back to base. Then I fitted out a fishing boat to the last nail as
Norwegian, and its skipper took it through the German controls into
their main fleet anchorage. One of our men, the only survivor of a
boat which was lost to a German gunboat 700 miles from base,
trekked for 5 weeks alone across Lapland in midwinter with only one
boot; he had to cut off eight of his own toes with his pocket knife
when they became gangrenous after frost-bite, but he eventually got
back here.

'As I said, there have been dozens of adventures like these in our
miniature unit. After two years of operations with fishing boats the
Germans got wise to some extent to what we were doing, and at the
same time the shortage of oil in Norway became so acute that there
were few boats left fishing. We lost half our strength of 80 men and a
dozen ships in a series of disasters in the early spring of 1943, and it
became obvious that we would have to give up the Q-ship principle

and come out into the open with ships fast enough to evade surface
patrols and heavily enough armed to see off any reasonable force of
aircraft. This was a problem because there was nothing in this
country which was fast enough, and small enough to get into our
hideouts on the Norwegian coast, and yet able to stand up to our
weather. However, when we had all but given up hope, the
Americans gave us three 110-foot 20 knot submarine chasers. I
rearmed them with power-operated six-pounders and a hefty AA
armament which we got from the British Admiralty, and we have
carried out well over 100 operations with them without losing one.
Since we got them it has been almost a full-time job for me being
engineer, shipwright, electrical radio and radar and gunnery officer
all rolled into one, and I have had quite a lot of fun and learned a lot
looking after a small self-contained and independent shipyard.

'Talking about adventures makes me mention mostly our failures,
but our successes have, I suppose, made all the sweat and the loss of
so many men worthwhile. I don't know how many thousands of
weapons and hundreds of agents we have landed, or how many
hundreds of refugees we have picked up and rescued thereby from
the Gestapo. But the greater part of the equipment for the
underground has passed through our hands – some went by air – and
the home front made themselves sufficient of a nuisance to keep 10
to 12 divisions of German troops in Norway instead of on other
fronts. And at 0001 on May 9th in Bergen (for example) 600 armed,
trained and uniformed troops emerged from nowhere. By next day
this number was doubled; and the Germans had not had the slightest
idea they were there. The same thing happened in every town in the
country from Tromso to Oslo, and the Germans were so staggered
that they assisted the home front to take over control of the country
without any complaint. When the first of our sub-chasers sailed into a
port after V-day, seven assorted German warships hauled down their
flags, and our crew marched through streets, lined with underground
men who had the town running perfectly normally.

'Well, as I said, my own part in it has been 100% unheroic,
because none of us three officers has been allowed to go across at all,
but you can understand how absorbing it has been. However, I am
heartily glad it is over. No one could deny that many Norwegians are
brave men, but they are infuriating to deal with in the long run, and
our private fight with the Germans has been paralleled all the time by
an equally tough political fight with undesirable elements in London.
Still, I have some good friends among the fishermen in spite of
everything, and I am not sorry to have been in a unit which I am told

has more British, as well as Norwegian decorations per head than any other in this war.'

Beryl's first letter to the Budget in 1944 had nothing of special war interest in it, but her first paragraph perfectly illustrated the way in which she managed to keep Felthorpe so very clearly in the thoughts of all the family who were away from home.

'FELTHORPE calling the Family – but it won't be a very coherent letter 'cos there's a most entrancing green woodpecker feeding very busily a bare ten yards away, and half a dozen pigeons are trying to make up their minds to settle on the oak by the summer house and thence on to the lawn where two jays are strutting already. The woodpecker (6 pigeons now sitting in the oak) really is the most marvellous bit of camouflage; with his head down and his back towards me, he is exactly the colour of our mossy lawn.'

At that time all the family was in Britain. David was recovering from a Christmas with Islanders and Norwegians.

'Something seems to have gone wrong with Christmas now; I suppose it's the war, but have people always got drunk at Christmastime? It is an incongruous way of celebrating the birth of Christ and I don't approve of it. As for New Year, I saw it in with a glass of milk and some digestive biscuits.'

Stephen was back at work and had had

'an appalling day, but most people's news is of appalling days so that I don't feel called upon to describe its horrors to an audience whose capacity for sympathy is doubtless exhausted.'

Helen was being

'Medical Orderly all this week because our regular MO is on her leave. It's great fun but rather hard work.'

Clare had left Benenden and was at Reading University; she had just received the news that 'this Dom. Sci. course is to be closed permanently from next year; they will give us no reason.'

At Marlborough

'George and I are quite mad but very happy; we've got no "living-in" help whatever now and we've found it utterly blissful having the house to ourselves.'

Christopher's first letter

'leaves me in hospital surrounded by pretty nurses, thoroughly enjoying life. Everybody swears my right lung has pleurisy and feeds me the fashionable M. and B.'

And Pat was able to write:

'all my rackets have come off. Tomorrow I go to the South Coast to rejoin the 9th Norfolk. Allah be praised.'

Pat had been very busy over the previous few weeks trying to get a new medical board and a satisfactory posting.

'I went to the Bn on Sunday and was welcomed as a prodigal son. The Colonel made it abundantly clear that he wanted me back and that as opportunity came, so would I receive promotion etc. I therefore came back to London to beat the medical racket.

'B. let me know that I was due for Chertsey, not Oxford, so I went down there today to see how the land lay. It started very stickily, but I knew what I wanted, so I argued and argued and refused to go away. Eventually I got the military registrar to concede my point that if the doctors were willing, I should have a medical board. I therefore went in search of the Chief doctor and told him I needed a Board. Why? Because the War Office had posted me (to Norwich Barracks!) but that I could not go unless I was raised in medical category. The doc. then looked at my arm (they think far more of it than does my family!) and put me through the exercises. My efforts at cheating were found out and he said that he would be prepared to recommend me Category C. I said that was no use, I wanted a B and eventually he seemed to be prepared to accept a "B, not for overseas duty" – I accepted this because I can easily get out of the condition later.

'First hedge jumped. Alas, they cannot board me without the War Office's authority, so I say I will go to the WO straight away. Usually you have to arrange an appointment but I decided just to arrive, and after a certain shuffling humility about my ignorance as to appointments, I was admitted. ("We like to be sympathetic to you people, Mayhew, but you must realize we're very busy".) Yes, they will authorize a board if the Medical will recommend it. Immediate telephone-message to Chertsey saying WO want an official recommendation, and so to tea.

'So – Chertsey thinks the War Office wants me re-boarded and the War Office thinks Chertsey wants me re-boarded. Will they tumble to it? Should be an interesting fortnight.'

He was appointed Adjutant of the battalion and recovered his Captaincy. He found that the job kept him very busy, particularly when the battalion moved to Shildon in County Durham.

He wrote with real enthusiasm about a church parade:

'They are usually very dull and tedious things, but this morning's was a wonderful show and everybody enjoyed it enormously. The CO and I saw the local vicar and arranged the service as far as hymns and lessons were concerned ("Go, sell what thou hast and give to the poor"). The Church was very attractive and warm, there was a choir in costume, candles, and an excellent sermon. I believe that that vicar could almost make us Christians.

'I went to supper with him last night. He's most interesting – very left-wing, but not in the least communist; he worked in the pits for 10 years and really has practical knowledge of what he teaches. He says "the mines must be nationalized" and when asked why, defends his statements from the point of view of the miner's psychology. Shildon was a depressed area pre-war, and his stories of the past and future Shildon are well worth listening to. He's rather taken the Bn by storm and for about the first time in history the men are saying "Let's have another Church Parade."

'I liked his summary of a certain Bishop – "Good as gold; fit for heaven; and no earthly use." '

Christopher had recovered from his pleurisy by the middle of February and had left Phantom to join Special Forces, a newly formed unit responsible for liaison in the field between the Army, SOE, and the Resistance Movement.

'I've accepted a Staff job at an Army HQ for the Second Front, one connected with my liaison job at the War Office. Not very heroic but it will at least take me across the Channel (if it's France we attack) and give me a strategic position for grabbing some of the 1944 vintage. I must somehow get re-boarded from C. but I think this will soon be possible.'

He had to say 'goodbye to London for a bit, and come down here to prepare for my Second Front staff job' but before he left he

'dined one evening in the Phantom mess in Richmond, and when the blitz in London began, was prevailed upon – without much difficulty – to stay the night there. They were all in very good form, and we drank rather a lot.

'I also drank rather a lot on Monday night when I stood Hugh Dalton dinner at Josef's in Frith Street. Unfortunately we drank Tokay and the evening cost me £4, but for that I was rewarded with much inside information on home politics (not fit for the ears of those reactionary Conservatives, Dad and Stephen).

'My last date in town was with none other than sister Helen. She looked me up at my office and apparently knew many of the senior officers in my department, having driven them round from time to time. It was an eerie sensation walking down corridors with her – some elderly and revered Colonel would appear round a corner, and just as I was preparing to bow humbly from the waist, Helen would let out a yell of "Why, it's old Pete" or words to that effect. Whereupon the Colonel would say "Hi-ya Helen" and slap her on the back. What it is to be a woman.'

Helen resolutely denied this story. She had decided that she wanted a change, an opportunity to use her intelligence again after two years spent mainly on driving. She applied to go into the Codes and Ciphers section which was in direct contact with the agents with whom they had been living and working.

She found the work fascinating, but sometimes deeply depressing when, for example, decoded messages were found not to contain the necessary security message at the end, usually meaning the agent had been discovered and that the Germans were using his wireless.

While doing this work she was promoted to the rank of Corporal.

Downe was once again experiencing heavy bombing; this time from the V1 'buzz-bomb' or 'doodlebug'. This was a pilotless bomb which flew low, with a very loud outboard-motor type of noise; it had the shape of a small plane and its main feature was that when the engine stopped the bomb glided to the ground and exploded. It had great destructive power, but many felt it less frightening than the bombing of an ordinary air raid because it was more predictable; it flew in a straight line and you could tell whether it would pass you on one side or another, it was also possible to tell, from the position of the bomb when the motors cut out, whether you were going to be in the danger-zone of the explosion at the end of the glide. It was also, except in towns, and subject of course to weather conditions, usually visible by day, and by night because of its flaming exhaust.　·

Uncle Bertie wrote about them from Downe.

'You may like to know we are still here at the moment of writing, since we are of course on, or under, the line of fire of the buzz-bombs. The things turn up at irregular intervals, and one feels that the siren-sounders don't quite know what to do about it. I think it's rather wonderful that they can give any warning at all; I fancy there is an alert on as I write: if so, it's been on for about six hours. Anyhow, it was the sight of two of them crossing the sky just now, and being shot at which put me in mind to let you hear of them.

'At night they look rather wicked, caught in searchlights and with their flaming tails. One is quite selfish about them; one watches one coming right overhead and thinks that if its engine stops one jolly-well dives for cover; if it passes over one merely thinks "well, that's all right." This has now happened during the previous sentence; the thing beetled along (but it was some way off), the guns opened up, and there was a distant thunderclap which just rattled my windows, though from several miles away.

'During previous raids my one instinct has been to get out and see what's coming: with the buzz-bombs this instinct does not operate, and like others I have spent comfortable nights, if somewhat disturbed, in bed. There isn't the variety about b.b. raids that there was about the other sort.'

Sadly, before the end of the V1 bombing phase in the autumn, Downe was badly hit.

'After all these years of escape, our village has suffered heavily in the past week. There has been only one fatal casualty, but miraculous escapes in dozens. Rows of houses are wrecked, the church is looking pretty poorly, and the official rest-centre was put out of action so that we, who have not suffered much as yet, had to become the rest-centre, and this placed WVS District Commander Eleanor Howarth in the business up to the neck. The Home Guard of course was turned out for assistance to Civil Defence who were seriously over-loaded, having their own troubles in the neighbouring townships.

'It may be mentioned that a rest-centre officer from outside commented fulsomely on the wonderful communal spirit of this village in contrast with others which, she said, are all split up into cliques.

'Life is full of interruptions and I have just paused to watch seven of these beastly things go over in a row: six got through and only one was stopped abreast of us and two or three miles off. Can any of you experts evade the censorship and tell me why the balloon barrage is so much more effective at one time than at another? Sometimes they hit and pop off all round, other times, as just now, they sail through the whole outfit. The phenomenon is so well marked that it seems there must be more than mere chance in it; but don't hand me out some highbrow theory or I shall probably deny it.

'Another pause while a single one goes through. They seem always now to be fired in volleys, so that this time I like to think that all the rest were knocked out somewhere to the South of us.'

As a result of the V1s most of the children of Downe were evacuated and there were only fifteen left in the school out of a normal attendance of fifty-four. This was the pattern all round London and once again Felthorpe became a reception area for evacuees; at that time there were forty-nine of them,

'i.e. people whose hosts are drawing government allowances for keeping them because they come from specified areas and under specified categories. On top of that there must be at least another score of relations and friends so that you can imagine there are not many empty rooms left. Yesterday I bought four prams for £10 and brought them home triumphantly. It's expensive, but will make all the

difference in the world to their trotting up and down the village to
meet each other, and I believe will go a long way to help them to settle
down.'

Beryl was writing on 7 June, immediately after 'D-Day', the
allied invasion of France, and by then all the family's thoughts
were with Christopher.

During the run-up to D-Day Christopher was at Second
Army HQ in a camp near Portsmouth. On one day he went up to
London for a medical board and was regarded A1, and on
another day he visited Pat who is 'only two or three miles away
and I have to admire his choice of camp-site. It is a most
admirable wood with tall trees (conifers – much the best for
camping under) with lots of room between them.'

Ten days before the invasion

'was a red-letter day for our Staff Section. Into our little
office-caravan climbed the Army Commander, and His Majesty's
Secretary of State for War, Sir James Grigg. Why they should thus
honour me I can't imagine. We had nothing to show them but they
plied us with questions for fully 15 minutes, the General tackling our
Colonel, while HMS of S cross-examined Jack and me. I say
"cross-examined" – actually his questions were remarkably naive and
Jack and I answered them with great promptness, happy in the
thought that almost anything said with conviction was sure to pass.
There could be no mistake about it – he was colossally ignorant of
our side of staff work. Lacking self-confidence among so many
soldiers, he was a bit pompous at first, but thawed later and showed
genuine interest and pleasant manners. A good old-fashioned civil
servant, rather than a leader of men. He wore a raincoat and a bowler
hat and looked quite ridiculous in the sun-baked fields, among the
battle-dress and tents.'

A letter posted on the day before the invasion showed his
increasing concern at the poor weather which could have the
gravest consequences for the invasion; but his concern was only
evident in his understatement:

'A horrid windy Sunday, making the tents flap all over the place.
My pending basket periodically empties itself all over the ground –
most exasperating. Let's hope it blows over soon.

'There's really no news, except that we are beginning to get a bit invasion-conscious these days. This is just to report that if there is an invasion ever, I shall be bringing up the rear, complete with library and deck-chair, and don't deserve a moment's worry or anxiety from anyone.'

'It's D + 4 and I've still got a couple of hundred yards to go to reach France. The weather has been letting us down, and my little recce party is a long way behind schedule. We're lying off shore, waiting for a chance to go in and land. At the moment some sappers are blowing up the last of the mines. Spurts of sand go up periodically, accompanied by sizeable bangs. There are lots of planes overhead – ours presumably as no one's firing at them – and more ships around than I can possibly describe.

'I landed soon after writing my last letter and found everything much as you probably imagine it – bomb damage, craters, dust, dirty-looking soldiers, excited civilians. People were de-waterproofing vehicles, digging slit-trenches, patching up roads, waving flags, putting up tents. Between the craters, Normandy looked lovely, good green trees and crops and pleasant contours. But its churches were much battered, one in particular which had had a Bofors turned on it to oust some snipers.

'The whole of the bridgehead is one big BANG from morning till night.'

For the first three or four weeks that he was in France his role with Special Forces was to liaise between the French resistance movement and 2nd Army HQ. News of sabotage, such as the cutting of a railway line behind the German lines, would be received by him from London and he would relay and interpret this to HQ Intelligence. This liaison service could sometimes be given in reverse; Army would – for example – ask whether the resistance could delay a German convoy and Special Forces would be able to find out the answer from London.

Christopher later realized that in the fluid state of the fighting it was quite possible for agents to operate close behind the German lines and that this had advantages over and above the London–Resistance link. He developed a practice of infiltrating agents through German-held territory to discover and report back information of immediate importance to the Army.

This needed careful planning, close liaison with 2nd Army

HQ and the full support of the local commanders and troops on the ground where he was operating.

On one occasion, hoping to increase his knowledge of conditions behind the German lines, he

'took a half-day off and went with a friend to a prisoner-of-war "cage" where he had to do some interrogations. Soon after we arrived, 300 new arrivals marched in with a heavily armed escort. They came from at least three different divisions, so must have been fairly typical of the German army. First came a dozen officers, very well-dressed and turned-out considering, and a thoroughly decent-looking lot. After them were about 30 toughly-built Aryans in camouflaged jackets, evidently from some élite formation – I didn't discover which, but the most striking of all were the 250 remainder. Never in my life have I seen such a wretched crew of human beings. Making all allowances for their having just emerged from a tough battle, they looked just the end. Some were much too old, some were much too young, some were too fat, many were too thin. Many wore heavy specs, most were flat-chested. An unlikelier lot to conquer Europe just couldn't be imagined.

'The interrogations were not very interesting to me, except that the prisoners were astonishingly ready to answer questions. They'd all been told, like any other soldier, to give Name, Rank and Number ONLY in the event of capture, but here they were spilling the beans as readily as if they were on our side, telling us everything we asked for and a lot more besides. It wasn't that they were afraid, nor that they wanted to let the Fatherland down, they just didn't seem to mind whether we knew or not.'

The American break-out from the bridgehead offered good conditions for infiltration, and in August he was

'lent to the Americans for a week or two, to try and help them out with the mass of work that's falling on their staffs. Much more goes on down here in the South than with the British Army, and it's all rather amusing. The first thing you notice is that American Staff Officers never write anything. "Personal Contact" is the slogan and at the top of their minute paper ("bucksheet") you sometimes find printed "Not to take the place of personal contact." I must say they play the game very well, and if you want to meet someone, even a full-blown Colonel, you're really welcomed into their office, and given all the time you want to say your piece. This is a great contrast with the British technique, which is to read your paper, write a long reply in sextuplicate, and refuse to meet you personally at any cost.

'There are pros and cons in both methods – slowness and lack of cooperation in the British Army, and muddles and inefficiency among the Americans.

'The American office work is atrocious. You can never find the paper you are looking for; the files consist of cigarette cartons and pin-up girls; there's never any stationery, or maps, or pens. Ink is unknown – only typewriters and pencils.

'Another feature of the American Way of Life is a heavy lunch immediately after breakfast, followed by starvation for the rest of the day. How they last out I can't imagine.

'Travelling is quite an adventure on the American sector. They are pushing ahead at such an enormous speed that sizeable pockets of Germans, still in fighting form, are left miles behind the forward troops. No one even knows where they, or our own troops, are, and a journey between a couple of Div. HQs is often quite an adventure. On one occasion last week my driver and I drove innocently up to a German road block – goodness knows why they didn't fire on us – perhaps they were as much surprised as we were, or more likely they'd abandoned the road block and gone further back. On another occasion we were bowling along in our jeep towards a farm when the farmer dashed out of a hedge, and ran down the middle of the track towards us, brandishing his arms in the utmost excitement. "Attention! Attention! les Boches sont ici." Stout fellow – and many thanks to him: we made one of the most rapid and panic-stricken military withdrawals in history.

'I also had an amusing time in Evreux (being one of the first in) which I will tell you about when the war is over, and an excellent journey by air just behind the battle lines, in one of those tiny "Austercub" planes you may have seen. We flew never higher than 1000 ft and never faster than 100 m.p.h. and could see everything going on below – columns of marching troops going up the roads; huge convoys of trucks and tanks; a Red Cross camp with the Red Crosses shining out miles away like beacons; groups of bomb craters round crossroads; areas of country miles wide simply plastered with big round bomb and shell craters, or with the jagged patches of light mortars and fragmentation bombs. It was all fascinating.'

Apart from infiltrating agents behind the enemy lines there was also the problem of picking up some of them from enemy-

held territory. This was Christopher's task on one particular
evening, about which he wrote:

'It is so seldom I have any warlike adventures to recount that you
may like a long letter about a rather harrowing evening I spent with
some Americans recently.

'By a series of appalling coincidences it had become my duty – you
will just have to guess why – to accompany a squad of tough
American paratroopers on a night patrol into no-man's-land. I went
as a kind of guest-artist, cast in an ignoble role which left the most
dangerous work to others.

'The plan was – we would cross 800 yards of flat country beyond
the furthest outpost till we came to a river. There we would divide,
half of us, including myself, lining the bank to give covering fire,
while the other half crossed the river, went 300 yards beyond, and
then came back again. All very simple it looked, especially as the
American Colonel assured us there were no Germans in the area.

'There were nine of us altogether, led by an American Captain
with an American Lieutenant for the river crossing. We left Regt HQ
in two jeeps, with a trailer carrying the boat and paddles. There was a
full moon, but it was drizzling steadily and the light wasn't too bad.

'After four miles we put out the jeep lights and our cigarettes and
went more slowly and quietly. Most of the regiment was now behind
us, and we had only outposts in front. After a time we met one, and a
sentry challenged us quietly from under cover. We told him not to
fire on us when we returned, and carried on. The track got worse and
worse – only jeeps with expert drivers could have got through. At one
point we found a newly felled tree blocking our path, and the
well-trained Yanks, suspecting an ambush, leapt out and took up
firing positions. But the American Captain soon saw that the trunk
was cut high up, obviously by a shell, so we just hauled the debris out
of the way, and drove on.

'The furthest outpost was in a blitzed house, by the side of a raised
road. Here we parked the jeeps, inflated the boat, made some final
plans and set out.

'The sky had cleared now, and it was bright moonlight. You could
see for miles. We crossed quickly over the raised road, crouched
down in the shadows the other side, and just watched and listened for
several minutes. Over on the left I can see a bend of the river shining
in the moonlight. Half right, over the river, two factory chimneys
stand out clearly. There is rising ground on the other side, just to
make things more awkward.

'On a signal, we get up and move forward 100 yards, making good use of a dry ditch. Then we lie down again. It is just like an OCTU exercise. Ahead we can pick out some horses; and when we get up again to move they stampede, flying around all over the place, their hoofs thundering fit to wake the devil. We lie flat again. I can hear my heart beating. It makes my breath come and go in little gasps. I can feel my adrenal glands working overtime. My nose clears miraculously, though I have a cold.

'Then on again – a long stretch across meadow-land. I find myself keenly noting any little hollow in the ground, and lingering a bit when we come across a dip. All this ground is commanded by the enemy on the other side of the river, 600 yards away, and in the still, dazzling moonlight it seems impossible that they shouldn't see or hear us. However, we go ahead safely, and reach a patch of roots 200 yards short of the river. Suddenly over on the left I distinctly see two men stalking us. I feel myself turning pale green. But they are a flanking party who got lost and are coming to rejoin us. Everyone breathes again, and we go on without incident to a little hollow by a raised road.

'The Lieutenant peers over the road, watching and listening for a long time, then comes back and whispers orders. The covering party takes up firing positions along the road. Then the advance party picks up the boat and runs across the road, lying low in the shadows on the other side. Then we watch them slowly edging their way forward to the river. There is a tiny sound of scraped rubber as they embark, and soon a shadow is moving noiselessly down and across the river in front of us. Everything is going like clockwork.

'They reach the other side. The American Captain and I look at our watches. Ten minutes past midnight. In 15 minutes all will be well. We give each other thumbs up.

'We grow colder and damper back on the road. I turn over on my back, and then nearly asphyxiate myself in suppressing a cough.

'Another five minutes passes. Then suddenly the whole operation turns from triumph to disaster. A vivid stream of m.g. tracer flashes across the river at us from straight ahead, smacking into our bank, flicking the turf up by our heads, ricocheting all over the place. Another m.g. joins in from slightly left. Flares go up all along the river for miles. Jittery Germans fire rifles and m.g.s. anywhere and everywhere, as fast as they can reload them. The American intelligence has been right out of joint: the area is stiff with Germans.

'The covering party cowers down in its hollow. We cannot possibly return this fire – it would be suicide to poke our noses for an instant

over the bank. In any case our men are already in the line of fire. So
we hug the ground, while a firework display fills the air immediately
above us. A flare drops actually in our hollow. Our two big personal
worries – will they start shooting from the right, where we have no
cover at all? and have they any mortars? Just one mortar would see the
end of us; the hollow is large enough to make an easy target, and
there's not a scrap of cover inside it. For several minutes we feel
miserable; but gradually it becomes apparent that there are no
mortars, and nothing capable of enfilading us from the right; and our
thoughts turn to the poor devils on the other side. As yet, there's no
definite evidence that they've been spotted: but the boat could hardly
be missed now, with the flares added to the bright moon. We hear the
Germans calling to each other "Have you seen anyone?" "Who is
that?" From the sound of it, they are scarcely less nervous than we
are.

'There is nothing to do but wait. After a bit, I cease feeling
frightened at all. God bless the stout bank in front of me, into which
the Germans are wasting so much good ammunition. I turn over on
my back and watch the tracer disappearing behind us into the
distance. One of the bullets snaps a strand of wire near the patch of
roots and a whole fence twangs noisily. It would be nice to be
comfortably in bed at home: but one should expect to be shot at now
and again, in a war. How far away was the nearest bullet in that first
burst? Eighteen inches or so. On the other hand, I wasn't looking
over the top at the time, so it couldn't have hit me anyway. Nor could
it have been me they saw. How lovely Venus looks, and the moon too,
– blast it. No clouds to the windward of it. It won't get any darker for
half an hour at least.

'After ten minutes the firing gradually dies down. One of the
American privates crawls round and whispers to his chief, "Say,
Cap'n, they'll never be able to come back this way tonight. Why don't
we scram?" I realize I've been thinking the same thing myself
subconsciously, not liking to admit it. But the American captain
decides to wait another ten minutes, – rightly, though there's nothing
we can do.

'I spend the time battling with my cough. My throat is so thick I
can scarcely breathe, but I dare not try to clear it. Then one of the
Americans suddenly coughs, loudly. The noise seems to echo all over
the countryside. All of us turn our heads towards him with the same
expression of agonized entreaty. Poor man, he is doing his best.

'The way back will be risky, but not frighteningly so. The worst
part will be crossing the skyline on leaving the hollow. Once behind

the roots we shall be poor targets from across the river, and there are evidently no Germans this side tonight.

'The American Captain signs us to get mobile. We crawl along to the right, and then double over the skyline singly, at 30 second intervals. It is a nasty moment, but no one fires at us. Then 20 yards of splendid ditch, a noisy scramble through the roots, and we can breathe more freely. A rapid crouching walk across the meadow-land, passing some dead and dying cows, and in no time we are back at the outpost.

'To our delight and astonishment, three of the five advance party are already safely back. They hid in the river and then swam back, returning to the outpost from a point further downstream. They say that one of the two others was wounded, but the fifth was last seen unhit and hiding in some undergrowth. One of them, whom I know quite well, does not talk at all. He is standing up rigidly in his sodden clothes, and I suddenly realize that he is too cold to move or speak. I tug his clothes and boots off and put my overcoat round him, then massage him till my arms ache. After a bit he comes to and goes to sleep. His companions, who swam back practically naked, are in a much better state.

'After making what arrangements are possible, the American Captain and I slither back to RHQ in a jeep. Shells pass airily overhead from both sides, long whistles and moans and distant crumps. Some flares are going down over a neighbouring town. A Mosquito roars overhead, plainly visible against the high moonlit clouds. It has been a very exhausting evening, and a failure. But we have nothing on our consciences. Two unsuspected m.g.s. wrecked our plans; and that is "just one of those things".'

Throughout the autumn Chris was moving forward with the Army, and being a very small unit of only six men and himself, he had great freedom of movement. He found

'The Belgian welcome far surpassed the French. In Brussels they still go completely mad at the sight of a British uniform. Strangers stop you in the street and insist on carrying you off for a drink. Shop-keepers refuse payment for the things you buy. You simply daren't ask anyone the way – in a second you are addressing a mass meeting.

'There can be little doubt the British race is remarkably well thought of in the ex-occupied countries. We are far more popular at the moment than we have ever been in the past or will be in the future. Naturally the welcome varies according to the circumstances of the Liberation. In Rouen I heard a lot of criticism of our bombing, also in Caen. American bombing is still more unpopular. But when you get to an undamaged town, the welcome is positively embarrassing. I revisited Leforest the other day (where I was billeted in 1939 and sang Christmas carols round the streets). Many of my old friends recognized me, and of course we had a tremendous party. The town had been remarkably lucky – no bombing, and Germans who behaved decently. There had been no resistance movement there which perhaps explains part of it.

'Out of the multitude of resistance anecdotes you hear every day, I was rather struck with this one: – A Belgian riding in a crowded tram lit a cigarette with a match and threw the match out of the window. A German SS man asked him for a light. The Belgian hesitated; then handed his lighted cigarette over. The German lit his cigarette with it and handed it back. The Belgian then threw the cigarette out of the window.'

In December he flew home from Brussels, strictly on business.

'But of course I managed a weekend at Felthorpe, finding the parents and the radiogram in excellent form. Dad has sprouted the most handsome head of thick silver hair you've ever seen in your life.'

While he was in France he had written about marriage:

'More Nuptials. Good old Pat, I thought I'd seen a vague, lost look in his eye way back at Portsmouth. He will, I imagine, make a good husband and father. Or will his children (juvenile delinquents to a man) bully him? Dear me, what a lot there is to family life. How brave people are to marry.

'Stephen, my dear cousin, all this impending matrimony brings us still closer together – the eternal uncles, in-laws for ever and aye. Or are you too going to get married? I have a four year plan for myself as follows: –

1945 Ask all female acquaintances to marry me. When that has failed
1946 Subscribe to the Bond St Marriage Bureau.
1947 An advertising campaign in the Matrimonial Gazette and as a last resort
1948 A house-to-house canvass in likely neighbourhoods.

Would you like to come in on it? It strikes me that working together would have many advantages – introducing each other to those who have rejected us, sharing the taxis, flowers, etc. Let me know.'

From Shildon Pat had moved with his battalion to a wood just outside Portsmouth which was to become a 'staging' camp for the troops that were going to be in the first assault of the invasion. He was not directly involved in this work, being responsible for the continuing administration of the battalion and for the gradual posting away of all the officers and other ranks until the battalion was finally disbanded. He had his own small camp of HQ staff where he was left entirely alone, with very few visits from senior officers. He wrote: 'Chris is of course "insecure" – here am I abstaining most carefully from describing my extraordinarily lovely camp, and he tells you that I am in a "coniferous" wood. His information would be invaluable to the Germans if they trusted him, but the family, knowing him, will not be in the least surprised to hear the trees are not conifers, but good English oaks.'

At the end of September his battalion had been disbanded and he had been posted to the Isle of Man as a Major and an Instructor at an Officer Cadet Training Unit.

In an earlier Budget Pat had expressed his concern about the future of the men in his Company:

'What is going to happen to all these men after the war? For nearly four years some of them have served and served and served – not themselves, not for their own profit. After the war will they still serve? Will the State cease to be worth serving? Will we rush madly back to a free-for-all existence?

'Wherever you look there are so many monstrous blemishes on the national life that you almost tend to despair that anything can ever be done. I used to believe that every man should concentrate on one branch of social life and try to improve it, but I can't see how they are separable. Wages, housing, health, crime, unemployment, pensions, education, insurance, class-distinction, morality – they all tie up. I can't help but feel that sooner or later the whole thing will blow up. What would you do with the man who thought his individual liberty of choice of greater importance than the welfare of the community.

What would you do with the man who hid his selfishness under the banner of "Freedom"?'

He was also very unhappy about 'class-distinction' – between officer and other rank, and within the ordinary civilian community.

'Is our "class" a permanent millstone round our necks? I don't mean the benefits, but the inequality it breeds in the relationships of men. I know some of the "poorer" group very well, but not entirely. Why not? I think because I have more money and an Oxford education – both admirable things! – yet both a barrier. The nearest I ever came to crossing it was while I was in the ranks, and often I curse the day when I took a commission. Yet, by holding a commission you can do more for the troops than you can if you yourself are a ranker. Can you ever have equality in relationship with inequality of rank?'

This letter brought an almost universal response from the members of the Budget. Uncle Bertie wrote that

'in regard to all the matters in which Pat, in a recent letter, deplored the lack of progress, I can at least say that in my lifetime there has been progress, however deplorably slow. I believe educational reform to be the root of the whole plant. Educate the people in what the advance of knowledge and research can do to improve their lot, and trust them to see that they get it, and to kick the backsides of ignorant politicians of whatever party until they do get it.'

David wanted to

'argue most strongly against Pat's Budget statements that sustained friendship is impossible between different classes. I have never found it so personally and find it less and less as I grow up and learn to see better beyond superficialities. In fact, since the war separated me from my old friends, the only valuable friends I have made are skilled workmen of various kinds and their wives and families.'

Stephen suggested to Pat that

'part of the trouble may be a personal difficulty arising from always having been implicitly or explicitly the boss?

'It seems to me possible that if Pat had tried some new approach – e.g.: personnel management in industry – he would have found an easier way down the mountain of society. As it is, does he not see a disproportionate number of the rock bottom in distress in his peacetime job, and does he not get at present a view of the English set-up forced into an unnatural mould?'

Christopher wrote:

'Your main complaint seems to be, dear brother, that class is a barrier to companionship. Never a truer word spoken. There are those who deny it but they are wrong. Even inside the Labour movement class is a great divider – though here it is the middle class who are the under-privileged.

'But your conclusions are surely wrong. You launch out against the upper classes for failing to behave as though this barrier didn't exist – you criticize their aloof, insincere and/or patronizing attitude and idealize working-class "naturalness" at their expense. But the barrier does exist, it cannot be walked through as though it wasn't there. I have often seen upper-class people behaving as though they were proletarians; it is a pitiful sight and is acutely embarrassing to everyone. It is right to try to overcome or minimize the differences, but disastrous to pretend they don't exist.

'One can go a long way in overcoming class differences by goodwill and tact, but the problem is fundamentally an economic and political one.'

Granted that there was a class distinction between the ranks in the Forces then Clare, who had now been called up into the Wrens, was at the very bottom.

'We have been on mess duty all this week and thank goodness it ends tomorrow; it really has been extraordinarily hard work.

'I am going to be a "Bomb Range Marker". I honestly don't know what this implies, except a little plotting. We work under Naval Officers on a Fleet Air Arm Station.'

The family was delighted that by working with the Fleet Air Arm Clare had added another Service to those in which they had a representative.

She was posted to Northern Ireland, to Eglinton outside Londonderry, and her job was to work as a member of a team of six, marking the hits that planes registered on drogues or on ground targets. Occasionally she was drafted to Portrush where the targets were mock-up boats.

It was one of the roles of the Bomb Range Markers to communicate with the planes in the air by RT, bringing them in and controlling their firing time. On one occasion a pilot ignored this and fired while they were still on the range, marking the targets.

'We have had a series of unpleasant incidents this week. It started a few days ago when one of the planes committed a dangerous and stupid mistake. It was a shocking accident, and we let go in no polite terms at the pilot and – as he rightly deserved – got him in a dickens of a row. All would have been well if the matter had been dropped there, but it wasn't, and as a result the pilot has been sent to be our Security Officer for a week. The pilot was the most abject person and obviously felt highly awkward at being confronted with us. It's going to be a difficult week for us, but I imagine much worse for him.'

It was not long before, like other members of the family, she was regretting that she could not get over to France to take part in the allied 'sweep' across Europe. She thought that it would have been possible if she had been doing 'practically any other job of work'.

Helen also was trying to get into Europe.

'Am feeling rather depressed at the moment because I practically landed a magnificent job yesterday – to drive madly in Paris for a mere six weeks on an emergency job, which would have suited my present frame of mind down to the ground, but the powers-that-be down here say that they don't think I can be spared from the office. Curse these Corporal's stripes! It's all very well your being proud of your daughter, Dad, but they are a handicap now!'

Helen was very well placed for keeping the family informed about Christopher's movements. In December

'I heard from a "secret" source that Christopher was coming home on the 7th so made a few expensive calls home to warn the parents, and contacted Dad when he was in London on the 6th. My source of information told me he thought Chris would have time to go home, so Dad went home on Thursday night and I came up to town on Friday for the weekend. I met Christopher in the office, surrounded by Majors and Colonels (to whom, incidentally, I did not say "Hyah" but whom I saluted with great respect).

'He was looking surprisingly fit, I thought, though perhaps a little thinner. He has exchanged his black beret for a khaki one and looks much less like Monty, which is a relief.'

'STOP PRESS.
Congratulations to MAJOR C. P. Mayhew.'

was a November PS to one of Beryl's letters, and this was a cause for celebration when Christopher got home in December.

Later there was further rejoicing when the following letter arrived:

'My dear Dad and B.,
'You may possibly see in the Eastern Daily Press shortly that I have been "Mentioned in Despatches" – a very minor award, and nothing to write home about, except you'd be annoyed if I hadn't told you first.'

Earlier Beryl had written:

'On Tuesday I gracefully retired after my second year as President of the Norfolk and Norwich Library; it's been quite fun. It's horrid retiring in November because the President sits with his (or her) back to the fire at Committee Meetings, and now I shall have to remove myself to a chair by the window just as the months get really cold!'

The hospital was very cold over Christmas because the boiler was not working and

'The absence of other heat has meant of course that the meagre supply of wood accumulated with such difficulty through the summer has been used up at lightning speed. The moderately well seasoned stuff cut before August was all burnt up the week before Christmas, now we are burning stuff cut up during October and November.

When that's finished, and I reckon we have about three weeks' supply, we shall have to struggle with stuff brought in and cut up about a week before we try to burn it. We really are very short of wood; a roaring fire in the men's room from 8.00 a.m. till 9.30 p.m., and a practically non-stop if smaller fire in the Nurses' sitting room day and night, with others at intervals in the study, and a big one occasionally in the hall, does get through an immense amount of wood in three years.'

Pat was now taken to task by Christopher for not having written more regularly to the Budget and he felt he had to make his 'first and last excuse for the weakness of my recent Budget letters'.

'When they disbanded the 9th we began to get a lot of letters from the ex-members, in which they all started to ask where their friends had got to, and one day as I lay in my tent in the "Portsmouth area" I thought, well, why not adapt the Budget and take all the relevant extracts from these letters and pool them into a News Letter? This would ensure that any people who wished to keep in touch with their friends were able to do so. I therefore typed out and duplicated Norfolk News Sheet No. 1 which was of only 35 copies, because at that time I did not know many addresses. A fortnight ago I had printed NNS No. 6 and found that I had to have 250 copies, and I reckon that an average of 4 to 5 ex-9th read each copy. At the same time as I started the NNS I said that I would answer any letters which might be sent to me personally and which asked for information about any individual; I have on average 4 to answer each day.
'At the moment the NNS goes to places all over England, France, Holland etc; Gibraltar, Sicily, Italy, Nigeria, Sierra Leone, Gambia, Egypt, Palestine, Nairobi, Kenya, India, Ceylon, Burma and the Navy! It is really becoming rather famous and is even observed by the Scrutiny Section of the Ministry of Information!
'Hence my dull letters, and if you regret them, please bask in the happy knowledge that the Budget principle is now worldwide!'

He was delighted to have had 'an amazing number of Christmas greetings from various ex-9ths including an airgraph signed by 35 of them in Italy'.

By January 1945 the end of the war in Europe was clearly only a matter of months away and the question of demobilization was beginning to be taken seriously. The order in which men were to be demobilized was determined by the number of 'points' allocated to them.

David assessed his chances and saw no reason

'to suppose I shall be demobilized by the spring. It's true that with five years service and thirty-two years of age, you get quite a lot of points; but I fancy that most of the Army will be home before they start on the Navy. There are about a hundred thousand landing craft, presumably, in the Channel, which someone with a cast-iron stomach and a pocket compass will have to take to the Marshalls or somewhere. Not that I want to do it. I wonder if anything like an adequate number of people want to go East? If not, there will be the most terrific rows when they start getting posted there after the Armistice in Europe. After five years in a uniform, any civilian soldier or sailor has a right to feel he's had enough for one lifetime.'

Christopher was back with the Army in Europe and by March he was in Germany itself.

'The German civilians have already convinced themselves quite firmly, that they are and always have been, fanatical anti-Nazis. "We were always against Hitler, but what could we do against the Gestapo? Hitler is mad; those who go on fighting are mad, the Nazis started the war. Would you like some eggs? Can we help you unload the truck?" As far as I can judge, they are not consciously acting – they'd be more self-conscious downing Hitler in each other's company if they were – but have genuinely convinced themselves of their innocence.

'The war isn't quite over yet. Numbers of incredibly brave and tough young Nazis turn up in odd places and make nuisances of themselves. Now and again one has some excitement travelling around. I had some m/gun tracer pass in front of my bonnet the other day on a main road two miles back from our spearheads.'

It was in March that the whole question of fraternization arose. Should British troops fraternize with German civilians? For most of the family this was only a theoretical question, but for Christopher it was a real issue, and he brought it up in the Budget.

'What are your views on "fraternization"? The teaching of Christ
on the subject just couldn't be plainer, not possibly; and I intend to
follow it to the best of my ability. The official attitude of the Army
and our government is the direct opposite. By radio, and by written
and spoken orders, we are exhorted not to be forgiving; we are
encouraged to believe that all Germans are devils and should be
treated as outcasts.

'At the moment I am temporarily separated from my staff section,
and am billeted in a German farmhouse. There are ten of us sleeping
under the same roof; the German farmer, his buxom wife, and two
small daughters; two foreign conscript workers – female Russians;
and two British officers and batmen. What would you imagine the
international relations to be like? Shut your eyes and imagine. The
German civilians have for years been cheering on their Army and
Gestapo, in their unexampled career of tyranny, plunder and murder
against the Allies. The Russians, newly liberated, have been torn
from their homes to do forced labour for the farmer. And we British
are under orders to treat the farmer rough; and really have no lack of
good reasons for doing so. And the farmer himself is no doubt under
orders to kill us British swine in our beds.

'The stage is therefore set, one might think, for grim drama as we
British enter the farmhouse. The Russians will throw their arms
round us and embrace us, crying a little. Then they will turn and rend
the wretched farmer. "Fascist viper!" they will cry. "Down with
Hitler! Long live the Soviet Fatherland!" We British shall stride
around looking victorious; and the farmer will cower in a corner with
his family behind him, thinking "Wait till tonight, you Jewish
pluto-democratic scum".

'In our case however, ordinary human nature held sway. The
farmer received us with polite reserve, which we reciprocated. The
Russians looked on shyly. The farmer's wife discussed feeding
arrangements with our batmen. Our welcome had about as much
hostility in it as we would be met with if we billeted ourselves in a
small English farm – hostility for the same reasons of inconvenience,
entirely non-political. Later on the atmosphere thawed; the kitchen
was full of noise as the German children showed off their English to
our batmen, and Russia tackled Germany over the card table. For the
British officers, the farmer's wife produced an irresistible strawberry
jam trifle, with real cream on top.

'What should we have done with that strawberry trifle? It was
clearly well-meant. Should we have accepted it? Or should we have
called to mind Oradour-sur-Glane, Warsaw, Auschwitz, Dachau, the

London blitzes, the starving of Greece, and the long list of personal
wartime tragedies; and refused angrily to touch it? I should be
interested in Budget views, not least from Pat.

'Of course the explanation of the odd situation is simple –
individuals do not behave like nations; and in any case ordinary
people judge nations on political grounds and individuals on personal
grounds. That is why our official anti-fraternization policy is doomed
to disaster. It's a positive menace in a way; because when our soldiers
see for themselves that nine tenths of ordinary Germans are decent
kindly people, they will think their military and political leaders are a
lot of fools, and may begin suspecting that the German nation is
decent and kindly.

PS Did you see – quite irrelevantly – that the Archbishop of York
stated in the House of Lords that Hitler should not be brought to
trial, but killed on the spot by whoever finds him first? I wonder
which part of the New Testament he would quote in support of this?'

This letter provoked replies which showed that there were
strongly held and different opinions.
Uncle Bertie believed

'the non-fraternization order to be right and wise, and, incidentally, I
thought Montgomery's statement of it one of the best war documents
I have read – a plain and temperate pronouncement of fact; so rare. I
take the order to be directed against the grosser excesses of
conquering troops, and possibly – though this may be unjust – to
Americans in the first instance. I can imagine sections of all the
armies, however, going on the blind with the natives if they have
anything to do it with, and individuals among any of the allied forces
finding a use for German no less than any other sort of women.
These things, I take it, are what it is mainly desired to avoid, together
with accepting too freely the view that the Germans lay down under
Nazism because they couldn't help it.

'If I were offered strawberry jam and cream by a German hausfrau
(and saw no reason to suspect its ingredients) I should probably
accept it with such dignity and grave gratitude as I could summon,
but that isn't fraternization is it? Certainly I should never have
construed the order as implying that we were to cut every German
dead, but that's a very different thing from answering their V-signs
or, on the other hand – and unless the occasion demands – smacking
the heads of all and sundry. Circumstances must alter cases, and, as

Christopher says, individuals do not behave like nations; nor, thank goodness, do nations always behave like politicians.'

Pat found the generalization difficult.

'In the last five years everyone – or the vast majority – has assumed one common idea. They all talk nowadays of "nations" or "armies" or "tons" of bombs; they generalize wildly and grow quite incredibly inhuman. We all ink in our maps and live in a world of black arrows drawn across the map of Germany or the Pacific; perhaps for ten seconds a day we think of the individual nonentities who are the cause of the arrow-moving. Of course we think of our families, but apart from that everyone else is an army, or a nation, or some other completely impersonal organization.

'I find this an unsatisfactory attitude; how then can I support non-fraternization? It is the supreme generalization of the war. I hold no brief for Germany, but cannot support this overwhelming generalization –

'The people get the government they deserve – this is maybe true, but you cannot possibly say that every person gets the government he deserves, it is ridiculous. From 1921–39 thousands of children in this country yearly were crippled with rickets and t.b. because our government was narrow-minded and selfish and incompetent. We all deplored it, but we did nothing about it as far as action went; but are we all equally guilty? The slum priest, the Sisters of Mercy, – equally guilty with the stock exchange gambler and the crooked landlord?

'We must first decide whether every man always gets the government he deserves. If the answer to that is "yes", then I for one would feel embarrassed to assume the role of Judge over any other nation. If the answer is "No", then the non-fraternization rule seems to me to be nonsense.

'Quite apart from the moral aspect, you have to consider the practicability. With this I entirely agree with Chris; anyone can breathe blood and thunder from a reasonable distance.

'Go and put another arrow on your maps!'

Dad was strongly in favour of the policy of non-fraternization and a letter from him was immediately challenged by Christopher.

'Many thanks for your anti-fraternization letter! – also for the newspaper cutting of Monty's orders on the subject. I see Monty says

that fraternization "would be bitterly resented by our own families",
which certainly seems true in your own case. Out here we discuss the
subject a lot, and, as in the last war, the soldiers appear to be more
moderate in their views than the civilians. It is much easier to hate
people at a distance, and to hate a nation rather than the particular
individuals who compose it. I wonder if your hate would last long out
here.

'You cheerfully underline the bit in the cutting about "the
Germans are planning to make fools of you again and to escape the
loathing which their actions deserve". My answer is – the Germans
never fooled me before the war and won't do so in future; but they
did fool the people who now cry loudest for their blood – the *Daily
Mail, Daily Express* and the prewar Tory friends of Nazism – all the
old, unbalanced "Hang-the-Kaiser" brigade, always ready to whip
up the popular prejudices of the moment.

'Anyway, who has the right to order someone to loathe someone
else? What right has the Army to butt into the realm of politics and
personal relationships? The Army authorities have strictly forbidden
us to shake hands, eat, or laugh with Germans. They are making
complete fools of themselves.

'Is it the German people you loathe? or the mass of German
individuals? If you were out here, would you loathe that old man in
the street there with the wheelbarrow with the crockery in? Would
you loathe the small girl with long fair hair who brought round some
eggs for sale yesterday? Would you loathe the refugee families along
the road trundling prams and babies through the mud and rain?
When you see some tired and washed-out mother on the verge of
tears would you say to yourself "she is planning to make a fool of me
again and escape the loathing her actions deserve"?

'You will say "they must be taught their lesson". But have you a
clear conception of the lessons they have already been taught? Have
you seen a blitzed town? London isn't blitzed. Norwich is practically
undamaged, a prosperous peaceful town. German towns are blitzed.
And that is only the beginning of Germany's sufferings. Even if we
tried to help them, we could not stave off years and years of misery
ahead.

'And what good does it do to hate them? Some people talk as
though hating Germany was a shrewd and constructive foreign policy
– as though we'd only got to grind German faces in the dust to secure
peace for Europe. But Germany is only a part – quite a small part
now – of the European problem. Not all wars have been caused by
Germany, not by any means, and when Germany is dust and ashes,

we shall still be shivering in our shoes. We must disarm Germany and keep her disarmed; compared with that, practically nothing else in our relations with her matters. Let us concentrate on that, and not get all mixed up about our personal relationships with individual Germans.'

The war was rapidly petering out and everyone was waiting, daily, for some final declaration of peace and victory. The future and all that it held was the uppermost thought in people's minds and this was centred, in part, on the expected dissolution of Parliament and a General Election. Many saw it as the most important election of their lifetime and many – including a large percentage of the Forces – would be voting for the first time.

Christopher was standing as the Labour candidate for S. Norfolk and was being helped by the local Conservative party which

'instead of putting up a young soldier with an agricultural background as candidate, has called down from the business circles of NE England an elderly Tory politician of the old regime, a pro-Munichite who actually belonged to the "Link" – an Anglo-German friendship organization patronized by Ribbentrop. He knows less about farming than I do. Goodness knows why they did it.

'Anyway the next step was for the farmers to get on their hind legs and say it was a disgrace; they are now in the process of appointing a young (comparatively) soldier-farmer as their own candidate. I think that if they both stand, there will really be a sporting chance of my winning!'

Many found it hard to hold to their earlier political allegiances. Uncle Bertie was

'in the throes of a mental political upheaval. I believe I have voted Conservative all my life, but unless something epoch-making happens between now and the General Election, I can't do it again. I can imagine some of my young readers saying fancy the old boy seeing the light at last; but where and what is the light? The Labour Party seems to me to be still half-educated or less, and I look in vain for any hope of inspired leadership in it, and only fear that when it comes to power, unless it accepts some measure of guidance from the young Tories (which is almost as likely as the millennium) the tail will wag the dog. As for the Liberals, the same applies, and they will never do any good until they throw up a Lloyd George without that nobleman's destructive capacity.'

Stephen found the prospects of an election

'both exhilarating and frightening. We must be going to jump into something, and whatever it is is pregnant in a big way with something more. Disaster, probably. As between the Conservatives and the Trades Unions, one of whom will presumably be on top, I can see nothing to choose. Both are old-fashioned, both perpetuate the class struggle, both are gagged by their own dated propaganda, neither has a hope of filling the great majority of the population with any sense of faith or enthusiasm. It is obvious that distrust of capitalism is the reason why the working classes in industry don't work and don't care, even in wartime; and why they fight so well when they get into the Army, which at least isn't run by capitalists. But the rot in the Unions is in the rank and file; while the top men drink tea with the employers, and settle things amicably behind the scenes, the rank and file trust nobody and haven't so far tried much for anybody. I know of course the sort of reactionary I shall be described as, as I've said it all before; but the only excuse for the workers in industry is "tout comprendre, c'est tout pardonner", which is no slogan to catch my vote anyway. Well, Liberalism for me; anything which hasn't wielded any influence in industry for a good long time has my support.'

Aunt Ellie had less difficulty.

'Personally I cannot vote for our sitting member; he is stupid, elderly and reactionary (and I really don't think his best friends could deny the truth of those adjectives). He was the sole MP to vote against the Beveridge report. So I shall have to be a Liberal, as up to date there doesn't appear to be a Labour man; and that's nice and simple.'

And so at last, after over five and a half years of war, the last German troops gave up further resistance, and 'Victory in Europe' was declared on 8 May 1945.

'How did you spend VE Day? [asked Pat] 'I expect – knowing the family, that we were all horribly sober and dull. I think about 60% of Douglas has been delightfully drunk; cheery, singing, good-humoured, but very drunk. We have exploded fireworks and hung flags, have had an OCTU service and sung famous hymns, have had drinks with the student officers, and a wife and infant party in the Mess. In the evening I listened to the various radio programmes and read in bed till midnight. I am now finally convinced that I am not good at parties.'

Clare was following the Campbell College band round the streets of a 'mad' Portrush, crowding thirty to a truck and touring the countryside, going to church, walking along the cliffs where there were six bonfires, with the Navy firing different coloured Very lights and rockets, and ending up at the local dance.

David was in the close company of jubilant Islanders and Norwegians, and he confessed to having had little alternative but to have been 'drunk in the line of duty'.

In Anglesey on business, Stephen was delighted to find the streets of Beaumaris 'festooned with the flags of the four victorious nations – Russia, America, France and Wales'.

Uncle Bertie recorded:

'Listening to BBC transmissions of VE and VE + 1 days, Ellie wished at intervals that she was there; I thanked God that I was not. Downe played up like the good village that it is. Flags and streamers sprouted all over it. Sports and tea for the children. The local "rich man in his castle" threw a sherry party, with sherry, drawing the line of the elect with unerring eye. The church crowded for 20 minutes thanksgiving. They burned Hitler, complete in coffin, on a bonfire – a work, perhaps, of supererogation but admissible as a symbolic act.

'I preferred the BBC concert: it is a pleasure to hear Land of Hope and Glory, Jerusalem, the Hallelujah Chorus done full blast and really well.'

From Felthorpe Hall, Beryl reported:

'The flag was flying bravely (and the right way up) on the roof, looking very jubilant. All the tables were decorated with vases of red tulips, bluebells, and white cowparsley, and looked most festive. The men had had an early cup of tea in bed, beer for lunch, and free cigarettes all round. The hospital had marched in a body to the Thanksgiving Service on the recreation ground in the morning, and we went to the Church Service at 7.30. And so to a sit-down supper for everybody in the hall, the King's speech at 9, and then dancing and singing till nearly midnight. Not so rowdy as in some places perhaps, but all very festive and, thank goodness, no after-effects.'

And finally, surely Uncle Bertie spoke for the whole family when he wrote on 10 May:

'Dear Budget,
    'It is to be hoped you will continue yet awhile, but I feel that I now owe you a last word of deep gratitude. You were a wonderful conception; but for you we must almost have lost touch one with another in the past five years.
    'If it is not too much to hope for, I would urge a selection from your pages be duplicated and held as a valued possession for us, and for those who follow us.'